Frank Samuel Child

An Unknown Patriot

A story of the secret service

Frank Samuel Child

An Unknown Patriot
A story of the secret service

ISBN/EAN: 9783337220150

Printed in Europe, USA, Canada, Australia, Japan

Cover: Foto ©Suzi / pixelio.de

More available books at **www.hansebooks.com**

AN UNKNOWN
PATRIOT

A STORY OF THE SECRET SERVICE

BY

FRANK SAMUEL CHILD

BOSTON AND NEW YORK
HOUGHTON, MIFFLIN AND COMPANY
The Riverside Press, Cambridge
1899

TO

THE MEMORY

OF

ELISHA CHILD

A MODEST AND HONORED PATRIOT OF 1776

CAPTAIN   TOWN-CLERK   DEPUTY

COMMITTEE-MAN ON WAR

CONTENTS

LIST OF ILLUSTRATIONS

AN UNKNOWN PATRIOT

CHAPTER I

THE GREAT WOLF OF NORTH CAROLINA

GOVERNOR TRYON set his heart on living in a fine house. "I'll build a palace," he said to himself. "It shall be the most stately and expensive mansion in all the American wilderness."

So he wheedled and flattered the people of North Carolina until the Assembly of 1766 voted him five thousand pounds sterling that he might begin the edifice. The following year ten thousand pounds was added by his minions and their servants in the legislature, and then the huge proportions of this provincial palace thrust themselves into the vision of his fellow conspirators and the amazed people of the colony.

The main part was brick, eighty-seven feet front and fifty-nine deep, with wings for offices and servants' quarters, these wings

being connected with the palace proper by a
covered curviform colonnade. The chimney
breasts for the council chamber, dining-hall,
drawing-room, and the elaborate cornices
were white marble. The great hall had four
niches for statuary. The furnishings of the
mansion were made on a scale in harmony
with the edifice. A handsome court stretched
between the palace and its wings on the front,
while the rear was finished after the style of
the London Mansion House.

Fifteen thousand pounds sterling was an
enormous sum for the tax-payers of North
Carolina to put into a house. It was a piece
of unparalleled extravagance. New York
or Boston never thought of such a thing.
Neither did the scattered, impoverished people of this southern colony. It was all Tryon's
doings. This was what he came to America
for, — to be the head man of his province, live
in prodigal style, and squeeze money out of
the colonists as you squeeze juice out of an
orange. Did not Providence open up the
world for the benefit of the adventurous Englishman? And had not the colonial governors appointed by king or queen made it a
point of honor (or dishonor) to line their
pockets and fill their coffers?

The poor farmers, planters, traders, were taxed, imposed upon, abused, and defrauded until they rose in armed resistance, — those sturdy, weather-beaten Scotch-Irish Presbyterians and their like. Tryon enjoyed it. He was a soldier-governor. There was a vein of ferocity in his nature which simply waited upon opportunity. Give the man a chance, and he would show the world how to deal with Indians or rebels. When it came to treatment of the Cherokees, he earned the bloody title which these thwarted enemies gave him, — "The Great Wolf of North Carolina." They feared and hated Tryon with diabolic intensity. When it came to treatment of the disaffected and seditious spirits of his colony, he was at the first wily and seductive. Bearded in his mansion by the people, he was compelled to give up the stamp-master for North Carolina. "We will burn your house, yourself, and your stamp-master together," said the angry multitude. So Tryon yielded, but it rankled in his heart, and he thought out plans of retaliation. "Bear down upon them for the taxes," was his word. "Double and treble your legal fees, your court exactions!"

It seemed almost impossible to get justice.

The man who paid the largest price was the man in whose favor a verdict was declared. These funds, secured by fraud and treachery, were divided among the servants and officers of the crown. Verily, Governor Tryon carried things with a high hand, and it gave him a famous reputation. He knew how to manage the white man and the red man. Did he not create a wholesome terror in the hearts of all that opposed him? Had he not succeeded in bending the colony to his will? Was he not doing well for the crown? Therefore was he called the best, the shrewdest, the most successful among his contemporary rulers of provinces.

Yes, what a brave and masterful campaign was that which he carried on against the Regulators. These burdened, harried men were driven to some kind of organization. They had submitted to injustice and cruelty until forbearance ceased to be a virtue. Banded together in order to resist further encroachments of the constituted authorities, they made a stand for liberty and justice. Tryon met them at Alamance River on May 16th, 1771, and there fought the first battle of the American Revolution.

The rebels were brave. Their hearts were

in the fight. But they lacked discipline and generalship. "Tell the governor we defy him," was the message they sent back when he demanded their surrender. "Battle is what we want." "The Great Wolf of North Carolina" fell upon the motley, untrained band, tearing them asunder and inflicting grievous wounds. The Regulators had made their stand, and the mighty Tryon scattered them to the four winds, accompanying his victory with such hangings, burnings, and confiscations as pleased his fancy or gratified his sense of fitness.

The hot breath of discontent and sedition carried across the sea had at length struck his Majesty the King of Great Britain in the face. These fires must be quenched. Was it not meet that a capable and conspicuous man like Tryon should be transferred from the remoteness, the solitude of the southern colony, to the centre of trade and power in the north? There were red men in New York, and they required a master to make them efficient allies of the crown. There were white men that must be held in check, disciplined, or put out of the way. Tryon knew how to do these things. He was well versed in the subterfuges and cruelties of such war-

fare. He could cheat a man or hang him,
burn his house and get him into prison, cut
off his ears or confiscate his property, with a
speed and sagacity commanding the widest
admiration.

So the king made him governor of New
York. Tryon transferred his household gods
and the treasure which he had squeezed out
of his southern victims to the rising metro-
polis of the north.

He was all grace and suavity when in-
ducted into this new place of trust. Having
learned several lessons in management while
quarreling with the people of North Carolina,
he put them into practice while conducting
the affairs of the northern colony, gaining
a fair measure of good-will. Many were the
flattering words which he spoke to his new
subjects. Hospitality, frankness, concern for
the general welfare, interest in all the things
of the passing day, a generous friendliness, a
wonderful tolerance of religious opinions, —
these were some of his characteristics, and
they gained him popularity. His despotic
will did not show itself. While he continued strict as a disciplinarian, he tempered his
severity with such reason and discernment that
people refused to credit the reports which followed him from the south.

"You know what they call him in North Carolina, don't you?" The speaker was David Hardy, a student in King's College. He was addressing his cousin, Duane Livingstone.

"I think I have heard. A wolf, is it?" And he turned inquiringly toward the collegian.

"'The Great Wolf of North Carolina,'" replied young Hardy. "I doubt not he deserves it. The 'Sons of Liberty' say he is a devil."

"Now, David, you ought not to speak that way about a fine gentleman like Governor Tryon. It'll never do for a parson to think ill of people. You must have more charity and believe less than half you hear, or you will be no fit man to preach the gospel of peace."

The tone of the speaker was gently satirical. He was three years the senior of his cousin, a traveled man of the world, engaged in business, and doing well, so that he might properly talk in this familiar and instructive way. Furthermore, he was a friend of the governor's. He had known the family in England when, as a schoolboy, he was invited to their home. He had visited them in Newbern after the great mansion was fin-

ished, and enjoyed the free, generous life
which there prevailed.

"Lies, David, lies," continued the callow
merchant. "You must meet his Excellency.
Although a born man of affairs burdened with
grave responsibilities, I call him the very soul
of courtesy, and he knows all about good
fellowship. My dear cousin, don't believe
the stories you hear. I tell you they are lies.
Come with me some time when I call upon the
family. They will give you a royal welcome."

"Duane," exclaimed the cousin, "I believe
you're an out-and-out Tory. You ought to
be ashamed of yourself."

"Now, David, my boy, don't get excited,"
cried Mr. Livingstone. "You must learn to
curb that high-strung Hardy nature of yours.
What's the use of maligning a man and
making yourself ridiculous simply because he
differs from you in his opinions?"

The question went unanswered, for a sudden light flared up into the sky: the old fire-
bell suddenly clanged out its tumultuous
noise, shrieking, groaning, muttering, roaring,
appealing for help, crying notes of warning,
waking all the echoes of the little city, filling
hearts with terror and foreboding.

The young men ran down the street in the direction of the fire. The houses poured forth their lively volunteers, adding to the racket and excitement. Men with buckets, ladders, all sorts of convenient apparatus, joined the motley throng.

"Where's the fire?" shouted a score of voices. At length the word was hurled up and down and across the town, "It's the governor's house. Governor Tryon's house is on fire!"

Fort George was at the lower extremity of the island, a rectangular stone-work strengthened with bastions at its angles, elevated on an artificial mound fourteen feet high, the main gateway fronting on the Bowling Green. It contained barracks for two hundred men, two powder magazines, and the Province House. The counterscarp on the eastern and northern fronts was used as a garden by his Excellency.

Duane Livingstone and David Hardy reached the spot in time to see flames burst from the upper story windows. They fairly ran against the governor, who had escaped from the burning mansion with his wife, whom he had hurried across to the barracks. Even as they met him, a faint cry from the burning

structure smote their ears, and a maiden
appeared in the window of a second-story
room. It was Tryon's daughter, cut off from
escape through the ordinary means of exit.
The governor was chained to the spot for a
second, and a groan of horror sounded above
the roar of flames and the din of help. Then
he sprang to the rescue of the girl, stood beneath the chamber window, shouted to her
that she must jump for life, reached forth his
arms to receive the down-coming burden, and
waited a moment in torturing expectancy,
braced for the fall against his breast. There
was the swift flight of the frightened maiden
through the air, the dark form silhouetted
against the glare, and father and child were
clasped in each other's arms. Then the building became a seething mass of contending,
wrathful flames.

"I wonder how he likes it?" remarked
David Hardy to his cousin, after they had
done what little service lay in their power,
and they were turning away homeward.

"Likes what?" asked Livingstone sharply.

"Why, likes to be burnt out. It's an old
trick of his, you know, to burn folks' houses
about their ears."

"Now, look here," — it was Livingstone

speaking, — "I don't know any such thing, and I don't believe it, either. People lie about him. He did n't burn the homes of those wild, seditious North Carolinians any more than you did. They were all the time fighting among themselves. He told me so. Tryon is a good governor, a fair man, a splendid soldier. Why can't you be just and reasonable, and give a man his due?"

"Well, Duane, there is no doubt in my mind that his Excellency Governor Tryon got a part of his due to-night. I saw his face when he heard the cry of his daughter. Great beads of sweat stood on his forehead. The lines of agony looked deep, like the furrows of old age. And when the girl sprang into his arms and they stood there together in their first sense of happy safety, I thought of the men and the women who had suffered even greater affliction and torment through the commands or the sufferance of this eminent person whom you call your friend. I confess that I felt resigned to any momentary distress that might press him sore to-night."

"A fine preacher you 'll make, young man, with such a spirit of wickedness in you. I marvel that you dare to think of the ministry."

"I wonder how he likes it! I wonder how he likes it!" David Hardy said it over several times, more to himself than to his cousin. He was revolving it in his mind, when at last he made his way to bed and fell asleep. "I wonder how 'The Great Wolf of North Carolina' likes to be burnt out."

CHAPTER II

A DEVIL OF A DREAM

THERE was talk in Fairfield when Master Hardy sent his grandson, David, to King's College, New York. What business had a Puritan New Englander in a Church of England institution? Some folks said that the old gentleman was losing his mind. The boy ought to have gone to Yale, where his father and his grandfather went before him.

But Jeremiah Hardy was as hale and hearty at fourscore as he had been at three; there were no more signs of losing his mind than of losing his tongue, as many a friend and enemy was prepared to testify.

The old schoolmaster had taken an interest in the new college, because his good friend, Rector Johnson, served it with such zeal, and Philip Livingstone was one of its stanch helpers. David studied there because his uncle paid all the bills and gave his nephew a home.

Master Hardy was poor, and when his son

Jonathan, who was a parson, died, and a little later this son's widow, leaving three orphans to the care of their grandfather, the old gentleman felt his straitened circumstances. He could live well enough and hold his own against the world, but it is hard for old age to assume the responsibilities of supporting or training a young family.

The schoolmaster took up this fresh burden uncomplainingly, refusing to accept any help from sons or sons-in-law. He was an independent spirit, asking odds of nobody so long as he enjoyed good health. When, one glorious morning, the life of his wife went out with the tide, the burden seemed doubled and trebled; yet there was the same brave purpose to do and endure unto the end, leaning simply upon the strong arm of the Great Father.

David was ready for college at thirteen, for his grandfather had spent a great deal of time over the boy. He was to take the place of his dead sire in the ministry, so Jeremiah Hardy poured the strength of his intellectual and moral life into the open vessel of this sensitive nature. But as the grandfather did not have the money to pay the boy's way, and Philip Livingstone did, being glad to do

it on condition that David became a member
of his family, affairs naturally took this turn.

It had been arranged for the young student
to read his course in divinity with the venerable pastor Hobart, but the good man passed
away before David returned to Fairfield.
Then followed the usual interregnum in the
pastorate, a period when all business waits in
abeyance upon the choice of a new minister.

Thaddeus Burr and other citizens were frequent visitors in Boston, and they heard high
words of praise for the son of the Rev.
Andrew Eliot, D. D. He was a tutor in Har-
vard College, a young man of rare attain-
ments, a gentleman of the best social position,
one combining in himself so many graces and
virtues that he evidently was admirably fitted
to succeed a minister of parts like Mr. Hobart.

On the 7th day of February, 1774, it was
voted in society's meeting that Mr. Elijah
Abel go to Cambridge and wait upon Mr.
Andrew Eliot, Jr., from thence to Fairfield,
and the messenger was requested to set out
on his journey at once, which thing he did,
returning in due time with the candidate.
The new man brought with him the intellectual spirit of Boston, a thing stimulating

and satisfactory to the people of the Connecticut town.

On the 2d of March the young minister wrote to his father, saying, "The church have this day met. They first sent a committee to confer with me about the ordinance of baptism, owning the covenant, the mode of administering the Lord's Supper, and of admitting communicants. After the committee had made report, the church proceeded, and by an unanimous vote gave me an invitation to the pastoral office. The parish are to meet next Monday. I am informed there is like to be the same unanimity among them as in the church."

But herein Mr. Eliot erred. It was many days before the sentiments and opinions of the voters in the ecclesiastical society crystallized. The fact that ninety-nine hundredths of a congregation are pleased with a certain candidate is enough to excite the suspicion or antagonism of some possible one hundredth in various queer parishes.

When the society's meeting was held, therefore, a fair degree of heat manifested itself during the discussion over Mr. Eliot. Ammi Barlow, a member of the parish, but not a member of the church, was the contentious

" one hundredth " part of the congregation in this case, — a very small and meagre minority, yet large enough to show strenuous opposition to the Bostonian. There was no reason for his course, except that he did not like the man. When asked to go into particulars, he hemmed and hawed, simply reiterating his charge that he did n't like him.

The final meeting was held on the 4th of April. After a free. expression of mind on the part of the voters, Mr. Barlow arose and objected to an election on that day. " I move that the meeting adjourn to a more convenient season." There was a murmur of disapproval. Men moved uneasily in their seats, shrugged their shoulders, and protested with numerous shakings of the head. At this point Mr. Hardy arose and addressed the meeting.

" Mr. Moderator," he said, "this electing a pastor has so absorbed me that I could not rid my mind of it. Last night I went to bed worrying, and for hours I did n't sleep. But finally toward morning I lost myself, and I dreamed a dream, and it was all about this very meeting. If no one objects, I 'll tell the dream."

Curiosity had been excited, for the school-master was not an ordinary dreamer. Evi-

dently the society's meeting was to be entertained, and things would take a new tack.
They all waited upon the dreamer with keen
interest.

"I dreamed," continued Master Hardy,
"that I was being carried away through the
air. I went down and down and down, until
I knew from the odor of things and the awful
heat that I had got into the neighborhood of
the infernal regions. The racket was tremendous, and all space was filled with big
and little devils. A sort of court stretched
into the distance, and I saw the Devil himself seated on a bench, surrounded by a vast
multitude of evil spirits, who came and went
like birds building nests or crows stealing
corn. Pretty soon a bright, lively imp flew
down from the upper realm and whispered
something in his master's ear. Then Satan
rapped on his bench for order, and shouted,
'Fellows, to-morrow the members of the
ecclesiastical society in Fairfield are going to
try again to elect that young Andrew Eliot
to be their minister. Now I hate that man.
He's an out and out fearless, energetic enemy
of mine. He takes every chance he can get
to do me an injury. I don't want him in
Fairfield. He'll make it harder than ever

for me to keep my hold on the few people in town that belong to me. What shall we do?'

"'Send some one there to get up a disturbance and split the parish,' cried a wise old minion of the Evil One.

"'Yes, yes. That's it,' shouted a thousand hoarse and angry voices.

"'I like your suggestion,' answered the Old Boy. 'Here, Beelzebub, you take Discord with you and settle the matter. Don't come back until you have got the whole parish at odds and everybody quarreling with everybody else.'

"So Beelzebub and Discord started for Fairfield. Before they got out of hearing - distance, I saw a fantastic imp fly quickly down to the father of devils and hold a short conversation with him. Then Satan jumped from his bench, waved his hands wildly, and shouted with a voice that sounded like a dozen hurricanes and a hundred bulls of Bashan rolled together: 'Come back, come back, COME BACK!'

"Beelzebub and Discord turned around and flew down to the place where Satan was standing, and all the wild multitude listened.

"'By Jove, fellows, there isn't any use in your going to Fairfield. It's a waste of time.

Ammi Barlow will be on hand, and he can do more to stir up strife and make things hot than a dozen of you devils.' There was a harsh, hilarious roar of assent, the very walls of hell seemed to shake with diabolic laughter, and the noise waked me up, and then I found myself sitting upright in my bed."

The schoolmaster sat down, and Ammi Barlow sprang to his feet.

"A devil of a dream is that! A devil of a dream is that!" exclaimed the angry opponent of Mr. Eliot. Down the aisle of the meeting-house he strode with rough step, making the floor shake and the windows rattle. Slamming the door behind him, Mr. Ammi Barlow disappeared from the scene.

When order was restored, a vote was taken, and young Eliot was elected to fill the vacant pulpit. He was to have an annual salary of one hundred and twenty pounds lawful money, with the use of the lot called Applegate's, and a supplemental sum of three hundred pounds in yearly installments of one hundred pounds for his settlement.

The result of the election delighted David Hardy. Boston was a hotbed of patriotism, and Andrew Eliot, Jr., was infected. Our young divinity student sniffed trouble; the new minister came from the district where conditions promised some interesting *dénoue-ment* any day. David had ideas concerning stamp acts, royal authority, and kindred matters. He thought quite as much on these themes as on the more sober, scholastic questions of free-will and divine sovereignty.

No sooner was the new minister settled than friendship bound him to young Hardy; no sooner were they reading the Greek Testament together and plunging into Puritan divinity than they gave themselves with kindling enthusiasm to the problems of political history.

It was a happy life which David Hardy spent, these days. He was a great scholar, and the short weeks passed all too swiftly in the pursuit of knowledge. Every incentive to achievement urged him into these broad fields. The grandfather was a man of books. Since retirement from the sovereignty of the rod, his days had been divided between hard, cheerful work on his farm and earnest, stimulating study. Master Hardy made a good atmosphere for the student.

David also had a twin sister, possessed of wit, intelligence, and learning. She was a restless, dare-devil spirit, otherwise she might

have been a scholar the equal of her brother;
but ambition in Desire's case concerned David.
He was doing well, and must be encouraged in
his pursuits.   So she made a willing sacrifice
of herself in order to advance the interests
of this brother.

Dressed in a blue copperplate gown, with
her sister Lois sewing by her side, she spun
at the wheel and joined in bright conversation
when the new minister and her brother sat
over their grave studies.   The subject might
be a regimental banner with the legend, " An
Appeal to Heaven," in golden letters, or the
scarlet coat and trousers, with a triangular
laced hat, worn by the old soldiers at Louis-
burg, or Andrew Eliot's old home in Boston,
on Hanover Street (built by Increase Mather
in 1677, and sold more than a generation
later to Dr. Eliot), or the Ministerial Army,
or any theological topic.   Desire had her
opinions, and was a keen, stanch defender of
them.   Life in the Hardy family was condu-
cive to intellectual vigor.

CHAPTER III

"THE stories of suffering in Boston are pitiful. It makes my heart ache." David Hardy was reading the Gospel according to St. John in the Greek, and Mr. Eliot was teaching him the art of exegesis. They were sitting in the parson's study, a sombre, dignified room, adorned with black walnut cases filled to overflowing with several hundred volumes.

"It seems unchristian for me to linger here in Fairfield amid all abundance, while so many friends in Boston are reduced to such unhappy extremities." Mr. Eliot interrupted the flow of Greek discourse. His mind insistently turned to the events of the day.

"We'll help them," exclaimed the divinity student. "You know our townsmen are already talking about it. I was up to Colonel Silliman's last night, and he said that Boston was passing through martyrdom for all New England and the colonies."

It was hard to stick to Greek, or theology, or the history of Puritanism, when every stage from Boston or New York brought news of agitation and resistance, or the story of fresh indignities on the part of insolent redcoats. The progress made by the young man in Biblical studies did not equal that in the knowledge and philosophy of political happenings.

The Rev. Andrew Eliot purposed to set David Hardy a good example in respect to abstinence from political excitement. "I do not practice visiting very much unless I am sent for," the new minister wrote to his father in October. "I am better contented when at home, and my best employment is in my study. I shall not meddle much with politics, though they are the chief topic of conversation among us, and yet I cannot avoid being engaged sometimes." The words were not dry upon the paper before minister and student were caught in the strong current of popular feeling, most ardent and zealous among their fellow citizens, in devices for the succor and heartening of the patriots in Boston.

One expression of town sentiment was shown by the following letter : —

FAIRFIELD, November 8, 1774.

GENTLEMEN, — The town of Fairfield by donations have collected 750 bushels of grain of various kinds which is ordered to you by Captain Thorpe, bound for Salem, which we wish safe to hand, and hope this little testimonial of our attachment to the common cause will comfort the hearts of all those worthy patriots in the town of Boston who have so manfully exerted themselves in the cause of liberty, as well as those poor who are suffering under the unjust and cruel operations of the unjust and cruel Port Bill. Persevere in your glorious opposition. We are not insensible of your sufferings, and hope we shall yet consider ourselves bound to afford you such succor and relief as our circumstances and your wants demand.

We are, with great truth and regard, your most obedient servants.

Signed by order of the town's committee on donations.

JONATHAN STURGES.

To be communicated to the committee of Ways and Means in Boston or Overseers of the Poor.

Boston responded with a fine letter of

thanks, saying that the testimony which the
patriotic inhabitants of the town of Fairfield
gave of their attendance to the glorious cause
of liberty afforded much comfort as well as
seasonable relief to their friends who were
suffering under the cruel rod of ministerial
tyranny and oppression.[1]

It was only a month later that a legal meeting of the inhabitants of Fairfield was held,
to consider the agreement and association entered into by the Continental Congress. An
enthusiastic approval was voted, gentlemen
appointed to coöperate in the work, a county
congress favored and representatives named,
and a committee of correspondence for the
town, consisting of Colonel Gold S. Silliman,
Jonathan Sturges, Andrew Rowland, Esq.,
Mr. Job Bartram, and Thaddeus Burr, Esq.,
elected.

This early swinging into line and casting in
their lot with the champions of liberty made
the people of the town a conspicuous mark for
the hatred and malice of the British. But
what of it? They must take their chances
with the rest of the revolting colonists. The

[1] Text of letter is given in *An Old New England Town*,
page 103. This acknowledgment of help was written on the
24th of November, 1774.

sea exposure might tell against them and the beautiful town get herself into difficulties, but these were not the days to sit down and be-grudge one's strength or property. A great stake was at issue. Even the boys and the girls were clear sighted enough to see the trend of things.

" Oh, Desire," cried Lois Hardy, the eleven-year-old witch in the schoolmaster's family, " I wish I was a man."

" Don't let grandfather hear you say such a thing," replied Desire, " for it would hurt his feelings. He thinks a woman 's the noblest work of God. And well he might, after liv-ing fifty years with such a saint as grand-mother. But, Lois, I wish I was a man too. I never see the militia on training-day that I don't turn green with envy. But, dear me, child, I ought not to talk so to you."

Desire Hardy had been the housekeeper in her grandfather's family since old Mrs. Hardy's death, and the maternal oversight of Lois was part of her daily task. It required a great deal of grace to keep herself in check, for Desire was a queer girl, evincing many of the startling characteristics transmitted from a line of extraordinary ancestors. But when the burden of training Lois was added to that

of looking after herself, Desire said that, had
it not been flying in the face of Providence,
she would have given up in despair.

The year had been one of great strain.
Not that the housework was too much for
the lithe, active maiden, for she had the help
of black Chloe, the slave, who was in every
sense of the word a member of the family,
devoted to their well-being.   It was mental
strain that taxed Desire.   She wanted to be
doing something for her country, but she
was a young woman, keeping house for an
old gentleman, looking after the clothes of a
twin brother, trying to manage a younger sister and keep on good terms with an ancient,
domineering, faithful domestic.   These were
trying circumstances in which to put a high-
strung, impetuous girl, who had known little
restraint on the part of a mother, and had
always been used to her own way in so far
as that was possible in a house with Jeremiah
Hardy.

"Lois, it seems to me sometimes that I
must die unless I get a chance to fight for
our liberty and honor.   There's David studying to be a minister, and he can't do anything.   It wouldn't make any difference to
me if I was a parson, I'd fight like a tiger if

any British soldiers tried to drive me into
paying unjust taxes. I glory in the spirit
shown by those old Regulators in North
Carolina, and I tell Duane so every time I
see him. It always vexes him, you know,
because he's such a friend of Governor
Tryon, and he says Tryon was in the right.
But we know better. Lois, I can handle a
musket as well as David or Duane. I made
them teach me a long time ago. And I can
fence and do all sorts of military tricks.
Don't you tell grandfather. How shocked
he would be! But I know, child, that wild
times are ahead of us. I expect we shall
have to defend ourselves, and I'm getting
ready to do my part. Lois, I'll show you
how to shoot, the first day we get a chance."

The eyes of the little girl shone with excitement.

"Do, please, Desire, I should love to handle the old musket and learn how to help
you when the British come." For there was
no doubt in the mind of these two girls that
war must soon involve them in its tragedy.
They had listened when Mr. Thaddeus Burr
and Mr. Jonathan Sturges told of the straits
in which the people of Boston were placed.
They had become familiar with scenes of the

blockade through the frequent narratives of
Mr. Andrew Eliot, repeated over and over
again by David.

So the winter wore away, and everybody
lived in a state of suspense and anxiety.
Fairfield kept in close touch with the New
England capital. Many of her citizens had
emigrated from that neighborhood or inter-
married with Boston families. There were
strong ties of blood and friendship binding
the two places together. The new minister
was a fresh bond of interest and affection.
There was also considerable trade carried on
between the Massachusetts and the Connecticut seaport, Fairfield being esteemed by
many people, and particularly designated by
the Records, as the second seaport in importance within the colony.

Communication with Boston was now uncertain. Thaddeus Burr had been appointed
by the Assembly to engage and employ, at
public expense, two news-carriers to perform
regular stages from Fairfield to Woodstock,
passing through Windham and Lebanon in
such manner that they were to arrive in
Hartford every Saturday. He was one of a
committee in the colony to look out for extraordinary and important intelligence, but

such a service was subject to many difficulties, and communication between distant
towns grew more and more infrequent and
expensive.

One Saturday morning in the spring of
1775 (it was April 22d), at about eight
o'clock, Colonel Gold Selleck Silliman and
Mr. Jonathan Sturges came over to see Mr.
Thaddeus Burr. They were members of the
war committee, and met for frequent consultation. The three gentlemen stood on the
front porch of the great mansion, their earnest
speech being noted by various passers-by, so
that a little group formed on the corner below
Mr. Burr's and waited for developments. On
the Green above, there was a semicircle of
children formed in front of the stocks, watching a culprit as he submitted to punishment
for some slight peccadillo.

The sharp impact of horses' hoofs upon
the half-frozen and slushy ground suddenly
diverted the attention of people on the street.
Down past Mr. Abel's and Captain Dimond's
a swift horseman came, his animal steaming
and sweating in the early sunshine, the messenger straining every nerve to speed his way
through the town. Opposite Mr. Burr's he
brought his steed to a sudden halt, and passed

into the hands of Colonel Silliman a sealed packet.

The messenger was Trail Bissell, who brought the news of Lexington.

" Yes," cried he, as Mr. Sturges looked inquiringly into his face. " The blow has been struck. The redcoats marched from Boston to Lexington and fired upon our militia, killing six men and wounding four others. To arms ! to arms ! "

Lois and half a dozen children ran down the street; the little group of men on the corner crossed hurriedly over; neighbors thrust their heads out of windows or ran along in the path of the messenger. It was not long before the bell of the Prime Ancient Society was ringing, and then men, women, and children flocked into the open, and told the news to one another with bated breath, flashing eye, and crimsoned cheek.

The paper put into the hands of the colonel read as follows : —

WATERTOWN, Wednesday morning
near 10 of the clock.

To all friends of American Liberty, be it known, that this morning before break of day, a brigade consisting of about 1000 or

1200 men landed at Phipps's Farm at Cambridge and marched to Lexington, where they found a company of our colony militia in arms, upon whom they fired without any provocation and killed six men and wounded four others. By an express from Boston we find another Brigade are now upon the march from Boston, supposed to be about 1000. The bearer, Trail Bissell, is charged to alarm the country quite to Connecticut; and all persons are desired to furnish him with fresh horses as they may be needed. I have spoken with several who have seen the dead and wounded. Pray let the Delegates from this Colony to Connecticut see this, they know Col. Forster, one of the Delegates.

J. PALMER,
One of the Committee.

A true copy of the original, per order of the Committee of Correspondence of Worcester, April, 1775.

Attested and forwarded by the Committees of Brookline, Norwich, New London, Lyme, Saybrook, Killingsworth, E. Guilford, Guilford, Brandford, New Haven.

To this document, later in the day, the committee added the following : —

FAIRFIELD, Saturday, April 22
at eight o'clock.

Since the above was written we have received the following by a second express: —

Thursday, 3 o'clock, afternoon.

SIR, — I am this moment informed by an express from Woodstock, taken from the mouth of the Express, then two of the clock afternoon, That the contest between the first Brigade that marched to Concord was still continuing this A. M. at the town of Lexington, to which said Brigade had retreated, that another Brigade had, said to be the second mentioned in this letter of the morning, landed with a quantity of Artillery, at the place where the first did. The Provincials were determined to prevent the two Brigades from joining their strength if possible and remain in great succour.

N. B. — The Regulars when in Concord burnt the Court House, took two pieces of cannon, which they rendered useless; and began to take up Concord bridge, on which Capt. —— (who, with many on both sides, were soon killed) made an attack upon the King's troops, on which they retreated to Lexington.   I am,   EB. WILLIAMS.

To COL. OBADIAH JOHNSON, Canterbury.

P. S. — M. McFarlane of Plainfield, merchant, has just returned from Boston by way of Providence, who conversed with an Express from Lexington, who further informs, that 4000 of our troops had surrounded the first Brigade above mentioned, who were on a hill in Lexington, that the action continued and there were about 50 of our men killed and 150 of the Regulars as near as they could determine, when the Express came away; it will be expedient for every man to go who is fit and ——

To this paper was added these sentences and names : —

"The above is a true copy as received for express from New Haven and attested by the Committee of Correspondence, from town to town.

"Attest : JONATHAN STURGES,
ANDREW ROWLAND,
THAD. BURR,
JOB BARTRAM,
Committee."

The entire document was forwarded to New York, where it was received at four o'clock, and immediately sent to Philadelphia, by Isaac Low, chairman of the New York Committee.

It was a day of tense feeling in the town. Every patriotic soul was fertile in loyal endeavors to get the train-band into marching order.

"Oh, Desire, Desire!" cried Lois Hardy, as she rushed wildly into the schoolmaster's house, "the redcoats have killed a great many of our soldiers, and everybody must go to the war. A man has just come from Boston with the news, and Colonel Silliman is going to call out our militia."

"Lois Hardy, what do you mean!" exclaimed Desire, as she stopped in the midst of her Saturday morning baking and gazed excitedly at the child. "Do you know what you are talking about? Is it really true? You run up to Mr. Eliot's and see if David is there, and go to the barn and ask your grandfather to come in. Oh, how I wish that I was a man and could start off this very minute and fight all the cruel horde!"

Desire passed the baking over to Chloe, donned her old camblet cloak and hood, and, without waiting for Grandfather Hardy or the return of David, walked rapidly up to the Green.

In an hour the alarm had gone abroad, and the open space in the middle of the town was the scene of feverish activity. People had kept their firearms in very good condition for several months, so that there was little furbishing to be done. But clothes had to be inspected and put into traveling condition, provisions gathered and made portable, — a hundred trivial matters attended to.

Captain David Dimon was here, there, everywhere, giving orders, consulting with Colonel Silliman and other members of the Committee of Correspondence, holding in check the restless spirits of his lively troops, trying to get things into such shape that they might start on their long march before evening.

The Rev. Andrew Eliot and Thaddeus Burr addressed the people in the meeting-house when there came a slight lull in the excitement. It was impossible for all to get within the walls, but the doors were wide open, and the multitude that surrounded the building caught now and again a sentence. When it came to the prayer, every head was bowed, and, amid a silence which was intense with suppressed emotions, the young minister from Boston prayed for the men who had made their brave stand for liberty at Lexington, and for the great fraternity of patriots in the beleaguered city and its neighborhood. Then he stretched forth his hands in benediction above the company of Fairfield soldiers who now went forth to share in the defense of home and honor, the firstfruits of love and sacrifice in behalf of their native land. What a prayer welled up from his patriot soul, mingling with the flame of heroic devotion!

It was April. The breath of spring kissed the worshipers. Then came sunshine, then shower. Was it not April in every soul? — the breaking up of deep, long-repressed feelings, the tears of a wild sorrow, the smiles of a glowing faith, a loyal heartening for the struggle?

The day was swiftly declining when Captain Dimon drew up his company in martial array, and they awaited the word of march. What clasping of hands, what multitude of kisses, what tender embraces said farewell and farewell! The shrill notes of the fife smote the air, there was a steady tramp, tramp of feet, great wavings of kerchiefs and hats, cheer upon cheer, a thousand good-by messages flying across the Green, then up and away moved the proud, defiant, handsomely equipped band.

Parson Eliot, Grandfather Hardy, Colonel

Silliman, Mr. Burr, and others followed along beyond Gold's bridge, freighting the air with their good wishes, loath to let the company pass out of their sight. David Hardy with his two sisters pushed on toward Newfield.

"I hope we'll have a chance at 'em," cried Desire, with vehemence.

"It will come in due time," observed David gravely. "I see before us years of conflict. And our beloved town will not escape the fire and the sword."

"Oh, David, do you think it? Will the war really come to Fairfield? Shall we have to fight here at home, see ships firing on us from the water, meet the foe face to face, in order to defend our rights? How I wish I might shoulder a musket!"

"Child, sufficient unto the day is the evil thereof. War is a horrible catastrophe. But we are in the right, and we'll fight until the day is won and justice is done to these insulted and oppressed colonies."

"I wonder what Duane will say now!" inquired Desire. "I warrant you he will uphold Governor Tryon."

"Well, that may be. I think it quite likely. Duane is very self-willed and opinionated. His years in England did him more harm than good. He acts so high and mighty sometimes that I have n't any patience left. And yet Duane is a fine fellow. I wish he did n't patronize me quite so much. Perhaps if I did n't wear his old clothes, it might be different."

"Now, David, he is n't so mean as to feel above you because you take his cast-off clothes. He 's too true a gentleman for that. But I do think that England has half spoiled him. Probably his friends there paid him a good deal of attention, for he has a winning way, and is excellent company. I suppose he was a sort of curiosity, a nine days' wonder, being a native of the western wilderness. A great many of those people imagine we are half savages here in America, you know. They can't believe their eyes when they see a gentleman who was raised in the colonies."

"There they go over the hill. They 're getting out of sight," cried Lois, as she frantically waved her hands and pointed to the disappearing train-band. The attention of her brother and sister had been relaxed for a moment.

"God bless them!" murmured Desire, tears filling the eyes, lips quivering.

"God bless them!" said David reverently,

as he shaded his face and peered into the gathering shadows.

"God bless them! God bless them!" It was Lois whose words crept into the stillness of the oncoming twilight, hushing the advance of the trio. A moment they hesitated, and then turned back, making a silent, swift way to the home of the schoolmaster.

CHAPTER IV

AARON BURR AND DOROTHY Q

PEOPLE must eat and drink, get their
night's sleep, take care of the farm, spin,
weave, knit, mend, look after every day's business, even when grim War stalks through the
land. So the old routine of life continued.

The first blow spurred the patriots to redoubled activity in their diverse employments,
for if there was much fighting to be done, a
tremendous amount of hard work must pre-
cede and accompany the struggle. The colonies were now cut off from commerce with the
mother country; stern necessity as well as
robust pride forced the Americans to restrict
their diet to home products, their wearing
apparel and a thousand other articles to home
manufacture.

David Hardy was running the farm while
studying to be a minister. This spring he
ploughed up a great number of acres, and did
an immense amount of planting and sowing.
Since the age and infirmity of his grand-

father, as well as the nature of David's profession, made it advisable for him to stay at
home, he was determined to offset these re-
strictions by an unusual diligence in tilling
the soil, so that they might have an abundance
to contribute in case the colonies needed supplies.

Desire was equally ambitious to do her part.
She, with Lois and Chloe, spun and wove, knit
and sewed, every hour that could be spared
from other labors; when extra help was required in the field, they turned their hands to
whatever task David suggested. The same
thing was observed among all their neighbors.
Few hours were idled away in vain gossip.
One must work to meet the emergency.
When one had something to say, it was
mingled with the service in household, shop,
or field. And there was a great amount of
talking done, for the crisis was uppermost in
everybody's mind.

"Desire," said Lois, one bright, blithe
morning, "they 've got company down at
Mr. Thaddeus Burr's. I saw the stage-coach
stop at the house. Two ladies got out, and
there was such a number of trunks and boxes!
I wonder who it can be!"

"As like as not they 're Boston people,"

answered Desire, as she gave a fresh impulse
to the wheel used in her spinning. "You
might run down after dinner, Lois, and take
that piece of linen which I finished last night
for Mrs. Burr. I'm curious to know if it is
somebody from Boston. We may get the news
about what's been going on there lately."

Lois stitched away faithfully upon the
undergarment which she was making.

"Desire, it would n't do us any good to be
rich now, would it, for we have got to wear
the things that we make at home, have n't
we? I mean everybody, you know."

"Lois, if we were rich, I'd spend it all for
the sake of my country. I don't know what
our soldiers will do, unless they starve to death
and go naked. Grandfather says he does n't
see where the money's coming from to pay
anybody. Even soldiers must be provided
for and their families supported."

"I'll finish this after dinner, Desire. I'd
like to take the piece of cloth down to Mrs.
Burr now." The child turned inquiringly to
her sister.

"Yes, I think it will be proper for you to
go now, if you want to. Be sure to see Mrs.
Burr and ask if they've heard from Boston
within a few days."

DESIRE . . . AT HER TASK

Desire continued at her task, and Lois sped up the street and across the Green. It was twelve o'clock when the child returned. She was out of breath, having come back as swiftly as her feet would carry her, and she was laden with news.

"It's Madam Hancock and Miss Dorothy Quincy that came in the stage. They fled from Boston, you know, and went to the minister's at Lexington in Mrs. Hancock's own coach. Finally, they had to leave there; they took the stage, and Colonel Hancock got a part of their clothes for them, and then they came on here, and Mrs. Burr thinks they will stay a long time. I saw 'em both, and they kissed me, and said what a sweet, brave girl, for I told them that you and I wanted to go to war; and they asked all about you, and want you to come and see them."

The child stopped to take breath, while Grandfather Hardy, with David, entered the kitchen.

"Why, Lois, what is the matter?" inquired the old gentleman. "Who are you talking about?"

"Madam Hancock has come in the stage to-day. She's going to stay down at Mr. Burr's. She was left all alone in her big

house in Boston, and the British insulted her
and threatened to burn her house down, so
that she had to leave everything and fairly
run for dear life. She says you never saw
such excitement. Her nephew, Colonel Hancock, has had a price put on his head. She
says there are dreadful goings on in the
neighborhood of Boston. And Miss Dorothy
Quincy's there, and she is a very lovely
young lady. I am going to see her real
often, for she invited me."

"Well, child," interrupted David, "what
did she say they were doing in the neighborhood of Boston now?"

"Oh, our soldiers are there and thousands
of other militia, and they're going to have a
fight and drive the British out; but Mrs.
Hancock is afraid they'll burn down the town
first, and she does love her beautiful home.
It's full of everything lovely, Miss Quincy
says, and it is such a pity to destroy it. But
if that is part of the price to be paid for
liberty, Madam Hancock says she'll pay it
gladly."

It was a most hospitable mansion to which
these ladies fled. Mr. and Mrs. Thaddeus
Burr were social leaders in the colony, and
lavish entertainment was one of their char-

acteristics. For years they had gathered
under their roof men and women of fame,
culture, and standing, many people of social
graces and intellectual attractions. John Hancock was a frequent visitor, one of Mr. Burr's
most intimate friends and trusted counselors,
and Fairfield seemed to him an ideal retreat
for his aunt and her companion. How little
did the venerable lady imagine that she had
looked upon Boston for the last time, — that
these feverish, eventful days in Fairfield were
destined to close the record of her life.

Desire and Lois Hardy paid their respects
to these honored guests the day after their
arrival. The stately courtesy of the Boston
madam had a subtle fascination for her
young admirers. There was heart in her
grace and affability, so that she won the two
girls, and with the months that followed they
became fast friends.

But the good lady had a diverting task in
the management of Miss Dorothy Quincy.

"David, you must see the Boston belle!"
exclaimed Desire, on her return from Mr.
Burr's. "She asked if there were many
young gentlemen in town, or whether they
had all gone to the war."

"I don't know why Miss Quincy should be

so anxious for male society. She ought to
be thinking of the Hon. John Hancock.
Mr. Burr told me they were engaged, and
his Aunt Lydia is trying to hurry up the marriage, I hear."

"You must have good ears, David. Why,
she has n't been here long enough to show
herself to our townspeople, and I don't believe they 've talked about anything but the
war ever since they came."

"Well, Desire, it does n't look well for a
young lady engaged to be married to be on
the lookout for gentlemen to flirt with. It is
setting a very bad example," answered the
virtuous student of divinity. "But then, I 'll
call upon Miss Quincy, and see that she has
some attention from our sex."

It was perhaps a week later that David and
Desire dropped into Mr. Burr's of an evening.

A great hall ran through the centre of
the mansion, — favorite sitting-place for the
family and their guests. The front and
the rear doors were thrown open, so that the
breeze played through the spacious room,
moonlight falling athwart the eastern entrance, a distant view of the Sound shimmer-
ing through the foliage of the trees in yard
and garden, the scent of roses being wafted

on the air with an occasional intermixture of
salt marsh odors. A monstrous lamp with a
monstrous globe emitted a mild light in the
parlor, which opened into the hall.

There were two or three groups of people
in the long apartment. Near the front door
stood Mr. Burr, Colonel Silliman, Mrs. Jonathan Sturges and her husband, with half a
dozen others. Several elderly ladies were
seated near the entrance to the parlor, knitting. But the circle which David and Desire
joined was one that had gathered around the
open doorway looking upon the sea.

Mrs. Burr led the latest callers to this
group. A gentleman was telling Miss Quincy
why he liked to visit Fairfield.

"You know this is the home of my ancestors. Why, half the people I meet trace their
lineage back to some of these old families.
My father was born here, in the Upper Meadows."

"Born here, in the Upper Meadows," repeated Miss Quincy quizzically. "What a
strange place to be born in!" A merry laugh
followed.

"I'll ride up there and show you the
place," said the young man good-naturedly.

It was at this point that David and Desire

were added to the company. In the dim
light it was almost impossible to distinguish
one person from another, but Miss Quincy
persisted that it was light enough, and the
moon was rising higher every moment.

"That voice sounds like Aaron Burr!" exclaimed David, as the speaker ceased.

"Quite right, Hardy. How are you, these
wild times of war?" Young Burr arose from
his chair, greeting David and his sister, whom
he had known from childhood.

"We are busily engaged in entertaining
Miss Quincy, at the present," said Desire
lightly.

"What a charming task! I came down
from Litchfield to help you. I was saying to
Miss Quincy that nearly everybody I meet
comes from this old town, or his father and
mother do. I'm going to show her where
my father was born, in the Upper Meadows.
You'll ride with us up to the place, won't
you? We shall be delighted to have your
company. And, David, you come along to
keep us in the path of sobriety and rectitude.
Since I left off studying for the ministry and
took to law, I feel the need of some such
oversight as David will exercise."

Aaron Burr was nineteen, a handsome,

buoyant fellow, gay as a lark, thirsting for adventure, brilliant in speech, and most winning in manners, — the beau ideal of a gentleman. When he went to Bethlehem at seventeen to study theology with old Dr. Bellamy, it was hoped that he might follow in the footsteps of his honored and lamented father, becoming a leader among the parsons and educators of the colonies.

" I could n't stand it, David," he explained to young Hardy. " The more Dr. Bellamy reasoned with me, the farther away I got from him and his teaching. I could n't be an honest man and preach what he preaches. Then I made up my mind that I was n't good enough to be a parson. After such an Aaron Burr in the ministry as my father, do you think I would tarnish the name and the office by being any the less a good, grand parson ? So I 'm fated to be a lawyer. But we did have great times up there at Bethlehem. The doctor seemed to think I was overmuch fond of the girls, and he was always talking about my being in love. Why, he had a dinner there last winter, and thirty ministers sat at the table, and I furnished the staple for the doctor's jokes all through the feast. Every grain of spirit in me was kindled.

But I kept my temper like a saint, and let him have his fun."

" Well, Aaron, I always thought you were a model boy, but don't drink cherry rum when you ride with the girls here, as you say the bucks and belles of Litchfield County do. It's a bad practice, and might lead to harm."

" There, I told you I needed your watch-care, David. Go with me to the war. Ogden and I have decided to offer ourselves on the altar of our country. Come with me as my chaplain. I *may* get into the company of my friend Samuel Spring. He's a sterling Christian patriot. But there will be room for you, and plenty of hard work to do, I'll warrant."

It was only a brief visit that Aaron Burr made at his cousin's, but it was long enough to divert Miss Quincy, and make her neglectful of her correspondence with the Hon. John Hancock. There were walks on the beach and drives back into the hills over long reaches of country. There were interminable talks about people and politics, as well as the sweet trivialities that circulate among susceptible youth, and pass for the wit and gallantry of love-making.

Desire Hardy was quite as much the object

of Burr's attentions as Miss Dorothy. The
two young ladies had become deeply interested
in each other. Desire was drawn to Miss
Quincy because she was not only a beautiful
and fascinating creature, but a belle in society,
a much-courted lady, one conversant with the
fashion and gossip of the day, the fiancée
of John Hancock, the wealthy Boston merchant, and now president of the Continental
Congress. Acquaintance with her opened to
Desire a vast realm of aspiration.

Dorothy Quincy liked Desire because she
found her intensely alive to everything that
was going on in the world, — one of the sym-
pathetic, quick-witted girls that respond easily
and naturally to every chance in life, a companion with a dash of originality, a force of
invention simply irresistible. Neither man
nor woman could feel solitary or downhearted
in the presence of Desire Hardy. She would
adapt herself to rich and poor alike, and was
quite as popular with humble folk as with the
best-educated and most refined individual in
town.

So the few days that Aaron Burr stayed
in Fairfield were among the gayest and happiest of the season. The war was on, and
news came back from Boston concerning the

doings of redcoats and minute-men; but
young men and maidens, howsoever patriotic
they may be, still remain true to nature and
think upon the gentler ways and means of love.

And Aunt Lydia Hancock was watchful of
the young people. While she might be won
by the frank homage and rollicking humor
of young Burr, and immensely entertained by
the fresh charm and ingenuous sprightliness
of Desire, yet she exercised a wise, constant
surveillance over the company, careful that
no harm came to her charge. So one day in
late June, the student of law mounted his
horse and galloped off to Litchfield.

"What a free-hearted, merry fellow he is!"
remarked Desire to Miss Quincy. "With his
gayety and youthful enthusiasm, there is a
spirit of real manliness which makes him infinitely attractive."

"Yes, he is a delightful young gentleman,"
sighed Miss Dorothy. "Do you really think
he will go to the war?" a secret hope that
perhaps he might return to Fairfield soon,
rising unbidden in her heart.

"Yes, yes; he'll go. How could he help
it? I have wished a thousand times that I
was a soldier, so that I could go too." The
young ladies were sitting on the front porch

at Mr. Burr's. It was the day after General
Washington had passed through town on his
way to Cambridge, June 29th. "They say
that our Commander-in-chief is a greater
fighter than General Putnam, but he looks
to me like a grand gentleman."

"Gentleman and soldier both, I think.
What a noble figure he makes as he rides
with his cavalcade of horsemen!"

"Ah! here comes Mr. Burr, and he's got
a packet in his hand. Perhaps it is a letter
for you." But Miss Dorothy was not wishing
for letters. She had received several from
her lover, and they remained unanswered.

"Did I show you my new stockings which
Mr. Hancock sent me from Philadelphia?
Come with me upstairs."

Another moment and they were engaged
in looking over the lovely things which Dr.
Church had brought her from the great trade
emporium of Pennsylvania. Spread out upon
the table was one of John Hancock's letters.

"Child, read it," said the fair Dorothy,
with a spice of mischief in her manner.
"Mayhap you'll wish to know how a great
lover expresses himself;" and she pushed the
precise, legible writing into the hand of the
curious girl. Desire read as follows: —

My Dr. Dolly, — I am almost prevail'd on to think that my letters to my Aunt & you are not read, for I cannot obtain a reply, I have ask'd a million questions & not an answer to one, I beg'd you to let me know what things my Aunt wanted & you, & many other matters I wanted to know, but not one word in answer. I Really Take it extreme unkind, pray my Dr. use not so much Ceremony & Reservedness, why can't you use freedom in writing, be not afraid of me, I want long Letters. I am glad the little things I sent you are agreeable. Why did you not write me of the top of the Umbrella. I am so sorry it was spoiled, but I will send you another by my Express wch will go in a few days. How did my Aunt like her gown & do let me know if the Stockings suited her; she had better send a pattern shoe & stocking, I warrant I will suit her. The Inclos'd letter for your Father you will read & seal & forward him, you will observe I mention in it your writing your Sister Katy about a few necessaries for Katy Sewall, what you think Right let her have & Roy James, this only between you & I; do write your Father I should be glad to hear from him & I Beg, my Dear Dolly you will write me often & long

JOHN HANCOCK

Letters, I will forgive the past if you will mend in future. Do ask my Aunt to make me up & send me a Watch String, & do you make up another & send me, I wear them out fast. I want some little thing of your doing.

Remember to all Friends with you as if nam'd. I am call'd upon & must obey.

I have sent you by Docr Church in a paper Box Directed to you, the following things for your acceptance, & which I do insist you wear, if you do not I shall think the Donor is the objection : —

2 pair white silk	stockings which
4 pr. white thread	I think will fit you
1 pr. Black Satin	shoes, the other
1 p. Black Calem Co.	Shall be sent when done.

1 very pretty light Hat
1 neat Airy Summer Cloak.   (I ask Docr. Church)
2 caps
1 Fann

I wish these may please you, I shall be gratified if they do, pray write me, I will attend to all your Commands.

Adieu my Dr. Girl, & believe me to be with great Esteem & Affection,

Yours without Reserve

JOHN HANCOCK.

Remember me to Katy Brackett.

"They are beautiful," said Desire, dropping the letter upon the table and taking the exquisite hosiery into her hands. "And Mrs. Burr herself never wore a lovelier hat, and the fan, — it is like a dream. I think Mr. Hancock will make a very domestic man."

"Yes," answered Miss Dorothy Quincy, with the slightest suggestion of impatience in her words, "I 've no doubt he 'll prove a thoroughly domestic person."

CHAPTER V

GOVERNOR TRYON sailed for England on April 7th, 1774, and remained away from his province nearly fifteen months. General Washington passed through New York city on his way to Cambridge the afternoon of June 28th, 1775. That very evening Governor Tryon returned to his provincial capital and resumed his governmental functions.

It was an odd coincidence that these two men should appear in town on the same day, and there was much anxiety on the part of many citizens in respect to a possible disturbance.

"I'm not a nervous man, you know," observed Duane Livingstone to David Hardy, "but I had a feeling that we might see lively times before midnight."

The cousins were promenading up and down the Battery, engaged in serious talk, although Duane was not so deeply involved in the conversation that he failed to notice

every bright face that met them, now and
again doffing his hat and making his most
respectful salutation to several gayly dressed
ladies that had come out to enjoy the sea
breeze and the gossip.

"How did it turn out?" inquired David.

"Oh, General Washington was greeted by
our citizens in the daytime and given quite a
hearty welcome, and sent on his way east with
more or less good wishes; while Governor
Tryon was welcomed at night and presented
with congratulatory addresses, and the city
was jubilant over his coming."

"A sort of double-faced people, you New
Yorkers seem to be," exclaimed the divinity
student.

"That's a mean thing to say, and it isn't
true. There are citizens that side with the
mother country, and those that side with the
colonies. I suppose the men that wish to
fight the British army greeted Washington,
and the men that don't were just as glad, if
not more so, to see Governor Tryon again."

"Probably you hurried to pay your respects to 'The Great Wolf.'"

David's tone and language expressed disapproval, although he was too mild a fellow,
with too much manliness and generosity, to
make hurtful speeches.

" My dear cousin, you thought you 'd give me a hard thrust then, did n't you? But bless my soul, it takes a man of a temper very different from yours to ruffle me. Of course I paid him my respects. Why not? Have n't I known the family for years, and visited them in England and North Carolina, to say nothing about New York? Why should I treat Governor Tryon otherwise than as a gentleman ? "

" Because he has n't the instincts of a gentleman in him, and is as hard, inhuman, and malicious as the Evil One himself."

David spoke with intensity. He was not one to mince words when thoroughly aroused. He had a good command of forcible speech. In these days of hot political agitation, he had thrown one side his native reserve and subdued manners, taking a firm, bold stand for liberty.

" That is your opinion, my young Puritan, but if he is any harder or more inhuman than those old fanatics that hung our ancestress, Anne Hardy, or if he has shown half the malice and downright cruelty that a good many of them showed, I wish you 'd enlighten me. David, the trouble with you is that you 're provincial and narrow-minded.

You're like your forbears. I don't suppose you can help it. You require change of atmosphere and associations. I thought that four years in King's College would do something for you, and it has; but you still need the broadening influences of a life beyond the confines of rigid, democratic Connecticut. We must take you across the sea on one of our ships, and give you a chance to see the world and get loose from the leading-strings of your provincialism."

"Duane, you're talking arrant nonsense, and you know it. There are people in New York, and a good many of them, too, your own family among them, that feel exactly as I do concerning Tryon, the awful injustice of the mother country, and the stern demand for the redress of our wrongs. How a young man of your parts, holding the position you do, and trained as you have been, can have the stomach to talk as you are talking passes my comprehension. The next thing will be your enlistment in the royal army, probably."

"Why, David, I never knew you to get so excited. You don't seem like yourself. I believe you're going daft on the subject of armed resistance to our mother country. Let's change the subject." There was a moment's pause to note the proud bearing of an English man-of-war as she moved around Battery Point and pushed her way into the North River. Then Duane continued, " So Aaron Burr has been in Fairfield again, has he ? I met him here in the winter. What a rollicking buck he is! and immensely popular with the girls. He has n't given up the law, has he, as he did the preaching ? I have thought that maybe he was unstable. Such gay fellows often are."

" I don't know whether he has given up the law or not, but I know that he is going to enlist and start for Boston in a few days. I like him, for he 's a patriot, and he 's got the courage of a lion. Desire said everything she could to encourage him in it."

" You don't mean to say that he 's been making love to Desire ? " Duane was now quick and spirited in manner, while a slight flush was perceptible on his cheek, as he turned keen, sharp eyes toward his cousin. " Burr is good-looking enough, and he has an amorous, taking way with him, but I can't see why the girls find him so seductive and fascinating. How long did he stay in Fairfield ? "

" Only a few days, but he knows how to

make hay while the sun shines. You ought
to have seen him with Miss Dorothy Quincy.
She's visiting Thaddeus Burr's with Mrs.
Thomas Hancock. She's engaged to marry
Colonel John Hancock, the nephew, you know,
and I think Aunt Lydia, as she calls her,
didn't have a comfortable hour while Burr
was in town, although she managed so that
they were never alone for a moment. Desire,
or the minister, Mr. Eliot, an old friend of
Miss Quincy's, or some of the Sturgeses, or
others were with them all the time. I think
Miss Quincy was charmed with Burr, and so
is Desire. She says he's the perfection of
a gentleman, and so entertaining. Well, he
is lively company. You know how the hogs
run loose in our streets sometimes. One day
we were all down at the Burrs', and Lois was
with us, and she had on a clean white dress.
Burr was always hectoring and teasing Lois,
and she was silly enough to stick to him.
One of these tame hogs came waddling along,
and Burr said to Lois, ' I 'll give you a sovereign, child, if you 'll ride that piece of live
pork from here to the Green,' and he pulled
a shining sovereign from his pocket. You
know he's got money, and he really is very
free with it. Lois never waited a moment.

She leaped upon the hog's back before Miss Dorothy, or Desire, or any of us had a chance to say a word, and off went the creature with all his might and main. I expected to see the child thrown from his back and trampled under foot; but she laid hold of his ears, and hung on like grim death. The creature squealed and waddled, and waddled and squealed, while Lois swayed from one side to the other like a ship heaving after a storm. We ran up the street to save the child from this madcap performance, but Burr was ahead of us; and when we reached the Green, Lois had slipped from the creature's back and had her sovereign in her hand, while Burr was shaking with laughter, telling what a brave girl she was, and paying all sorts of flattering compliments to her. Lois's dress was a sight to behold, but she had won her money and come out unharmed, and she was off home before we had time to say a word. Burr reveled in the telling of it" —

"Well, I think such a thing is disgraceful," interrupted Mr. Duane Livingstone. "What did grandfather say?"

"If he'd seen her with her besmirched dress, I think he'd have given the child a dressing-down not soon to be forgotten, for she is full of capers, and tries our patience almost beyond endurance; but Lois showed him the sovereign, and told him in her own inimitable way how she had earned it, so that he was made to feel she had done rather a smart thing. He winked at the caper, and solemnly shook his head, and told her she must n't ride any more hogs."

As the young men continued their walk and conversation, it was evident that they excited more than a passing interest.

"David," exclaimed Duane suddenly, as he noticed how much attention was paid them, "I believe we grow to look alike. It never struck me so forcibly before. I declare, now that we happen to be dressed in the same sort of clothes, we appear like twins." And as he spoke, the two young men gazed at each other with lively concern, for it was true that they were as near alike as two peas in a pod. "You've become a mighty handsome fellow, David." The country cousin smiled.

"That's a kind of back-handed way to boast about your own good looks, is n't it?" David's eyes twinkled merrily.

"Take it as you please," laughed Duane.

"I don't think I'll urge you to stay long in town hereafter when you come down to visit us. Folks will get you and me mixed. They won't know 'which from t' other.' Perhaps I'd better stop sending my clothes to Fairfield. Our dressing alike may complicate matters. You'll be making love to some one of my girls, and she'll think it's I."

The boys were now in a jestful mood.

"Duane, if you don't give me your old clothes, I shall have to go stark naked. These are hard times, and the war makes us poorer than ever."

During all these years when the Livingstones had helped David Hardy, there had never been a thought or feeling of envy or condescension between the cousins. Duane was glad to give, and David quite as glad to receive. Although they were divided by four years, yet they had always cherished a hearty affection for each other. The trend of political events was the first occasion of serious disagreement. But underneath any expression of present hostility there throbbed a deep, genuine spirit of brotherliness.

"I'm going back to Fairfield with Sam Smedley," observed David, taking a new tack in the conversation. "Come up and spend a

few days with us. I'd like to have you meet
Miss Quincy, for she's very fond of society,
and we don't want her to get lonesome. Sam
Smedley is a great sailor, and very much of a
man, too.   You ought to hear him talk about
the war.   He's looking for a chance to ship
on some privateer.   I tell you he is bound to
stir up the enemy when he gets a chance."

" David, your mind is too much on war for
a man of peace. I advise you to read more
theology and less politics. Is Miss Quincy
as hot-headed on the subject as you are ?
Because if she is, we might come to hard
words."   And so the conversation ran along
in various channels.

Two days passed, and when David Hardy
had finished the business which brought him
to New York, he returned home in the company of young Smedley and his cousin Duane.

CHAPTER VI

THE summer of 1775 was a season of tense life in Fairfield. The soldiers, patriots, theorists, politicians, — representative men of western Connecticut, — held frequent conclave at the county seat. Early in the summer, Gold Selleck Silliman was appointed colonel of the Fourth Regiment of militia. Governor Trumbull had written to General Gage asking for an explanation of the course which he was pursuing in Boston. Thaddeus Burr and Jonathan Sturges took counsel with the governor in respect to the condition of the shore towns and the necessity for their protection. The sea-dogs of the colony were invited to play the watch over the enemy along the Sound, and encouraged to do any handy job of privateering that came in their way. The train-bands drilled on the Green day after day, getting themselves into good trim for the hour of need.

The male population of the colony in **1775**, between the age limits of sixteen and fifty years, subject to military duty, was about twenty-six thousand. Perhaps two thousand of them were disaffected toward the service, sympathizing with the royalists. Fairfield had its Tory element, the Rev. John Sayre, rector of Trinity Church, being one of the most conspicuous figures, around whom rallied the major part of his parishioners.

John Adams spoke the truth when he said that Connecticut was doing everything that could be done by her men, both for Boston and New York. All sorts of supplies were prepared and forwarded to the Continental soldiers. A full quota of militia took to the field. Whatever form of assistance was demanded on any side, Connecticut did even more than her part. The enthusiasm of liberty had swept over the colony, nerving her people to the most strenuous action.

Yet domestic life and the social amenities were not neglected. It was a gay season in Fairfield, despite the fever of war and the hurly-burly of politics, for Miss Dorothy Quincy was a luminary which shone with no uncertain radiance, and she had various satellites basking in her light, reflecting something of her own glory.

There was hardly a family or dignitary of eminence in the colony that did not take the pains to render proper homage to the fiancée of his Excellency John Hancock, the President of the Continental Congress. So it was a round of modest yet lively festivities, amid all the strain and turmoil of the growing conflict.

"It seems almost wicked for one to have such a good time," remarked Desire to Miss Quincy, one perfect evening in early September. "But it is delightful to have you with us these months; the summer has come and gone with the speed of a bird shooting through the air."

There had been a rapid succession of walks and drives, little boating parties, evening companies, now and then a jaunt to New Haven or some other near-by town, and the thousand trivial gayeties that made up the round of mild dissipation in colonial society.

"Now the autumn has come, and soon you will leave Fairfield and return to the fascinations of high life." Desire spoke in a sweet, sad, minor tone of regret.

"But I shall never forget these happy months of freedom," replied Miss Quincy. "I have reveled in all the sweets of friend-

ship, and grown to love this old town and its
people with a strange passion."

"I suppose it will be especially dear to
you, too, for the reason that you are married
here?" Desire looked inquisitively into the
face of her companion.

"Yes, I think so, although it is hard to be
driven from home when one is preparing for
one's wedding. But Mr. Hancock has been
very kind and obliging, sending me everything in the world that I need, buying silks,
satins, laces, linen, and a thousand necessaries
with the taste and judgment of the shrewdest
woman in the world. And then Mr. and
Mrs. Burr have acted like my own kith and
kin, putting their whole establishment at my
service, entering into the spirit of the occasion almost like my own parents."

The fair Dorothy was immersed in dry
goods as she spoke. All the dressmakers in
town were at her service, the house of her
host being converted into a huge shop filled to
the full with these workers and their fabrics.
For the wedding was to come off the latter
part of the month, and the women were straining every nerve to have the lady decked out
according to the latest mode.

How those last days hastened !   Invitations

in the name of Mr. and Mrs. Thaddeus Burr
went hither and yon. The mansion was be-
comingly adorned after the Boston style.
The trousseau was finished, — a most elegant
outfit, worthy the lady for whom it was prepared and the bridegroom who had taken
such an unusual part in selecting it. Then
came the twenty-eighth day of September.

It was a gala occasion for the town. War
may sound its tocsin, yet people will marry
and give in marriage. Men will toil and moil
with dumb persistence, and turn on the instant with bounding heart and beaming eyes
at the bidding of Hymen. The fret, weari-
ness, uncertainties of strife, may dog our steps,
but no sooner do we catch sight of Love than
all else is forgotten and we yield ourselves to
its intoxication. Boston may suffer the pangs
of starvation and the encroachments of her
enemies, New York blow hot and cold between patriot and royalist, the unprotected
colonies along the coast invite the onslaught
of British tars; nevertheless, it is quite the
fitting and timely thing for the President
of the Continental Congress to turn one side
from the stress of public duty, the strain of
private care, and take unto himself a wife.
She will cheer and comfort him in his need.

She will brace him for the great struggle which must be waged. She will animate him with fresh spirit and enthusiasm.

It was a famous company that gathered for the nuptials of this highly favored pair.

"You ought to have seen them when they arrived from Philadelphia," cried Lois, who noted every detail of the important affair, and counted it as one of the brightest days in her life. "There was Mr. Hancock's great coach in all its fresh, fresh" — she hesitated for the right word — "grandeur, and four beautiful, prancing horses; and there were some other coaches filled with people; and there were many men on their gallant steeds, making a fine show in their gay colors. Oh, it was glorious!" The child was describing the scene to her grandfather. "And I've seen I don't know how many people that have come down from Boston way; and Governor Trumbull's here and some men from Hartford. Why, the town looks like training-day, and everybody is dressed in such beautiful clothes."

The day was dreamy and poetic, for a soft haze hung above the landscape and sifted the lazy sunshine down gently upon the blithe, brilliant company.

Burr House

THEY WERE MARRIED IN THE GREAT PARLOR

They were married in the great parlor of
the mansion, and the Rev. Andrew Eliot, Jr.,
old-time friend of the Quincy and the Hancock families, performed the simple, brief
ceremony.

"Well, it's next to being in Boston to
have a Boston parson officiate on this occasion," observed Mr. Adams.

"And I warrant you that we shall enjoy a
richer feast than any bridal party in Boston
for many a month," said Governor Trumbull.

"Oh, Desire," whispered Lois, who had
been smuggled into the house by special
request of the bride, and placed where she
commanded a large sweep of vision over the
guests, "did you ever see anything so fine?
There are all the colors of the rainbow.
That lady in the corner must have made
her gown out of blue sky. Oh, how lovely!
And look at Madam Hancock in her stiff
purple satin! Isn't Mrs. Burr magnificent
in velvet and lace? She seems like a queen.
And who is that woman with the wonderful
gown of pink, and her head sprinkled with
diamond dust, and her breast sparkling with
gems? And oh, Desire, do see what gloves
the ladies wear, and the ruffles and scarfs
and ribbons and chains and jewelry! Isn't

it the brightest, splendidest scene you ever saw? Why, I see sunsets and flowers and the blue sea and the green meadows and the gray of the clouds and a hundred other colors in the people's clothes. The men are quite as shining and glorious as the ladies, I think. Look at their red and blue and yellow vests. And how beautiful are their small-clothes! Oh, the stockings, the buckles, the white ruffles and old lace, the elegant, many-hued coats! Some of the gentlemen have such big wigs, with such big bows behind, and see, a good many don't wear wigs, but have their hair tied up in a queue, with a bigger ribbon and " —

" Lois, Lois," whispered Desire, " folks will hear you, and they 'll think we 've never been anywhere before. You must be quiet."

" Oh, Desire, it is like heaven, I think. I feel as if I was reading in the book of Revelation. And what a regal gentleman Mr. John Hancock is! How much do you suppose his clothes cost? I 'd like to ask Dorothy Quincy."

" It is n't Miss Dorothy Quincy any more, Lois, remember. She is Mrs. John Hancock now."

This whispered conversation was taking

place while the congratulations were being said
and the company was waiting for the feast.

"A very pretty show, my dears, is n't it?"
It was Duane Livingstone speaking in subdued voice to Lois and Desire; "but I've
seen many a brighter one."

This remark was received by the younger
of the sisters with incredulity. It did not
seem possible to Lois that anything in all the
world could be more brilliantly attractive and
elegant. Desire listened to the young gentleman's whispered comment philosophically, and
then answered : —

"I suppose you refer to some social func-
tion held by your friend, Governor Tryon, in
the Government House?"

There was mischief in the answer; for Desire had learned to despise the courtly representative of the crown in New York, although
Mrs. Thaddeus Burr had assured her he was
a gentleman of good presence and pleasing
manners, and had made himself very agreeable
when she met him in Hartford at Governor
Trumbull's, in Fairfield as her own guest, and
in New York when he was host at an evening
party.

"David has prejudiced you," said the
cousin.

"Well, there is Mr. Sam Smedley; let us ask him, since he's running up and down the Sound and knows about everybody along-shore and in the city."

The bronzed young sailor named approached the little group.

"We were saying that Governor Tryon is a fine example of the old English gentleman. You agree with us, do you not, Mr. Smedley?"

Desire spoke with a demureness and repose infinitely charming, although a telltale flash in her eyes might have warned the observer that smouldering fire lay hid beneath the sweet, calm exterior.

"Who was saying it?" The man of the sea spoke with gruffness. "Not you, Miss Desire, I warrant me."

"Come, come," interrupted David Hardy, as he pushed his way to them. "All the belles and bucks are drinking to the health of the bride. Let's away and share the jollity."

"That sounds like a divinity student, doesn't it?" cried Duane.

"It isn't original with my brother," observed Desire. "That's the way Aaron Burr talks. 'Bucks and belles' is one of his favorite phrases. David has become hilarious on this great occasion, and he has fallen into the form of speech peculiar to a very worldly companion." Desire was brimful of fun and mirth, for here were several young gentlemen waiting upon her, and she could see that others were edging their way in her direction and must inevitably join the group.

They all moved into the current that had set toward the refreshment tables, and soon the contagious good cheer had raised them to such a pitch of liveliness that they made for the lawn, where they might find ample space for the exercise of their merry hearts and glad voices.

Lois, meanwhile, flitted from room to room, or from group to group, sipping the sweets of gossip and jovial fellowship, as caprice dictated, observing every feature of the kaleidoscopic pageant, talking with the numerous servants that vied in their eager wishes to make all happy, taking the opportunity more than once to dash into the crowd of interested spectators that thronged the street, in order that she might explain something to a mate or friend whom she spied, or distribute goodies from the wedding feast.

The honorable President of the Continental Congress bore himself with remarkable suavity.

A very dignified gentleman, punctilious and a stickler for the proprieties, on this red-letter day he unbent and beamed and rejoiced with a luxury of abandon that startled his old friends. And well he might for once give way to such jocund impulses, for he was now wedded to the lady of his choice, and all peril of break or disaster had passed.

Miss Quincy was a person of such charms that many lovers flitted about her like moths around a lighted candle on a summer's night. This courtly suitor had been not a little annoyed and vexed by a certain lack of response and lover-like devotion on the part of the Boston belle during his absence in Philadelphia. The sly gossips had intimated that Dorothy Q. was a flirt, and that she did more than pass the time of day with several of these ardent admirers. Now that he was to keep her under his daily care, his fears went to the winds, and his heart beat with a new, riotous joy.

Yes, he could afford to be happy and cast the stiffness and stateliness of his lofty position one side for the day.

"Is n't he delightful!" said Lois to her sister. They had greeted the bride and the bridegroom a second time, and both John Hancock and his wife had given the two girls

several resounding kisses upon their fresh
and lovely lips.

"Yes, Lois, he's really an ideal bridegroom, — ideal from our point of view. He
does n't save all his sweetness for the bride.
They make a regal-looking pair. Why did n't
you kiss the bride?"

Desire was now teasing her cousin Duane,
who stood on her right, while David had
moved over to her left, and Lois leaned
upon her arm in the front. They made a
remarkable group.

"Colonel, there's a picture that vies with
the beauty of the bride and the grandeur of
the bridegroom."

Mr. Jonathan Sturges was speaking to
Colonel Silliman, a listener to Captain Samuel Squier, Mr. Job Bartram, and Dr. Allin
engaged in war talk.

"Did you ever see such a striking resemblance?"

As Colonel Silliman spoke, the knot of
people about him gazed upon the little company to which he pointed. It had often
been remarked that Desire and David looked
so much alike that it was a matter of clothes
alone which enabled people to distinguish
them. But when a third person, this New

York cousin, with a resemblance quite as striking, was put in line with them, and the handsome group received a sort of finishing touch from the child Lois, whose features were likewise characteristic of the Hardy lineage, it was a picture long to be remembered.

The brother, sisters two, and cousin stood engrossed in bright conversation and gay banter, while person after person noted them, looking with warm heart and kindling eye upon the rare quartette. For the schoolmaster's grandchildren made many friends, doing not a little to enliven and adorn the society in which they moved.

"They are very interesting young people," observed Mrs. Andrew Eliot the senior. She was speaking with Aunt Lydia Hancock. "I doubt me if we could find in all Boston better-looking or more attractive children and youth."

"Yes," replied the serene lady, "I have become very fond of the girls. And I know your son thinks highly of David Hardy. Mr. Duane Livingstone is almost a stranger to me, but I hear excellent reports of him. Aaron Burr admired him, and told us how popular the young gallant was in New York. But I have not asked concerning your husband to-day."

Mrs. Hancock was not the only refugee

seeking a home in Fairfield. The wife of the
North Church pastor and four of his children
had fled to the hospitable town, bringing
friends with them.

"I know I put you under difficulties," Dr.
Eliot wrote to his son in April, when Mrs.
Eliot was starting for Connecticut by the
overland way, and the children had embarked
on a ship from Salem, "but you are the only
asylum I have."

The faithful man remained stanchly at his
post through the siege of his native city, and
many were the kind offices which he performed for friend and foe alike. Meanwhile
the other members of his family were scattered, and communications became infrequent
and beset with trouble.

"Did the coach bring you tidings of Dr.
Eliot?" inquired Mrs. Hancock.

"No, I have received nothing from him
these two weeks. But I do not fret. He is
in the Lord's keeping, and doing what he
deems is his plain duty. He'll be cared for.
I think we all learn to be brave and trustful,
these days. It will take a great deal of courage and devotion to carry us through the
struggle, but I believe that God is with us.
Of whom shall we be afraid?"

Colonel Abraham Gould bowed deferentially to the ladies as he passed, tarrying for a moment to pay his respects.

"Madam, this is a happy day for you." He addressed Mrs. Hancock. It was reported that she had been exceedingly anxious to see Dorothy Quincy wedded to her nephew.

"A most happy day, I thank you, sir," replied the lady. "And Fairfield becomes dear to me. Would that every city of refuge for the people of God might be as lovely and hospitable as this town."

"You honor us, dear madam. We shall not forget your gracious words."

Mrs. Hancock acknowledged the gentleman's courtesy.

"And may I express, esteemed lady," — Colonel Gould was still conversing with Mrs. Eliot, — "our deep sympathy for you in this enforced separation from your eminent and greatly beloved husband. I trust that he keeps his health amid the worry and trial of his arduous duties. And I trust that while you mourn this enforced exile from your home and husband, you do, nevertheless, in some measure receive compensation for it by staying with your son."

"You are very kind, my dear sir, and the

many expressions of good feeling on the part
of your people I deeply appreciate. I am
comforted by the tender solicitude of my son,
and everything is done to mitigate my distress. But, sir, my sufferings are nothing,
and I glory in them, if so be there shall come
liberty and justice to the colonies."

"Madam, such sentiments are noble and
inspiring. They enable us to gird our loins
for the conflict, assured that we are sustained
by those more precious to us than life. I
believe that God will give us the victory,
although the price must be not only our service and substance, but a vast amount of distress and much spilt blood."

A slight commotion on the street drew the
attention of the guests. Madam Hancock
hurried down the front porch into the yard
in pursuit of Mr. Thaddeus Burr, and Colonel
Gould with Colonel Silliman accompanied her.

"I beg your pardon, gentlemen. My anxiety
may be needless, but I remember that General
Gage has put a price upon the head of my
nephew, and has made more than one attempt
to captivate him. It was only by the good
providence of God that we escaped from the
enemy while staying with our beloved cousins in the parsonage at Lexington. And

methinks some traitor in our midst perchance
might conspire to turn our rejoicings to-day
into terror and lamentation."

A report had gone abroad that the British
were on the watch for the President of the
Continental Congress, and that it had been
planned to take him prisoner before the bridal
party left town. The commotion on the street
was caused by the cantering of a swift messenger, who evidently came bearing dispatches of
importance.

No sooner was he dismounted than the
festivities suddenly ended. Danger seemed
to lurk in the air. Governor Trumbull, Mr.
Quincy, John Adams, the gentry of the town,
and the startled guests that had gathered
from all parts of the colony awaited the rapid
approach of Mr. John Hancock, for the communication was addressed to him. His wife,
in all the splendor of bridal array, tripped
lightly down the steps and followed him
where he stood amid the throng of excited
friends and observers. He broke the seal of
the letter, scanned its contents, then with
flushed face addressed the company that
pressed upon him : —

"You will pardon me, gentlemen, if I withdraw to my chamber and attend to public

affairs of great moment. I will meet the
governor and his council and the Fairfield
Committee of Correspondence for immediate
consultation."

" Desire, Desire, I think the British are
coming ! " cried Lois.

The gentlemen had retired to an upper
room in the mansion, where they were soon
closeted in counsel with Colonel Hancock.
The festive appearance of the town changed
to a martial aspect. The wedding guests
hurried away, getting into their coaches, or
walking to their homes in town, or galloping
down the King's Highway to the lower villages, or hastening along the shore toward
New Haven.

When the massive, shining coach of John
Hancock drew up in front of the Burr homestead, the bride and bridegroom entered the
capacious structure, the outriders and the
postilions took their places, the guard of
honor arrayed itself in all military splendor
to the front and the rear, while an escort
of private citizens and guests brought up the
end of the procession. Thus with haste and
good wishes, amid anxieties and prayers, the
honored gentleman and his beautiful wife
started upon the journey.

CHAPTER VII

THE UNITED AMERICAN COLONIES ARE FREE AND INDEPENDENT STATES

AFTER the evacuation of Boston by the British, Washington came back to New York, passing through Fairfield April the 12th. There were greetings on the part of the town Committee of Correspondence and a brief halt at the mansion of Thaddeus Burr, where the Commander-in-chief of the American army took the opportunity to pay his respects to the aunt of the President of the Continental Congress. Both Desire and Lois happened to be present when General Washington arrived, while David was one of several young men that escorted him through the town.

"I have a message for your Excellency which I am instructed to deliver in secret."

Desire addressed the Commander-in-chief as they stood for one moment apart from the other members of the company. His eye kindled with interest and admiration. Desire shone with a beauty that was the revelation

of a lively, intelligent spirit, expressive of
rare, fine character, interpreting with startling facility the moods and dispositions of a
generous, intense, high-minded young woman.
She was impulsive and fearless, quick to adapt
herself to circumstances, a keen wit and a
shrewd observer, gifted with all the subtle
intuitions peculiar to her sex, possessed of a
certain masculine force and aggressiveness
that often imperiled her own peace and that
of her friends. Yet there was an honesty
and straightforwardness about her, a loyalty
to principle, an enthusiasm for right, which
kept her out of mischief and preserved her
from many a trial that now and again seemed
imminent.

Washington was an excellent judge of
human nature, while swift to respond to the
charms of a woman. And he detected in Desire
something other than a beautiful face and
winning manners. There was a depth of soul
and purpose revealed to him, a delicate sense
of responsibility, a vital concern in affairs,
that commanded instant confidence. She did
not wish to draw attention to herself, or profit
by any interview with the man who held
in his hands the destinies of the American
colonies. Washington became aware of that

fact while she preferred her simple request. Here was a person capable of serving her country, and she had something of importance to pass over to him.

"With your permission," — Desire bowed to the host and hostess, — "I am to serve General Washington with a cup of cold water fresh from the well."

"And with your permission," — the Commander-in-chief bowed very graciously to Mr. and Mrs. Burr and the company, — "I will go with the young lady and draw the water with my own hands."

There was a tone of authority in his words. The two passed down the long hall, Desire turning one side to get a silver mug. Then they walked to the well. The bucket was attached to one of the old-fashioned sweeps; and while the general pulled down the cumbrous instrument so that the water gurgled into its receptacle, Desire bent her head and peered into the darkness, speaking hastily and pointedly to her eager listener, — ending her address by giving him a little packet, which she transferred with the cup into his hands, and which he quickly slipped into his breast.

It was a warm, enervating April day, one of the sweet precursors of the on-coming summer, and the crystal waters were refreshing after the march from New Haven.

There was a strange sparkle in the eyes of Desire as she accompanied General Washington back into the mansion. And it was with matchless grace and gentleness that the great man took her hand in his when he came to say good-by, and, lifting it to his lips, reverently craved God's blessing upon her.

" Was n't it lovely ! " exclaimed Lois, who had been a sharp witness throughout the whole scene. " Why did n't he kiss my fingers ? I 'd have been glad to have him kiss my lips, as John Hancock did. Would n't you, Desire ? "

But her sister was absorbed in thought, and there came the fitful play of light and shadow upon her face.

" Child," said Madam Hancock, " General Washington is a courtly gentleman, but you shall visit me in Boston and meet many a northern man with manners quite as fine. And yet methinks it would sound hypercritical and vainglorious to speak in these terms among your Fairfield gentry. I find no better, nobler exemplars of Christian courtesy or true manhood than here. The lavish hospitality of these old friends, their

extreme politeness and beneficent friendship,
shall I ever see their match?"

"Ah, madam, I grieve that you leave us,
for we have learned to love you, and many
are the happy hours which Lois and I have
spent in your company."

This was on April the 12th.   Three days
later, the lady, while engaged in final preparations for her return to Boston, was seized
with apoplexy and passed away.

"Oh, Desire," cried Lois, "to think that
Madam Hancock must die when she was
planning so much for the enjoyment of us all
and for the help of the colonies!"

For the good lady had possessed an ample
fortune, and her affairs having taken a favorable turn, she had proposed to furnish some of
the sinews of war and share more generously
in the protracted conflict.

Thus there came changes in the life of the
Hardy family.   At the beginning of the war,
the grandfather died, so that heavier responsibilities were thrust upon David and Desire.
There was the farm to manage and their support to get out of it.   There were the slaves,
Minto and Chloe, a constant care and cause
of vexation, in spite of their services.   There
was Lois to train and instruct, a most trying

task, for she was fain to imitate Desire even
to the point of fault and folly.

"I 'm glad we have only two slaves," cried
Desire one morning, after a tiff with Chloe,
who now felt that, since Grandfather Hardy
was dead, the burden of domestic affairs fell
upon her. "If we owned as many as Colonel Silliman, I should die of vexation and
wrath."

"Why, how many belong to the Silli-
mans?" inquired Lois.

"Ten or a dozen. And I heard the colonel tell Mr. Eliot the other day that if he
had stuck to his law business and let farming
and slavery alone, he would have been worth
a good deal more money. He was advising
Mr. Eliot not to buy a manservant. And I
agree with him. I don't think we ought to
own folks, any way. Negroes have souls the
same as other men and women."

"Let 's free Minto and Chloe," said David
quietly. He had been reading Greek while
the girls were speaking.

"David, you could n't drive either of them
away. They think they 're the responsible
parties here now, and I heard Minto say to
Chloe the other night, 'Chile, we 's got to
look after 'um; they 's an awful 'sponsibility,

but it's de Lo'd's will.' Feeling like that,
do you suppose they'd leave us?"

The brother and his sisters were seated at
supper one June evening when Sherwood
Spalding entered unannounced. He was
a Tory friend of the Hardy family, a member of Trinity Church, and a hot-headed
loyalist.

"What do you suppose your fanatics have
done at Hartford?" he blurted out, not waiting for a reply. "They've resolved that the
delegates of Connecticut in the so-called
Continental Congress be and are hereby instructed to propose to that body to declare
that the United American Colonies are free
and independent States; absolved from all
allegiance to Great Britain. Heavens! they
must have all gone stark mad!"

"Have they, have they?" exclaimed Desire excitedly. "Hurrah for old Connecticut!" and she waved her kerchief above her
head as she sprang from the table.

"Hurrah, hurrah!" echoed Lois, loosening
her white apron and unfurling it like a flag.

The child had a mind of her own, and
she was free to assert her independence when
Desire ordered her to the doing of this or
that task. She was not to be domineered

over by her sister. Nevertheless, Desire was the inspiration and pattern of her life, and Lois adored her. A flame of patriotism had been kindled by the enthusiasm of Desire, and every fresh expression of interest nourished it. So when the elder sister gave way to a jubilant hurrah, the younger one followed.

" You girls don't know what you 're about!" shouted the visitor angrily. " Why, these colonies can no more take care of themselves than dogs can fly ! "

" They can't, eh ? " exclaimed David, whose spirit began to show itself. " I 'm thinking that Connecticut has sense and backbone enough to look out for herself, my British friend. Other colonies may not elect their own governors and transact their own affairs, but that 's what we 've done for many a year, and more than that, every one of the thirteen provinces is capable of doing the same thing."

" You 're all Radicals here. You don't know on which side your bread is buttered. I tell you it 's idiotic for the colonies to resist the mother country, and the day will come when " —

" You 'll eat your words and be a mighty sick man," interrupted David.

It was true that Connecticut had sent on

the instructions described, and it was only a few days before the Continental Congress issued the Declaration of Independence. Events were following one another in quick succession. Howe had laid Falmouth in ruins, and made every true New Englander feel that the die was cast; it was now war to the knife. As the eastern colonies were free from immediate peril, they spent their resources in assisting neighbors.

It proved a fine record which Connecticut was making. At the very beginning of hostilities, she sent several of her sons to take Ticonderoga. Then her troops responded heartily to Washington when he held the British army blockaded in Boston. Governor Trumbull continued active and alert in every emergency, so that men and substance were forthcoming whenever solicited. These things made the Tory citizens of the colony angry and offensive.

"I suppose you 've been reading Paine's ' Common Sense,' " said Spalding contemptuously.

"Yes," answered Desire, "and I like it. The man knows whereof he speaks. I don't wonder that it has had such an immense circulation. Why, thousands upon thousands of copies have been scattered through the colonies. Perhaps it has influenced the Continental Congress itself."

"Oh, very likely," continued Spalding, in the same sneering tone. "That and 'Mc-Fingal' are great books. You'll keep them by the side of the Bible, won't you?"

"They say a Connecticut man wrote 'Mc-Fingal.' Whoever did it, I am proud of him," exclaimed Desire, with spirit.

"Perhaps David is the writer, and his modesty restrains him from confessing."

The guest was evidently anxious to abate the acrimony of the discussion and get into the good graces of his hearers, now that he had delivered himself of the news and his choler.

"Sherwood, have you heard the latest definition of a Tory?" David put the question, and challenged by a glance the young fellow.

"I don't care what the definition is. These colonies belong to Great Britain, and she is ready to do the fair thing by them. If it had n't been for a few hot-heads like Samuel Adams, our difficulties would have been amicably settled."

"A Tory," continued David mischievously,

"is a thing whose head is in England and whose body is in America; its neck ought to be stretched."

"And I suppose that you would like to be a committee of one to stretch it, hey? Try it, David. Try it."

"Well, you boys can settle matters to suit yourselves," said Desire. "Lois and I must do our stint of spinning to-night."

So while the young men exercised their gifts in a spirited match of word-sparring, the sisters worked, listened, reflected, until Lois, tired of the confinement, ran out in the twilight for a breath of fresh air.

"Have you heard the news about the Defence?" exclaimed the child, as she came hastening into the house.

The Defence was the new brig which the General Assembly had ordered to be constructed in January, 1776, Benjamin Huntington, of Norwich, and Captain Seth Harding being the commissioners to look after the matter. She had a keel of eighty feet, a beam of twenty-seven, a depth of hold of twelve, her burden being two hundred and sixty tons. The vessel having been finished in May, and manned, had sailed for the neighborhood of Boston harbor. Captain Harding was in com-

mand, and two Bartrams and Sam Smedley
were lieutenants.

" Mrs. Smedley has heard from her husband, and she says that while the brig was
cruising near the entrance of the harbor, they
had a fight, and took two transports, both
armed. Nine men were wounded on the
Defence, but they 'll all get well, and I don't
know how many soldiers were taken prisoners;
and the very day after this fight, the Defence
caught another transport with a lot of redcoats, and they 're all prisoners, too. Is n't
it glorious?"

Sherwood Spalding slipped quietly away to
learn if the story was true, while the Hardy
family joined in fresh jubilations.

CHAPTER VIII

ONE LIFE TO GIVE FOR MY COUNTRY

MR. DUANE HARDY LIVINGSTONE assumed an unenviable position. His family were ardent patriots, but the impression went abroad that the young man was either on the fence, or an out and out Tory.

Tryon was now attending to military affairs, and the subtlety, vindictiveness, and downright cruelty which had won him the name given by the Cherokees were forcibly illustrated.

The Great Wolf of North Carolina turned his eyes on Connecticut. The war game which he was playing in New York not only required some diversion, but Connecticut seemed to him in need of chastisement. She had given a helping hand to New York patriots on numerous occasions, and she was doing more to harass the British and prolong the struggle than any other colony, with one exception. In the affluence of her support and encouragement, she had sent a great portion of her sons into other States, so that her own shores and towns were meagrely equipped for defense, while the amount of supplies which she had furnished was almost beyond credit.

"I hate those Connecticut Yankees!" observed General Tryon one day, in a frank talk with Duane Livingstone. "I'll teach them a lesson that they'll not soon forget."

The young man moved nervously and held his peace.

"They're the meanest, slyest lot of rebels in all the provinces. And they are so sleek and cunning in their pious talk about rights and freedom that I am aching for a chance to flay them."

Still the general's auditor made no reply.

"It seems to me, Livingstone, that it's time for you to be doing something for your king and country. You're a little too much on the fence, my boy. Come, join my staff and bravely show your colors."

"Well, general, you'd hardly expect me to look with favor upon any incursions into Connecticut, would you? All my mother's family are Yankees, and I have hosts of friends among the gentry of the colony."

"Gentry be damned!" exclaimed Tryon hotly. "They're a blasted horde of unrepentant renegades."

"Did n't you enjoy their hospitality more than once? Have n't you met several of our Fairfield people and found them among the most genial and refined in the colonies?"

"Man, what do I care about their being genial or hospitable? They 're in arms against their lawful sovereign, and they ought to be humbled and whipped into subjection. I 've been a-watching 'em many a month. Think of the bold miscreants coming down here and smashing Rivington's presses and carrying things with such a high hand in this city! And there is n't a move made in all this section on the part of the rebels that the Connecticut men are not in the forefront of it. They tell me that almost half of Washington's army comes from the cursed colony."

It was not long after this outburst in the presence of Duane Livingstone that a warning word was passed all along the shore towns. It reached the ears of the governor, who, in his generosity and eagerness to help Washington, had well-nigh stripped Connecticut of her troops. So there was renewed activity in every village, the train-bands multiplied, and the Green once more became a scene of incessant military drill.

In Fairfield a coast guard was voted and set nightly in the following manner: Four to patrol from Saugatuck River to Cable's Mill, four to patrol from said Mill to Sasco River, four from Sasco River to Mill River, four from Mill River to Pine Creek, six to patrol from Pine Creek to Ash Creek, so called, and in the town streets, and four at Strathfield. They were to be paid three shillings for their services. It gave the people a slight sense of security, and enabled many a family to sleep at least half the night.

The times were hard, indeed. Smallpox raged in the neighborhood, so that pesthouses had been erected and filled with victims of the contagion. Then the poor, anxious citizens that escaped the pest were subjected to inoculation and forced to retire from the village, living their allotted period in isolation, Thaddeus Burr among them, for no distinctions were made in these matters. In addition to decimated ranks and prevailing disease, there was the incessant strain of providing the necessaries of life for the inhabitants of the town and the soldiers doing service abroad. The taxes were heavy, the currency poor. Luxuries had been given over, and the necessaries often followed. To

cap the climax of distress, this message concerning the fell purpose of General Tryon
was widely circulated.

General Washington had been in great
need of accurate information all these months
in regard to the movements of the British,
but the Secret Service was a branch of patriotic sacrifice that did not appeal to many men.
It was not so much the perils connected with
it that held volunteers aloof, as an indefinable
sense of disgrace.

Connecticut was foremost in this order of
merit and achievement. Nathan Hale had
been in Fairfield on various occasions, so
that he was known to several of the citizens.
Only a few days after the Declaration of
Independence, Desire met him at Colonel Silliman's. A little later, he was engaged in his
memorable services on Long Island. And
then one day came the story of his tragic
end.

It was late September, in the twilight of the
22d, that Duane Livingstone galloped up to
the Hardy homestead and shouted for Minto
to come and take his horse. David, Desire,
and Lois ran hastily into the dooryard when
they heard his voice, for they were sure that
he brought news. Every traveler these days

was a newsbearer, and the stay-at-homes took possession of him the instant that he appeared.

" What is it, Duane? " called out David. " No bad news, I hope."

" The royal army holds New York; the Continental forces have withdrawn; General Tryon had an enthusiastic reception when he returned to his headquarters; and last night a good part of the city was burned to ashes."

" What did you say? " cried Desire. " You don't mean that all the city is destroyed. Where is Aunt Esther? Did your house burn? " and the voice of Desire betrayed her agitation.

" Yes, the old mansion is gone. We have another house into which we can move, but the family thought it best to leave the city until things are more quiet than at present; and what place shall we fly to if not Fairfield?"

" Yes, come and welcome. There is room for you all," said David, with genuine heartiness.

" Oh, it's mother and the servants that we feel more particular about. The rest of us can take care of ourselves. We'll be here, there, everywhere, — only it's pleasant, you know, to establish headquarters and feel that,

when other resources fail, there is one place
to fall back on."

They were now walking into the house and
paying Duane those slight attentions which
a weary traveler loves. But while the preparations for supper went on, the conversation
continued without break.

"How did the city get on fire?" asked
Lois.

Duane hesitated before making a reply.

"Well, Tryon and the loyalists say that it
was set on fire by the rebels."

"Duane," interrupted David, "don't talk
about rebels to us."

"Oh, well, no offense intended," the cousin answered. "I don't believe the report.
I think it was accident that started the fire.
And then we had no conveniences to stop it
when once it had made headway. Why,
everything was out of order,— buckets, ladders, and the whole paraphernalia of the fire
companies. We could do nothing with the
flames. They seemed bound to eat up the
whole town."

"Probably Tryon himself set the city on
fire. Like Nero, he wished to see a great
conflagration, and then it was easy enough to
lay it to the slaves, or the Whigs, or the cut-

throats that are always hanging around in times of trouble."

" Now, David, you 've no right to say such a thing. It 's absurd and unjust."

" Is there much suffering ? " inquired Desire, whose cheeks were flushed with the glow of excitement.

" Not as much as there will be later, you know. The weather has been fine ; the suffering will come after the frost and the storms begin their work. But it was pitiful to see the awful destruction of property, and hear the cries of the woe-begone women and children."

" Oh, war is a terrible thing ! " exclaimed Desire. " The horror of it deepens every day."

" You 'd think so, if you had seen what I saw this morning," said Duane, with quivering lip and whitened face.

" What was it, Duane ? Tell us about it."

It was Lois speaking, with the intense, morbid curiosity of childhood.

The cousin had now seated himself at the supper-table, and the sisters were doing all in their power to make him comfortable, even Chloe flying around with unusual swiftness in her zeal and concern.

"I think you know Captain Nathan Hale, don't you?" Duane spoke with measured tone, like one striving to repress the emotion that threatened to overpower him.

"Yes, he was here only a few weeks ago to see Colonel Silliman. We've met him half a dozen times in the past few years. A splendid fellow he is, too, a clear-headed, pure-hearted, high-spirited patriot. Why, when he left his school and went into the service, he gathered all his pupils together, and talked with them about the necessity of standing up for the defense of their liberties; then he prayed like a very saint, I've been told, and having said good-by, threw himself, heart and soul, into the fight."

It was Desire that spoke. Duane lifted a hand to his brow and wiped away several drops of sweat that had appeared. Doubtless his fast ride had heated him overmuch, or was it the sign of anguish?

"Captain Hale was a spy."

Again Duane struggled to master himself. There was a stillness like death in the room. Desire, David, Lois, Chloe, and Minto stood motionless in their places, watchful of every change in his expression, alert to catch each word of the narrative.

" They made him a prisoner, two or three days ago. He had compromising papers upon him, and confessed that he was a spy."

Desire laid hold of the table to balance herself, for a kind of faintness began to creep through her limbs, while every bit of color left her lips and cheeks.

" What did they do with him ? " cried Lois, with shrill, pathetic voice.

There was another pause, long and solemn.

" They hanged him this morning," said Duane huskily.

As he uttered the words, Desire swayed over against the table, then slipped unconscious to the floor. In the excitement, both the young men forgot their own emotion. It was an unheard-of thing for Desire to faint. Chloe wrung her hands, screaming with terror, "Oh, the poor chile is dead! " Minto was paralyzed at the sight, and stirred not a muscle. Duane bade him bring water, while David bent over his sister, lifted her from the floor, put her upon the kitchen settle, and began to chafe her hands. She came to herself in a moment, but there was an expression of tense pain, a look of horror, that remained.

" No," said Duane, when further questioned, " they did n't give him any trial. He

was n't even allowed to see a minister. I
was told that they destroyed the very letters
which he had written to his mother and sister." Again the beads of sweat appeared
upon the face of the narrator. " It was by
the merest chance that I was present at his
death. I was on my way to see a man about
some private business."

" Did n't the redcoats let him say anything
or send any messages to his friends ? " This
was David's inquiry.

" He said," responded the newsbearer, ' I
only regret that I have but one life to give
for my country.' "

The sentiment came like a life elixir to
Desire. The flush returned to her face and
the sparkle to her eye.

" It was a noble sacrifice," she said.
" Men will honor him for it ; his name shall
long be remembered. I glory in such consecration and faithfulness. Would to God ten
thousand young men in the American colonies stood ready to imitate his example, if
needful ! "

" Perhaps there are many that do," quietly
observed David.

The family had now recovered from the
first shock of this startling tragedy, and they

were gathered before the great fire on the kitchen hearth, engaged in earnest talk, which lasted long into the night.

Two or three days passed, and the Hardy home was filled with the New York kindred.

Meanwhile, Desire grew serious and thoughtful, a change noted by all her friends, probably the result of war, anxiety, and hard work.

But if this woman patriot felt the strain of life, and appeared careworn and aged, none the less did changes mark the common experience of the people in the colony. Every piece of pewter in Connecticut was run into bullets. They were trying to make salt down at Horseneck. The old copper mines at Simsbury had been transformed into a prison. Tories from one and another colony, Benjamin Franklin's son, the royal governor of New Jersey, among them, were sent for safe keeping into loyal Connecticut. Home manufacture of every description multiplied. Long Island was subject to frequent maraudings, and finally the people of Fairfield frowned upon the sale of stuff taken in such case from their neighbors across the Sound. The Defence with a small fleet of vessels, little and big, did lively work upon the shipping of Great Britain that ventured within reach.

The towns held meeting after meeting in order to devise fresh means of enlistment or enlargement for the army, voting to pay the soldiers from out the town treasury, take care of their families, and do a generous part in clothing everybody concerned. Through all the months of these ceaseless activities, there ran an undercurrent of fearful expectancy, the eye of General Tryon being still fixed upon Connecticut.

The Livingstones had returned to New York, and Duane was a bird of passage plying back and forth between city and country.

His was an anomalous case. He seemed to continue friendly with both parties in the conflict, although not especially at home with either. He was not committed to the royalists, yet he was seen among them as "a hail fellow well met." He went now and again on some private business into the Continental army. It was known that at least on two occasions in the second winter of the conflict, he had had interviews with General Washington.

It was said by several acquaintances that Duane manifested a remarkable zeal for trade, and that the reason why he refused to commit himself might be found in the fact that he was making money. The standing

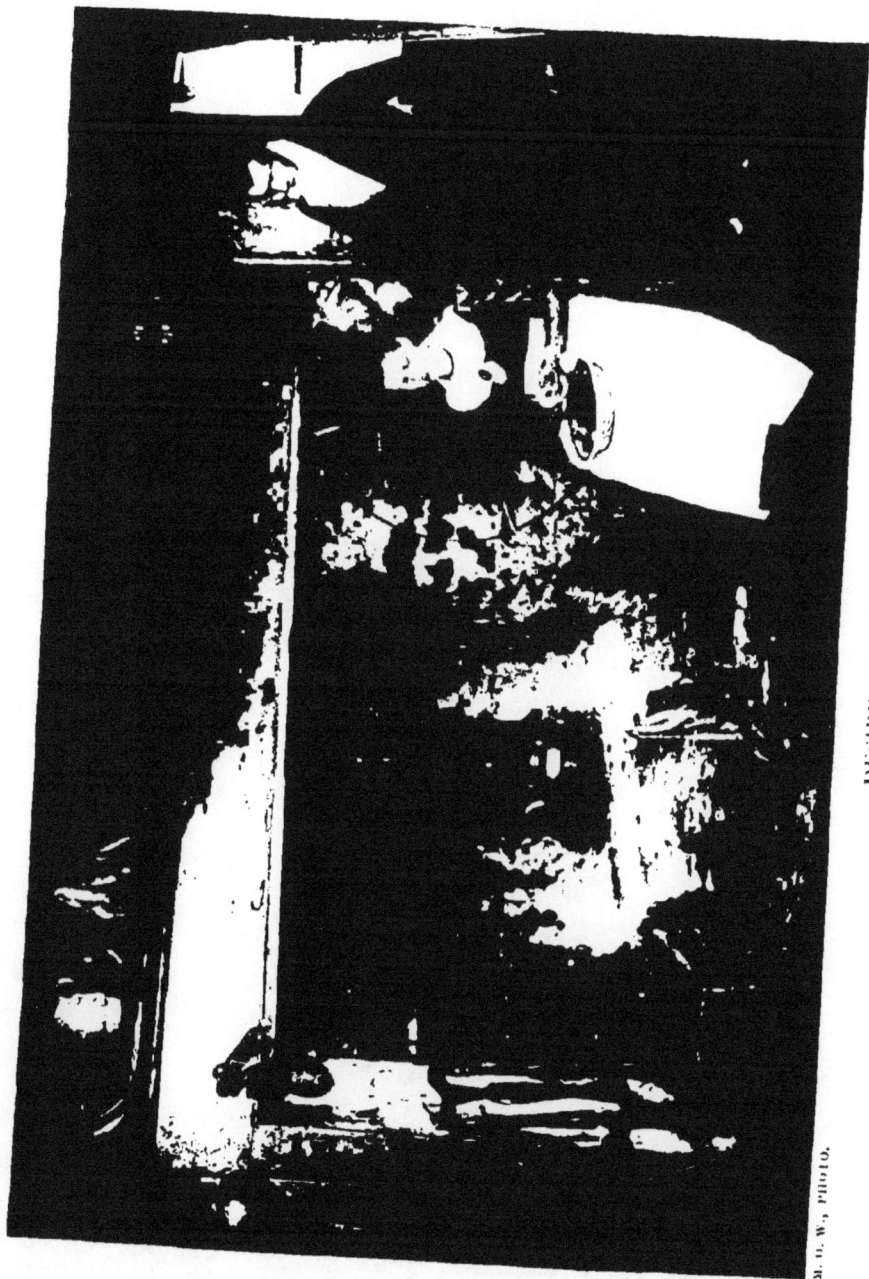

DESIRE AND DUANE

R. B. W., Photo.

and patriotism of his family kept him in touch with the Americans, while his old-time friendship with Tryon enabled him to move freely among the royalists.

Desire was the only person beyond his immediate family that placed absolute confidence in the young man. Duane was known as a fellow of mettle, so that his peculiar position did not subject him to the accusation of cowardice. He had so much native *bonhomie* and good humor in his make-up that it was possible for him to steer a safe course through the political breakers which encompassed him, if anybody could do such a feat. Nevertheless, there were not a few people among the Americans and the British that looked with suspicion or disapproval upon him.

"I suppose that I must keep my own counsel and hold my peace," observed Duane to his Cousin Desire.

It was on the 24th of April, in the year 1777. The two were standing under the trees back of the Hardy cottage. No one observed them but old Chloe, and this discreet soul was as close-mouthed as one could wish. A few minutes later, when the shades of evening thickened, Desire was alone.

"David," said the girl, as she entered the
house in search of her brother, "I want you
to ride with me to Colonel Gould's and General Silliman's."

In the December session of the General
Assembly, 1776, the militia of Connecticut
had been divided into six brigades, David
Wooster and Jabez Huntington being made
major-generals, and Colonel Silliman one of
the six brigadier-generals. To the latter was
given the special task of looking after the
shore towns and protecting them against any
incursions of the enemy.

"David, you are to give this slip of paper
to Colonel Gould while I am talking to Mrs.
Gould and the children."

The brother and sister were on the horse,
Desire riding behind upon the pillion. David
assented.

"And this other scrap you are to hand
to General Silliman. I shall enjoy a little
chat with his wife, and perhaps we may leave
you in the room together. You are to say
that he may depend upon it."

In both cases the directions given by Desire were followed, and within two hours the
young people were home again.

That night the coast guard paced a watch

of tireless vigilance, but nothing out of the
usual order occurred.   The Sound was almost
devoid of sails when the morning dawned.
Peace seemed to brood in the calm waters
and the welcome sunshine.   But there were
many anxious eyes gazing in the direction
of New York, miles and miles up and down
the shores.

It was early in the afternoon that a fleet
of twenty-six British vessels was observed
making a proud way east.   David had spent
the morning patrolling the shore as far down
as Norwalk, and he it was who first discovered the approach of the foe.   The instant
that the fleet hove in sight, and he was able
to note the number of vessels, David wheeled
about and made for General Silliman's headquarters, ten miles distant.   Tryon might
strike Norwalk, Fairfield, or New Haven, or
he might lay waste all these shore towns.
They were not only exposed to the enemy,
but they were helpless and at his mercy.
The best that could be done was to arouse
the country and face the hostile force with
such opposition and embarrassment as the
militia were able to give, trusting the issue
with God.

CHAPTER IX

To the surprise of the coast guard and the few straggling militia-men on the lookout, the enemy made for Compo Beach, on the eastern side of the Saugatuck River, not far from its mouth. Could it be that they had chosen this point as a favorable starting-place for some widespread work of devastation ?

There were some two thousand redcoats, thoroughly equipped for their nefarious mission. They landed a little before sunset, formed in marching order, and pushed six or seven miles back into the country before they halted.

Months earlier, David Hardy had yielded to the martial spirit of Desire and his own patriotic instincts, and enlisted in the militia. He was not able to leave Connecticut and wage war in neighboring colonies, as many of his friends and neighbors were doing. (In 1775, the Department of the North had twenty-eight hundred men in the field, and

twenty-five hundred of them were Connecticut troops ; and when Washington lingered
in the neighborhood of New York, more
than half his army of seventeen thousand
men came from David's native colony.) Yet
he was glad to bear arms in behalf of coast
defense, although the profession which he
had chosen was one of peace, and a minister
with a musket in the ranks was an exception, not the rule. Washington had offered
to make David Hardy a chaplain, as he did
the poet Joel Barlow, David's friend, at a
later period in the war; but it seemed best
for him to stay at home and render his service in other forms.

He was not cut out for a soldier. David
was brave and strong, he was imbued with
the most exalted sentiments of patriotism;
but he was absent-minded and given to absorbing meditation. On more than one occasion he had tried the soul of Desire almost
beyond endurance. With the best purposes,
and moved by a genuine enthusiasm for liberty and self-government, he might be suddenly diverted to some abstruse problem in
philosophy or theology, and for the time
become utterly oblivious to an imperative
duty. He was not born for action so much

as for study and contemplation. And yet one could not find a more companionable fellow so long as he was jogged into consciousness of his surroundings and the task set him to achieve.

"I'm always afraid that David will get to wrestling with free-will, or divine sovereignty, or some other awful question, and forget to keep his eyes open, or drop his musket, or let slip some great opportunity," observed Desire on several occasions. This was a congenital defect, and during childhood it had occasioned many a chastisement. There was a period, when at college, that his friends hoped this peculiarity might be eradicated, but since his study with Mr. Eliot and years of independence on the farm, the habit had asserted itself with old-time force. When Desire wished to make sure that an errand was done, or a service rendered according to orders, she either accompanied her brother, or devised some extraordinary means of reminder.

"Now, David, keep clear of theology and Hebrew roots. Do, please, get them out of your mind. You must hold yourself screwed up to the fighting-point so long as the redcoats harass our shores."

Desire spoke with a tremor in her voice.

She was fearful lest he might become involved in trouble or fail to obey orders. He had notified General Silliman concerning the approach of the foe, and he was now going back among the hills to summon the militia and arouse the people.

All night long he ranged the country, galloping from farm to farm and village to village, sending on the words of warning or command, taking his full part in gathering the train-bands for the coming fray, carrying his message to General Wooster, and reaching at last New Haven and General Benedict Arnold.

When the morning dawned, western Connecticut was alarmed, and hundreds of the "Minute-men" were moving toward Danbury.

It was a night of anxiety and widespread alarm. But toward the sunrising, Desire, who had been active through the dark in attending to a score of trivial errands, ordered out Minto and the old horse, and hastened after General Silliman, to tell him that she had reason for thinking Danbury was to be the first objective point; and as this seemed probable because of the large amount of military stores gathered there, the word was given to make that neighborhood a rendezvous for the militia.

It rained in the afternoon, so that General Silliman was not able to marshal his troops with rapidity, and when evening came, Tryon and his forces had entered Danbury. The destruction of the three thousand barrels of pork, sixteen hundred tents, a thousand barrels of flour, two thousand bushels of grain (more or less), and numerous other articles, like wine, rice, army carriages, rum, did not take a long time; and as that was the ostensible object of the foray, it was natural to expect that the enemy would withdraw. But Tryon had something else in mind. For months, he had harbored a grudge against the patriotic citizens of Connecticut. No small part of the harassment formerly inflicted upon him was owing to the assistance given Washington and the rebels by Governor Trumbull and his militia. Here came the first chance to deal a rough and cruel blow.

When David reached the outskirts of Danbury, the noise of reveling was borne broadcast on the night air.

"It was hideous," he explained to Desire on Sunday morning. His sister had crossed the country with Minto on the old farm horse, and found David in his soldier gear, mud-bespattered and weather-stained like some veteran in the service. They were following the British, who had left Danbury and made toward Ridgefield.

"I knew Tryon would never rest satisfied with the destruction of military stores. For months, he has been intent on burning the shore towns. And no sooner did he finish the supplies than his drunken crew began to insult the women, abuse the children, and breathe out threatenings against the village. I never heard such stories of goings-on before. And toward morning the wretches began to fire the houses and stores."

The brother and sister were standing on one of the hills to the west of the place. The signs and sounds of war came to them from every side.

"But, David," interrupted Desire, "you will have to go on with the militia, won't you?"

"Yes, yes, we're going in pursuit of them. But, Desire, I've been a-thinking this morning how to reconcile God's sovereignty over these brutes with their free-will acts. It never struck me with greater force than to-day. I" —

"Oh, David, don't get to thinking about it at all. You must go ahead and fight the miscreants. It makes my heart bleed to see it. Go, David, go in the strength of the Lord. I'm running down into Danbury, or what's left of it, to see if there is anything that I can do, and by and by Minto and I will ride home."

As Desire spoke, she sought to brush off some of the dirt from the clothes of her brother, then, giving him a hearty kiss and a " God bless you," sent him forward with scores of scattered men, who hurried without regard to order in the direction of the retreating enemy.

Desire reached home late in the evening, a tragic figure. She had stayed in Danbury long enough to mark the horrors of such a scourge as had swept over the village. Meeting some acquaintances made homeless on that day, she persuaded them to go with her and accept a temporary shelter. Sympathizing with them in their misery, she sought by every encouraging word to sustain their drooping spirits ; but it was hard work, and the stern realities of war pressed upon them.

It was evening when Desire and her companions reached Fairfield, the evening of the blackest day in her remembrance. For well-nigh all the male inhabitants had gone in pursuit of Tryon and his horde, so that the place was absolutely without defense; and should the invaders swoop down suddenly upon it, there was nothing to do but fold one's hands and gaze upon whatever work of ruin they might choose to do.

Few people in that part of the land laid their heads on a pillow Sunday night, for the next move was uncertain, and it was felt that however brave and ready the Connecticut militia might be, they did not have the numbers or the equipment to cope successfully with the much larger forces of the enemy.

It was a night of extraordinary strain for Desire. She felt that she ought to be with David, and yet duty seemed to indicate that her place was at home. How she longed for news! What wild fears tortured her!

"I'm sure they must have done hard fighting this afternoon." Desire was talking with Lois and Chloe. "I heard the roar of musketry and cannon before we left Danbury. Oh, will the day never come?" And then she turned to the spinning-wheel, so that her mind might be diverted.

At midnight, a messenger came into town saying that there had been a battle at Ridgefield. Tryon was reported to have changed his course of retreat, made for this village built on ridges overlooking the Sound, and there turned upon the militia.

Toward morning, David appeared. He had been dispatched on business to Holland Hill, and General Silliman gave him permission to stop a few moments in Fairfield and describe the condition of affairs.

"Oh, tell us, David, all about the fight. Did you kill anybody?"

It was Lois that made the inquiry, with both hope and fear in her voice. It seemed an awful thing to shoot a person, even if he was an enemy of one's country; then again she reasoned that every wretch who ravaged the coast, preying upon the colonists, ought to be shot dead in his tracks. The child was tossed to and fro between conflicting emotions.

"Yes, Lois," replied the brother, who might now be aptly termed a cross between a divinity student and a soldier, "I killed my man."

David and his hearers shuddered. It was not the kind of answer anticipated. Desire had no doubt respecting his ability to carry messages and attend to various details of preparation and management. She had even

dared hope that he might hit two or three
redcoats in the legs or arms, so that they
would be unfit for fighting. David was a
capital shot. But she had not dreamed of
his taking human life. It did not look well
for a minister of the gospel of peace to kill
a man. Was not David the same as a minister? He had read and studied several years
with Mr. Eliot. When the war ended and
affairs settled down to normal conditions, he
would take a church.

"Why, David Hardy!" exclaimed the
startled child.

"The Lo'd hab mercy on us. You's sure,
Massa David?" And Chloe gazed awe-
stricken upon him.

David was a distressing object to behold.
His clothes were not only soiled and disar-
ranged, but were torn and blood-stained. He
had lost the wig which he usually wore — one
of Duane's handsome extravagances, — and
his military hat. The young man had black
circles around his sunken eyes, his face being
unshaven and drawn with deep lines of pain.
He was well-nigh fagged out, having taken no
sleep for three nights, and half starved, since
a scarcity of provisions prevailed, and there
had been scant time to search for food.

"I could n't help it," said David, with hollow voice and deprecating manner. "Likely as not, the fellow's face will haunt me to the day of my death." As he spoke, David unconsciously put his hand over his eyes, as if he wished to shut out some hideous vision that persisted in rising before him.

".You were doing your duty, were n't you, David?" Love and trust were in the words which Desire uttered.

"Yes, yes. If I had n't killed him, he'd have killed me."

There was an instant revulsion of feeling. Any pity or regret that might have been detected a moment before disappeared. There was a sudden flaming of passion in the faces of his hearers. Desire flung her arms about her brother and clung to him, as she gave way to her emotion. Lois sobbed hysterically, crying, "I wish you'd killed them all, the devils!"

"Bless de Lo'd! you's safe an' soun', chile. Bless de Lo'd, bless de Lo'd!" And Chloe wiped her eyes, clapping her hands in joy and thanksgiving. "Come, honey, you's hungry. Sit right down and old mammy'll feed ye."

Breaking the thread of conversation, Chloe pushed David into a chair before the kitchen table, and set before him a very feast of good things.

It was only a few moments that he stayed, long enough to satisfy the cravings of hunger and give a brief account of the state of things in Ridgefield; then he was off for the scene of conflict.

It was late the following afternoon that the sisters had gone to the house of Mrs. Gould, to inquire if further report had come. This lady with her children was waiting anxiously for the return of some soldier or messenger who might ease their minds and gladden them with good news.

" David saw us a few moments last night," said Desire. " He brought a message from General Silliman. Oh, Mrs. Gould, war is horrible. When will it be over ! "

" There was a man tried to shoot David," interrupted Lois, " and David killed him."

" Did he? did he ? " The children were all talking at once in their excitement.

But what is that down the street, printed against the evening horizon ? A cavalcade of soldiers, surely. And some one leads the middle horse, and the rider seems strangely stiff and unresponsive. Is it a wounded man that they have set bolt upright, and are his comrades

riding close by his side in order that they
may aid or support him? His sword dangles
carelessly in its place, and the crimson sash is
bound in orderly way across the breast. He
has returned from the fight, and he looks
neither to the right nor left. It was love that
first distinguished the martial figure.

"My husband, my husband!" cried Mrs.
Gould. But as the little company approached,
it grew evident that not all was right. The
watchful spouse observed no lifting of the
hand in salutation. A rigid posture and a
blindness to surroundings foretold some dire
calamity.

The friends veiled their faces in the presence of awful tragedy. Colonel Gould had
given his life for the love of country. This
last march from the hills over west to the
stately home of his illustrious ancestors had
been a dead march. Stark and cold, astride
the horse gayly caparisoned, this noble gentleman and grand patriot, having fought his
fight and finished his course, left to family
and successors the inspiration of an honored,
lofty character, and the treasures of many
good works well done.

It was late the next day before David
returned, grimy and aged with war.

"We did the best we could," said the young soldier. "We drove them to their boats. If the country had n't risen in arms, they 'd have swept over us like a tornado, and destroyed everything they could lay their hands on. I 'm thinking they did n't find it the easy task that they expected. And we 'll make it hotter for them another time."

"You had a real battle, did you, David, and men were wounded or dead in the streets and fields?" Lois was eagerly watching every change of expression in her brother's face.

"Yes, child, but the noise and confusion was so great, and there was such a lack of discipline among our troops, that I found it hard to keep track of the fight. The regulars had all the advantage, and they moved like a piece of clockwork, although the amount of rum they drank at Danbury was enough to paralyze a host of common men. General Wooster fell, you know. I think a good many of our men were dazed. It was the first time they had ever seen war in earnest, and it was difficult to hold them together and make them obey orders. I heard General Wooster try to rally them, shouting, 'Come on, my boys, never mind such random shots.'

It was while he was in the van, urging the troops forward, that he was wounded, and they say he will die.   And there was Colonel Gould in the thickest of the fight rallying his men, and he fell " —

" Yes," cried Lois, " we saw them when they brought his body home on his horse; and poor Mrs. Gould is heartbroken, and the children wailed so you could hear them down the street."

" God pity them ! " said David fervently.

" What did Colonel Dimon do ? " inquired Desire.

He had seen lively service, having been on Montgomery's staff in the expedition to Canada in 1775.

" Oh, he had command of the barricades in Ridgefield, and fought like a tiger.   He's a great soldier.   He chased the redcoats to Compo, and picked off many a straggler. And General Arnold was a hero.   But I never saw a man go hither and thither like General Silliman.   He seemed to keep the whole thing in mind all the time.   He must be half dead for want of sleep and rest."

" They 've gone over to Long Island, have they ? " inquired Desire.

" Yes, I think the fight is over, although

they may try it again. We must be ready for them, however, but in my opinion they 'll go back to New York."

" If they don't ? " Desire looked eagerly at David.

" General Silliman thinks the next place to suffer will be Fairfield. But we 're going to ask the governor for soldiers to help us. You see Governor Trumbull is such an obliging man that he sends all our troops to Washington, and so leaves us almost unprotected. That 's what they 're all saying about him. It seems to me that Connecticut is doing more than her share of the work. I don't complain. I 'm glad to have her do all in her power, but it is n't right to hand us over to the tender mercies of Billy the Butcher ! "

" Good name for old Tryon, is n't it ? " exclaimed Lois. " He was in his element when handling pork at Danbury, was n't he ? — Billy the Butcher ! "

" It was the Sons of Liberty in New York that gave him the name," answered David. " Does n't it fit him to a *t?* The Sons of Liberty have made it lively for Tryon ever since he came north. I was talking with Mr. Jonathan Sturges, secretary for the order

in Connecticut, you know ; he says, we owe
this secret organization a great debt of gratitude for their splendid services.   Colonel
Lamb, who was wounded at Compo, is one of
their most active members.   They're going
to bring him to Fairfield for some of you girls
to nurse.   It's only a few days ago that he
sent his wife and family away from Stratford
back into the hills of Litchfield " —

"Well, David," interrupted Lois, " I'd be
a Son of Liberty if I was a man, and I've no
doubt Colonel Lamb and the New York
patriots are doing their best, but I'm proud
of Connecticut.   It's the greatest colony in
the world," she continued, in her childish
enthusiasm.   "How I would like to be governor some day !"

"You'll have to rest satisfied with being
a governor's wife," said David, as he patted
his young sister on the head, and bent his
weather-beaten face down to kiss her.

"It must have been an awful sight, as you
followed along the path of the enemy's retreat," observed Desire.

"It was, it was," answered her brother.
" Broken fences, burning buildings, castaway
garments, patches of blood, here and there
a broken musket or some other weapon, dead

horses and demolished wagons, waste supplies, or half-stripped corpses, — it makes one heart-sick."

"But it's the price of liberty, David," the older sister continued, with solemn voice, "and in spite of these horrors, the hand of the Lord is in it."

CHAPTER X

"WELL, young man, you had a safe return from Connecticut, I see." General Tryon was speaking to Duane Livingstone, as they stood on the Battery facing each other.

"I don't know what you mean, your Excellency." An expression of surprise and annoyance crossed the speaker's countenance.

"I mean, sir, that I saw you both at Danbury and Ridgefield. If I may judge from the character of your actions, you have at last declared on which side the fence you stand; and "— with an oath —"if I do my duty, you will be placed under arrest as my prisoner this very day."

"You are evidently laboring under a misapprehension, General Tryon. I have not been absent from New York any day the past two weeks, a statement which I can prove by any number of witnesses you may desire."

"Then you must have a double," said the governor harshly.

" Well, I have a cousin in Fairfield who does bear a resemblance to me. It is possible that he was the man you saw. I have not heard from the colony since your return."

The choler of Governor Tryon abated, his voice assuming a more friendly tone.

" Well, my man, it behooves you to keep yourself in good company, or I may have something of a serious nature to say to you one of these days."

The general was still somewhat crusty, and they parted on terms not especially cordial.

General Tryon *was* mistaken. Duane Livingstone had been in New York when the stores at Danbury were destroyed ; but it was not later than two hours after this interview that the young man succeeded in leaving the city and galloping away toward Fairfield.

" People seem to be a good deal excited along the shore," said Duane.

It was early in May, nature all alive with the impulse of spring, and the day fragrant with the first apple blossoms.

" Had you seen what we saw, it would n't surprise you to find our folks restless and suspicious."

It was Desire that answered, and they

were walking under the trees in the orchard. All unconscious to herself, she was now and again reaching up to some low - hanging bough, breaking off beautiful clusters, half buds, half blossoms, weaving them into her hair, or thrusting them into her belt, or pressing them against her bosom, an act significant of sweetest, subtlest witchery.

"Desire," said the cousin, with look and tone of the most ardent lover, "you are very beautiful."

"And is that the way you flatter yourself?" She spoke in a light, provoking way. "For you know very well that everybody says you and David and I look near enough alike to be triplets."

"Desire, you 're no more like me than white is like black."

"I know it," she answered. "How deceitful looks are! What was it the Lord said to Samuel when he admired Eliab and was going to anoint him king? 'Look not on his countenance . . . for the Lord seeth not as man seeth; for man looketh on the outward appearance, but the Lord looketh on the heart.'"

"You 're a great Bible scholar, almost as wise as my mother, Desire. You ought to follow up her teaching and see what you can make of me. Heavens! how I wish this war was ended. It blocks everything. Why, I never come to Fairfield that it does n't take all the planning and manœuvring I can compass. I run such a gauntlet of sharp eyes that one might think I was the Foul Fiend himself let loose for a short vacation under the watch-care of every man, woman, and child between here and my native city."

The young man was evidently appealing to the sympathy of his hearer.

"Well, I think you run too great risks. It is n't wise or necessary for you to come so often. Something dreadful will happen. Then Aunt Esther will say that your blood is upon our heads. I know she considers it foolish for you to go back and forth every week or two."

"Now I think that's very unkind." Duane spoke with feeling. "Is n't my coming to Fairfield the only happiness that is left me these days? You know that nearly everybody in New York regards me with indifference or suspicion. Why, General Tryon himself accused me of being at Danbury and Ridgefield; said that he saw me there, and was now glad to know on which side the fence

I was. That's pleasant, is n't it ? Of course
it was David he saw. Confound this family
resemblance ! I suppose I shall hang for it
one of these days, unless the war ends soon."

"Oh, Duane, Duane, don't speak like
that !" Desire placed her hands upon his
shoulder, and looked seriously, beseechingly
into his face. " I don't like to have you run
unnecessary risks. There are enough perils
for us all without courting needless ones."

" Desire, I care nothing for perils, so long
as you give me the assurance of your love."

" Duane, this is not a time to talk about
love, unless it is love of country. Did n't I
tell you what one of our Connecticut parsons
said to the maidens in his congregation ?
' Have nothing to do with a man that will
not take up arms in defense of liberty ! '
Many a young woman has sent her lover into
the war. I believe in the greatness of our
opportunity, the grandeur of our destiny.
When I hear the patriots talk that come to
Mr. Burr's or Mr. Sturges's or General Silliman's, when I see Washington (I 've seen
him twice, you know), and Mr. Adams (he 's
stopped here several times), and Colonel Hancock, and Benjamin Franklin (he 's stayed
here overnight too), and all the brave, noble

men that visit our town, and hear them discourse with eloquence, and tell about the
deeds of courage and the wonderful sacrifices
of our men, I am all aflame with a passion
for liberty. Can I think of aught else?
Why can't I go to war and do something
worth naming for the success of our arms?"

Clad in her simple gown of homespun linen,
decked with fresh apple blossoms, her face
illumined with the glory of a real consecration to the cause of American independence,
who could withstand such enthusiasm?

There was a moment's pause.

"Have you heard from Aaron Burr lately?" Duane regarded his companion with
close scrutiny.

"Yes, I've seen him since you were here,
and I've had a letter since the attack upon
Danbury. I grow proud of him every time
I am told how he bears himself. Why
should n't we be glad that he shows such
spirit? Is n't he our cousin? — is it second
or third remove? Well, what difference does
it make? I wish there were a thousand more
like him. And he does write the gayest,
brightest letters that you ever read. General
Silliman does n't know yet that it was Aaron
Burr who saved him and his battalion from

being taken prisoners when the enemy gained
possession of New York.   All the rest of the
army had retreated, but General Silliman was
holding his post.   The redcoats had landed
between him and the other divisions, and he
was cut off from communication with the
Continentals.   Burr saw the danger, galloped
over to General Silliman, and told him to save
himself and his men, but General Silliman
said he had been ordered to hold that post
until he was commanded to withdraw.   Then
Burr galloped behind one of the hills, and
soon returned with an improvised order for
him to move on the instant, and he did.   It
was a bold, reckless thing for Aaron to do,
but he can do that kind of a thing when
other people would fail.   When General Silliman wrote to his wife from the camp four
miles below King's Bridge, I remember that
he said his way was hedged up, but the Lord
opened it.   So you see it was Aaron Burr
that the Lord used to open the way."

"Very interesting," said Duane, when Desire finished her story.   "I wish you were as
loyal to all your cousins as you are to Aaron
Burr.   He's very good in his way.   I rather
like him, but he makes love to every girl that
he meets in all his campaigning.   I hear of

it from a dozen sources. I suppose he finds it diverting and restful after such prodigious valor in the field.''

" You ought not to speak in that way, and you know it. I suppose he does admire the ladies. That's nothing against him. You do, don't you? "

The exalted look on Desire's face had given place to one of annoyance. She was ready to jest with her cousin and entertain him, but her heart was in the great struggle for freedom. Circumstances had favored Desire with a large acquaintance among the patriots of Connecticut and some of the other colonies. It was not alone that men like the Adamses and Trumbulls and Hancock and Quincy stayed long enough in town to impart their own zeal and faith to the people that they met, but it was quite as much because a notable galaxy of young heroes shed more or less of their radiance in the neighborhood, inspiring their associates to lofty sentiments and actions.

When Nathan Hale set forth on his perilous adventure as a spy, it was whispered that he came to Fairfield with a letter introducing him to the Committee of Safety, requesting them to furnish him with a whaleboat properly equipped and any other necessary help, and see that he was carried to whatever point he desired. Rumor said that the letter was written by Washington.

The young man had met Desire and David when he was teaching school at Wethersfield. When the struggle began, it was known to them that he gladly cast in his fortunes with the colonies. He left Fairfield in September, after a memorable interview with the brother and sister. His manliness, nobility, utter self-abnegation, and the frank gratitude that he was permitted to die, if need be, for his native land, made ineffaceable impression upon the young people of the Hardy family.

Then Aaron Burr had not been without his influence upon them. He was one hard to resist when once his powers were exerted on behalf of any cherished plan or interest, and he was quite as ardent and intense in his patriotism as in his love-making. The presence of such a man in a community is sufficient explanation of any extraordinary spirit.

Among the friends of Nathan Hale was a college contemporary named Benjamin Tallmadge. The two had been correspondents since college days, and Tallmadge was eager to throw himself into the conflict. He likewise was a frequent guest in town, known to David and Desire, finding in them congenial helpers in numerous schemes of patriotic service.

" Captain Tallmadge has been to see us since your last visit," continued Desire. " He grows more interesting as he gets deeper into public affairs. His accounts of the service are the most fascinating narratives I ever heard in my life. He was telling me about the tumble he got last October when General Washington removed his army up to White Plains. He was on horseback, crossing the Bronx, when Mr. Trumbull — the chaplain, you know, you 've met him at General Silliman's — sprang up behind him with such force that he and his accoutrements, with the chaplain himself, were all carried pellmell into the river. In the scrabble to reach the other side of the river, they were delayed, so that the Hessians came up and thought they had caught a prisoner or two ; but at that very moment our troops swooped down that way, and poured such a destructive fire upon the Hessian column that it wavered, and Captain Tallmadge had the chance to make for General Washington's headquarters, where he informed him about the situation of our soldiers on Chadderton's Hill, — a very narrow escape, and I don't know how many he has

had. General Washington seems to like him.
The captain's been spending the winter at
Wethersfield with his Second Regiment of
Light Dragoons, training and breaking horses
for the coming campaign."

"Well, Desire, you are well informed on
the fight. I suppose you correspond with all
the young gallants that visit you and David
so long as they stay in the army?" There
was a shading of vexation in the tone of the
inquirer.

"I suppose you think it's very bold and
unmaiden-like for me to write a letter to Aaron
Burr, or Captain Tallmadge, or Colonel Dimon. Well, Duane, I'll relieve your mind.
I let David do the writing, and I dictate. Is
that proper?" Desire looked amiably at her
cousin.

"Oh, I suppose, so long as David does
your letter-writing and puts his own name to
it, nobody can find any fault. But, Desire,
you must remember now that grandfather is
gone, and you are the woman of the homestead, that it isn't wise or safe to go against
the proprieties. Your good name is too precious, and there is no telling what advantage
might be taken of any mistake or carelessness."

Desire looked troubled. It was not pleasant to be lectured by her cousin. She felt that it was undeserved, and yet her protests were unspoken; for she feared that Duane might possibly have an inkling of certain risks which she had run in the discharge of what she esteemed her duty. There was a shadow of mystery clinging to the home of the Hardy family these days which one and another neighbor had secretly observed.

The brother and sister had manifested trivial eccentricities, and a certain freedom was given them by public opinion and sufferance. David was good, his neighbors remarked, but he was not a safe dependence. In scholarship and moral integrity, in kindness, hard work, and lofty purpose, he set a worthy pattern; but he was not always practical, and he had a way of losing himself that proved embarrassing to everybody concerned. All the time that Desire and her cousin were talking under the trees in the orchard, David had stood by the barn door, his hand grasping the horse's bridle, his head bent forward in severe and exacting thought. It was evident that some grave problem vexed him.

Minto, the old slave, was a faithful soul, but he lacked the brains to manage a farm.

So long as David directed him and stayed in his company, Minto did well; but when left to himself, there was a ludicrous failure. Chloe, to be sure, was always ready with her advice, and able to help in field or garden; still, it was poor service, and since the schoolmaster had gone, it seemed harder than ever to make ends meet.

Desire was brave and trustful all the time, schooling herself to see the bright side of things, yet it grew plainer every day that affairs must take a favorable turn, or the Hardy family would come face to face with poverty.

"Desire, Desire!" It was Lois calling in the distance, as she ran in from the street. She was bringing news, and her face betrayed pride and exultation.

"Desire, Mrs. Smedley's had a letter from her husband; he's a captain now, and he's taken I don't know how many prizes. One had three thousand barrels of provisions."

The cousins hastened toward the house, as the child shouted the good news.

"David, David!" she called, in shrill accents. "Do you hear? What are you standing there with that horse for, when I've got something exciting to tell you? Mr. Smedley is a captain, and he's taken the Snow Swift, the Anna, and the bark Lydia with ten guns, and the Grog (isn't that a good name for a ship that carries rum between here and the West Indies?). Mrs. Smedley's wild with joy."

"Glad to hear it, glad to hear it," answered David, as he dropped the bridle and ran toward the house, having been awakened from his state of absent-mindedness. "Why, there's Duane. Where did you come from, my gallant? What is the latest word from New York?"

CHAPTER XI

"I AM very anxious to obtain a true account of what is passing in New York." This was the summer of 1778, and General Washington was talking to one of his aids, the Continental army being encamped at White Plains. "I wish you could fix upon some officer at Danbury in whose discretion your correspondent would be willing to confide," continued the general. "It would be better for the correspondent to reside in New York, and mix with and put on the airs of a Tory, to cover his real character and avoid suspicion."

"I think that a satisfactory arrangement can be made, sir," was the reply of Major Tallmadge.

A few days later, the young officer was a guest at the house of Mr. Jonathan Sturges in Fairfield.

The Secret Service in war has a curious fascination for the daring soul, although it involves the spy in many personal trials. But a proud man does not like to engage in work that subjects him to the hazard of common infamy. His good name is too precious. However honorable may be one's motives and methods, a stigma often attaches to this particular form of conflict. Major Tallmadge therefore found it an exacting task to get reliable and efficient men who would take these awful risks.

At this time, there was no more convenient point alongshore for making secret incursions into Long Island, a hotbed of Tory sentiment and machination, than Fairfield. The whaleboat was a favorite means of action in these frequent and lively adventures. This popular craft was thirty feet in length or thereabouts, narrow, and made short at both ends, with arrangements for a crew of eight or more oarsmen. Well handled, it became very useful on many occasions.

When Captain Hale left for Huntington in September, 1776, on his fatal mission, it was a whaleboat that bore him across the Sound. When Captain Abraham Parsons attacked the fortified church at Brookhaven, held by a little company of rampant Tories, in August, 1777, he collected something like one hundred and fifty men in Fairfield, provided them with muskets and a brass six-pounder, and carried them over to Long Island in a sloop and six whaleboats. Major Tallmadge was pleased to avail himself of the whaleboat service repeatedly during the intermittent weeks or days that he stayed in the neighborhood of Fairfield, watching the course of events and entering into secret communications with the enemy.

"I keep one or more boats continually employed in crossing the Sound on this business," he remarked to Washington, when reporting on the success of these mysterious enterprises.

Sometimes the brilliant young officer stayed on Greenfield Hill, where the wide, unobstructed view enabled him to use his glass and resort to signals. No important blow had been given the enemy for several months, so that there seemed an especial need of such information as might open the way for some decisive movement on the part of the patriots.

Tryon continued to prophesy evil against the shore towns, observing to Livingstone that his work of chastisement had simply begun. He was biding his time, and when the hour struck, he proposed to inflict even severer blows upon the helpless, unprotected Connecticut villages. On the last Sunday of August, 1778, a great fleet passed Fairfield, — the day that Lafayette was a guest of Thaddeus Burr. In writing to a friend in Philadelphia, requesting him to send two bottles of Maredaunt's Anti-Scorbetic Drops by the first post, Mr. Burr refers to passing events.

"The latest accounts we have from Rhode Island are Friday evening last, by the Marquis De La Fayette, aid-de-camp, who arrived at my house on Sunday evening on the way to General Washington. He informed me that the determination there was to hold the ground we had got, that General Hancock had gone to Boston to make provision for marching the French troops from there to Rhode Island, that the Marquis was to set out for Boston on Friday to take the command of the troops, that it was agreed that all the French fleet which were in a condition to put to sea were immediately to return to Rhode Island, that General Sullivan had imprudently given out in general orders some reflections upon the French nation and Count D'Estaing, of which I suppose even you will hear. I am much concerned for our army and the Island and wish to hear that they

were safely off ; otherways I am afraid many
of them will be made prisoners. . . . Last
Sabbath at noon passed us a fleet of war a
hundred sail, with a fine wind, which, I think,
must arrive at Rhode Island before the French
fleet; should that be the case I fear the consequences. But God hath done great things
for us. I hope for the best. We are often
disappointed when our expectations seem well
founded."

It was this coming and going of the fleets
and the frequent appearance of men-of-war
that excited the people alongshore.

On the 2d of January, the town had voted
to approve the Articles of Confederation and
Perpetual Union agreed upon by the Continental Congress, and expressed the desire
that the Assembly of the State authorize their
delegates to ratify the same in Congress on
behalf of Connecticut.

As Fairfield was the headquarters of General Silliman, who had charge of the state
militia for the defense of the coast, as it was
the centre of what military activity existed in
that part of the country, as the large part of
the whaleboat service radiated from this port,
as the leaders of opinion, the chief conspirators in rebellion (using the language of the

HEADQUARTERS OF GENERAL SILLIMAN

Tories) held frequent conclave in town, Fairfield became the particular object of General
Tryon's venom.

The first thing to do was to spirit General Silliman away. A few renegade Tories
volunteered to make him prisoner, among
them a former employee of the general, a
man familiar with his habits and domestic
arrangements.

The Tories of the section, and, for that
matter, of the State, became intensely bitter against the patriots. The Rev. John
Sayre, rector of Trinity Church, and other
men of his parish, had refused to sign the
articles prescribed by Congress, so that strong
feelings had been excited. On one occasion,
the house of the rector had been surrounded
with more than two hundred armed men,
indignant that his sympathies went with the
British, and that the strength of his influence
was boldly given to the party of oppression.
It was the condition of his wife on that wild
day that had restrained his neighbors from
taking strong measures of rebuke. Later,
Mr. Sayre was banished to New Britain, being
allowed to return after seven months' absence,
and remain within specified limits, under conditions of territorial imprisonment.

Other Tory families in town were likewise ostracized, or subjected to various hard
ordeals. It was a matter of necessity. Numerous individuals had secretly joined the
Redding Association, a fraternity of royalists
pledged to work for the triumph of British
arms. These men were all enemies in a town
that was aglow with enthusiasm in behalf of
liberty, and they were plotting against their
neighbors and holding communications with
General Howe or General Tyron.

For months, the Church of England service
was suspended. When, on Mr. Sayre's return, a handful of people met in their comely
house of worship each Sunday morning, it
was simply to hear the Scripture lessons with
a brief homily, and join in the saying of the
Psalter and the singing of familiar hymns;
for the liturgy was omitted, since it contained
prayers for the king. These people did not
venture to mutilate their petitions by any
omission of his Majesty's name.

Every movement of a Tory citizen and his
family was watched with eagle eye, yet the
schemes and doings of the patriots were disclosed by cunning Tory neighbors. There
were times when wrath and indignation
waxed so hot against these unpopular ad-

herents of the king that life itself hung in
the balance, while tar and feathers became a
hated popular mode of punishment.

Sherwood Spalding continued his attentions
at the Hardy homestead. He was in a strait
betwixt two, his love of Desire and his love
for the royal cause. A friendly, ambitious
fellow, he was devoting a part of his time to
an attempted intimacy with David and his sister, and many other hours to secret relations
with the British oppressor.

Desire had spent pleasant hours in his
company, for he was bright, merry, ingenious, bringing the latest gossip with him,
always inventing some fresh plan of entertainment. But he was simply their friend, a
man they liked, one that contributed to their
enjoyment. Desire had told him more than
once that they must remain on this footing
of neighborly association.

As the struggle between the colonies and
the mother country went on, a change was
noted in the young man. He grew restless, moody, suspicious, observing both David
and Desire with a scrutiny that annoyed the
latter. She became convinced that he was
an active agent of the royalists, although the
evidences were scant and vague.

Yet Desire would not break with him. She parried his questions when he pried into the affairs of the patriots; she gave him now and again some home-thrust in the heat of political talk; she wormed all sorts of insinuations or warnings out of him; she so managed to lead him on, or drive him into a corner, that he was repeatedly obliged to take back his words in confusion, involving himself in telltale contradictions. It was a bold game that Sherwood Spalding was playing, and Desire was the only person that unraveled its cunning, all unknown to the young man himself; on her part it was intuition rather than evidence. The game which Desire Hardy was playing proved to be even bolder and more perilous, although she played it with marvelous wit and delicacy.

"General Silliman is a great man among us," Spalding said sneeringly, in conversation with Desire. "Some day it will be said, ' How are the mighty fallen.' "

"Has he ever hurt you?" inquired Desire, with assumed indifference.

"Well, if he has n't done me an injury, he 's abused a good many folks that are true to the king."

"He was conscientious in it, my friend,"

explained Desire, in a quiet, modest way.
" There is no better, nobler man in the State
than General Silliman, a most rare exemplar
of Christian humility."

" He 's as proud as Lucifer in his ridiculous authority, and I shall be glad to see him
taken down. Don't talk to me about his
humility."

The young man reddened with the remembrance of some fancied slight or severity on
the part of the general in command of the
local troops.

" Oh, your anticipations are altogether
groundless. I suspect, Mr. Spalding, some
little miff has engendered ill-feeling on your
part. I 'd like to know how General Silliman could be touched these days by the
enemy ; " and Desire smiled in a most provoking way.

" You think there are not enough good
subjects of the king familiar with this neighborhood to slip up to his house some night
and take him prisoner, eh ? " said Spalding,
with rancor. Then the color left his face as
he continued, in a low, constrained tone, " But
then, of course that 's impossible, for he 's always on the lookout. I suppose he has a score
of men on guard to warn him of danger."

It was Saturday evening, the last day of April, 1779, when this conversation occurred, and no sooner was Sherwood Spalding gone than Desire prepared to ride to Holland Hill. Saturday night was holy, for the Sabbath began at sunset, but war minimizes such distinctions, and gives liberties to the most strict sects.

Minto brought the horse to the door, David mounted, Desire sprang up behind, and away they sped into the shadows of the night.

General Silliman was at home, for the morrow was communion Sunday, and he was the senior deacon in the church. The holy bread had been prepared that day, and the ancient silver cups and tankards polished for the service.

"It is very kind of you, Desire. I thank you for the warning." The general had received her message, and was now revolving it in his mind. "Perhaps the coast guard ought to be increased, and it may be wise for me to keep a sharper watch over my premises. But the hour is late to-night. On the morrow, I will speak of it to the brethren. After all, your fears may be groundless."

"Sir, I believe that you are in peril. I

have reason to think that General Clinton would be pleased to have you for his prisoner." She spoke with great earnestness.

There followed two or three moments of whispered consultation, then the young people returned to the village.

It was moonlight, quiet and lovely, suggestive of peace. Yet the inmates of the Hardy homestead did not rest. They were haunted with strange visions. Desire peered into the ghostliness of the night many times; twice she called David, saying that she heard guns, that loud voices came floating down to her from the hills to the east. A few minutes before two in the morning, the sounds of a galloping horse smote their ears. David ran out upon the street to intercept the rider, then hurriedly returned to get his musket and tell his sister that the attack which was feared had been made. General Silliman was now a prisoner, and the few members of the train-band in town were called to go in pursuit.

But it availed nothing, for the deed was done, and the captors away with their prisoner, before any alarm could be given.

Desire hastened with Minto through the gloom to Holland Hill, that she might comfort the terrified household.

" We were all asleep," said Mrs. Silliman, in telling the story of his capture. " William had been sick with chills and fever all day, so that he had not lifted his head from the bed. Suddenly I heard an awful banging at the door. They were hurling rocks against it, trying to break it in. My husband awoke and sprang for his muskets, running with them to the front window. He thrust one musket through the window-pane and tried to fire it, but there was only a flash in the pan. Then there was a dash for the window by the assailants, the sash and glass were broken into fragments, and the men were in our room wrestling with Mr. Silliman. He saw that it was vain to resist them, and tried to hush their wild, discordant cries and imprecations, saying that his wife was present in bed, appealing to their instincts as gentlemen. At length, they consented to go into the adjoining room while he dressed and made his hasty preparations to go with them as their prisoner. While waiting for him, they fell upon William, and compelled him to rise in his weakness and become their prisoner. They also took what pieces of silver and small objects of interest they could find. By this time, my husband was ready, and they hastened with him and William down toward the shore."

She was a brave and trustful woman, this narrator of the incident, although her agitation was still manifest, and the horror of the hour lingered upon her.

"Then they came by boat, and they will carry General Silliman across the Sound," exclaimed Desire.

"Yes," was the reply; "I fear that our alarm was too late for any rescue. There were eight of the captors, and their haste makes me feel that they must have put off from some ship nigh the harbor, or mayhap they used a whaleboat and are bound for the Long Island shore."

With the dawn of the morning, the news of General Silliman's captivity spread broadcast.

It was an excited congregation to which the Rev. Andrew Eliot preached on that 1st day of May, 1779. The church silver, over which the general had thrown a loose piece of cloth when the enemy entered his bedroom, had been saved from their sacrilegious hands and brought down to the meeting-house for the service. Never did it seem more precious or beautiful than on that sad, solemn day.

Deacon Silliman was a prisoner, and could not
wait upon his sacred office in the sanctuary,
yet every touch of the lip to the chalice
passed from communicant to communicant
was a reminder not only of the sacrifice on
Calvary, but of the later sacrifices made in
the name of liberty and righteousness by
God-fearing men like their absent friend and
leader.

It was an incident ominous with meaning
to all the shore towns. For nearly five years,
the citizens in the southwestern part of Connecticut had looked to General Silliman for
protection. He had given himself heart and
soul to the task, preferring to take the hum-
bler rôle of a state militia-man, serving under
Governor Trumbull, than the more conspicuous position of an officer in the Continental
army.

Peculiar dangers beset his native colony.
Its wide exposure to maritime depredations
and its voluntary poverty in respect to trained
and tried soldiers (the great majority serving
in other States) proved very alluring to the
enemy. But General Silliman had done excellent service, being vigilant, energetic, work-
ful, and a good disciplinarian; winning the
esteem and confidence of his men, keeping

in close touch with every forward movement, contributing not a little to the success of various campaigns in contiguous territory.

It was felt on the day of his capture that affairs were approaching a crisis for Connecticut. The news carried sorrow and dread anticipation all through the State. A fresh appeal was speedily sent to the governor for adequate patrol both on sea and land. Every preparation for incursions of the British was made that circumstances permitted. But when all had been done, Connecticut remained at the mercy of an invader.

CHAPTER XII

It was a singular position in which Desire Hardy was placed. Had it not been that she was a young woman of remarkable force, her situation would have proved extremely embarrassing.

People made great allowances for her. She was motherless, and the innumerable restraints which maternal care imposes had been lacking since childhood. She did much as she pleased. The gentle counsels and loving confidences that bind mother and daughter together, helping to refine and shape the child life, were almost unknown to Desire.

When the grandfather left the home and his control was withdrawn, it threw this young woman back completely upon her own resources. For while David was a man of sterling integrity, good judgment, and rare worth, he was not the man to hold authority over a sister like Desire. She was the real master; he did her bidding with a cordial acquiescence and fidelity that made their home life thoroughly peaceful, if it did not result in large crops from the farm or an abounding prosperity.

It was a happy relationship which existed between the brother and his twin sister. David was never asked a second time to do any service for Desire (that is to say, in case he heard the request), for her expressed wish was enough to send him to the ends of the earth. He had such faith in her goodness, discernment, affection, that he did not question her wishes unless it was clear to him that unwittingly she misinterpreted facts.

He had observed that she made frequent use of her pen. Writing letters was not a common thing among the majority of people. It was a luxury. Postage burdened a· poor man, and there was little occasion for correspondence. "It costs four shillings to write you in Boston," said Mr. Eliot to his brother.

Nevertheless, David was the cordial ally of Desire in this extraordinary piece of extravagance, writing freely to Duane Livingstone and Aaron Burr, receiving in exchange letters brimful of news and merrymakings.

It did not surprise him that Major Tallmadge came often to the house; that whenever he stopped in Fairfield, a part of the brilliant officer's time was devoted to Desire and himself. They discovered in him a most genial humor; he came freighted with all the patriotic ardor and hopefulness of the day. It was delightful. So when Tallmadge asked the privilege of writing to him with an inclosure for his sister, David was pleased.

Sometimes, the major would simply say, " Tell your sister to read such and such a verse in Scripture," or " Tell Miss Desire that it is late for the arbutus," or " Tell her it is sweet to die for one's country." Such sentences seemed very matter of fact; there was a quaintness and humor about these messages that amused David. At other times, the letter would consist of an inclosure for Desire, David straitly passing it over to his sister. But the great part of the correspondence on Major Tallmadge's part was directly with David himself, generally concluding with a request to hand the letter to Miss Desire, that she might also read its contents.

After General Silliman was captured, Sherwood Spalding left town. A week later, David and Desire received from him a request for news. He was staying over at Judge Jones's, on Long Island.

There had never been a thought of impropriety in the mind of either brother or sister concerning this writing. The history of the letters would be interesting, if it was recalled. Many were the adventures connected with their going and coming. Some of the missives were carried by public post. Others came by the hands of private messengers. A few reached their destination by unnoted agents. Possibly an Indian was the intermediary, for there were four descendants of the savage tribes left in Fairfield at the period of the Revolution, or some witch ally may have served as mail carrier, according to the fancy of Lois.

One thing David observed which puzzled him. Desire always assumed care of the letters and, as he supposed, preserved them ; but one day, when a long one had come from Duane Livingstone, after the brother and sister had read its contents, David saw Desire tear it into shreds and burn it on the kitchen hearth. He pondered the matter. Letters were precious. One liked to read them to friends. If one did not read them to friends, it was pleasant to keep them and reread them on some later day.

" Do you burn all your letters ? " inquired

David, in a troubled way, as Desire hurried into the little front room where he was working away at Puritan theology.

The color forsook her cheeks, and there was the slightest tremor in her voice as she replied:

"Yes, David. If the British took the town, do you think I'd like to have them running through our little correspondence?"

"Why, I never thought of that, Desire. But you were always wiser than I. You do quite right, I am sure."

"Yes, David, quite right; although it's nobody's business what we do with our letters, and we won't talk about it, will we?"

She was bending over David, arranging his wig, which had been twisted to one side.

"It's a strange life we're living, Desire, isn't it?" He leaned back in his chair as her arm fell across his shoulder.

"David, these are strange times. I am strange to myself. I never dreamed that one could love his country as I have learned to love this our native land. David, it sometimes seems to me that I must shoulder a musket and fight for our rights. Do you think it is unmaidenly? Would it be wrong for me to play a man's part in the conflict, if that were possible? It's well enough to talk about drinking liberty tea and denying one's self imported luxuries. There is some satisfaction in spinning, weaving, sewing, and knitting so that our soldiers shall be clothed. And I'm glad to toil on the farm, if need be, and help plant and reap and do anything that will feed our men and fit them for service. But, David, I have actually thought that I would like to go to war and take my part in ending this awful conflict."

"No, Desire," exclaimed the brother, her spirit of enthusiasm quickening him, "I'm the one to go to war. I'll go to-morrow, if you say the word."

David paced the floor in his earnestness.

"Oh, that I might give myself!" Desire exclaimed. "No, David, you cannot go. We should starve. Some one must stay at home to guard the shore. And, David," — she looked into his face with sweet deprecation and whimsical dissent, — "you are not made for a soldier. You live too much in the higher regions. You get lost too often in the realms of pure spirit. It takes a good part of my time, brother, to keep you in order and hold you down to earth."

Even as she was addressing the young man, she observed that his mind began to wander.

There was a telltale, absorbed expression stealing into his face. As Desire ceased speaking, there was deep silence in the room. She gazed upon him with the kindly indulgence, the pathetic solicitude, that a mother sometimes bestows upon a dreamy, heedless child.

"What's that you say? What? What?"

David was slipping back to consciousness of the present, and getting a fresh hold upon the thread of discourse. He had been absent only a moment, but it was a graphic proof of the sane conclusion reached by his sister.

" Poor child," continued the brother, as he came into full possession of himself again ; " I fear that your training has been wasted on me. No, Desire, it looks as if I should do no one any credit. I believe I'm queer. It's an awful thing to have a witch for an ancestor, is n't it ? " David laughed skeptically, and printed a kiss on his sister's forehead.

" I suppose we're both queer, and of the two, I'm the queerer. But, David, how can we help it ? I don't see why a woman can't be a patriot and do as much for her country as a man. One's country belongs to the women as much as to the men, does n't it ? I've heard how the ladies of Philadelphia

have raised such a great sum of money for
the soldiers; how a woman in Maine ran
twenty miles to carry her husband his powder
horn which he had forgotten (she ought to
have hit him over the head with it when she
caught up with him); how Emily Geiger ate
the note she carried to Sumter when she was
taken prisoner; how Nancy Hart put on the
uniform of an officer and made the other
women dress in soldier clothes, so that the
redcoats, when they saw them, withdrew because the fort was well manned; how the
women of Groton put on men's clothes, and
defended the bridge, and took the Tory messenger prisoner, and sent him to Colonel Pres-
cott. I've heard about these and a hundred
other daring deeds of women patriots. Why
can't I do something that will count in the
struggle? David, I've a mind to borrow
some of your clothes and try my hand at
service."

Her listener was again wandering in his
mind. Something which she had said awakened old associations; he was thinking of
certain grave metaphysical questions that
had puzzled him three years ago. Perhaps
it was well that he lost the last words of his
sister, for they would have given him pain
and anxiety.

It was a real home, the abode of love and trust, where these young people lived. They attracted to them the best society in town, the wit and wisdom, the youth and gayety, the adventure and enthusiasm, of their little world. One was certain to find the brightest company at the Hardy homestead. The lawyer, the soldier, and the traveler resorted thither to tell their tale and bask in the sunshine of Desire's charms. The parson, the doctor, the school - teacher, the town clerk, the young collegian, and the old controversialist frequented the house, ostensibly to talk with David and sharpen their faculties by some lively speech upon the questions of past, present, or future.

Every patriotic soul was made welcome, and there was sure to be a second, a third, an oft-repeated coming. For it must be noted that a rare and delectable freedom prevailed in this house presided over by a young student and his fair, brilliant sister, — a freedom, in truth, that never transgressed the bounds of decorum, yet a freedom that was expansive and vitalizing.

The lively, magical patriotism of Desire drew every officer and many of the rank and file in the train-band to her charmed circle.

One might have thought the homestead was
a recruiting station, observing there such
numbers of men belonging to the soldiery;
or perhaps the headquarters of the town militia. It was a veritable centre of martial news
and movements. One was certain to meet
some comrade in arms, or learn some facts
concerning the war, whenever he dropped in
to greet the young people. Yet the visitor
never detected any lack of maidenliness in
Desire, and never left her presence without
paying homage to her subtle, gracious fascinations.

Did an officer wish to instill courage into
the soul of some country lout, he led him
within the realm of Desire's bewitchment.
It did not require many minutes for her to
inspire him with warm and manly devotion to
country.

Every wounded man transported to Fairfield was cheered and strengthened by her
tender offices. They had brought Colonel
Lamb from Compo after the raid on Danbury.
He was seriously injured while in pursuit of
the foe, and Captain Deming took him to his
own house. Here Desire waited upon him
like an angel of mercy. When Colonel
Dimon, another victim of the Danbury fight,

suffered through the summer of 1777, Desire
was the same faithful, delicate minister of
comfort. There was nothing demanded for
the sake of a sick or wounded soldier that
she hesitated to do. The men learned to
look to her and David with a trust and affection that was its own sweet reward.

Yet Desire felt that she was doing little or
nothing for liberty. Albeit her heart was
given to the great cause of civil rights and
national independence. She had no heart left
to give to Sherwood Spalding, Aaron Burr,
Duane Livingstone, or any other man living,
so long as the conflict waged.

Major Tallmadge succeeded in getting the
New York correspondent that General Washington wanted. Neither the Commander-in-
chief of the American army nor his shrewd
and efficient field officer Tallmadge knew who
this secret, invaluable agent was, the correspondence being conducted in a way that made
it next to impossible for the secret to leak out.
Major Tallmadge found a person he could
trust implicitly. This person simply agreed to
be a medium of communication, and arrange
with other trusty individuals to keep him informed concerning the situation in New York.
The secret intelligence was generally com-

municated by way of Long Island. It often
came into the hands of Major Tallmadge at
Fairfield, or was forwarded to him in cipher.

One lowery night in June, a whaleboat, with
its crew of sixteen oarsmen and two closely
muffled passengers, shoved off from Black
Rock and shot into the misty gloom. Huntington was the objective point. Not half a
dozen words were spoken in crossing the
water, for the men had received their instructions. They were as familiar with tides and
winds, fogs and points of land, sunken reefs
and similar things, as with their own door-
yards.

They reached the appointed rendezvous in
good time, the two muffled figures stepped on
shore and disappeared in the darkness, while
the crew, having drawn the boat into a thick
wood that ran down close to the shore, and
having done everything to conceal their where-
abouts and make themselves comfortable for
the night, stretched out under the inverted
craft and fell asleep. They were to remain
hidden until the next night, when at two
o'clock in the morning the orders were to
have the boat in readiness to receive the
secret passengers and return to the Connecticut shore.

It was a dreary, perilous tramp through the deep wilds of the forest which the two unknown began, but they pushed eagerly forward, in order to get into hiding before the break of day. There were no words wasted between them. Occasionally, they rested a moment to make sure that they were on the right track. They seemed reasonably familiar with the course, and the slight obstacles that presented themselves were quickly surmounted.

The first gray of the morning, with the cheerful twitter and sweet melody of the birds, found them sheltered in a tiny hut of logs and bark, completely embowered amid a small growth of hemlock. Here they rested, and it was not five minutes before one of them had thrown himself down upon a fragrant bed of fresh-cut boughs and dropped asleep. The other waited until certain that all was unobserved, then stole softly forth into the dim light of the forest, walked to a piece of rock projecting from the sharp descent, bent down above a mossy bed that covered a portion of the rough surface, pressed the hand into the damp, soft lichens, and drew forth a letter. Thrusting it into the bosom, this figure hurried back to the well-hidden rustic bower, and soon there were two people wrapped in profound slumber, buried in the friendly interior of a vast forest.

No signs of human life appeared during the day. The woods resounded with the merry pipings of gay bird songsters and the busy animal creation. The bower itself now and again swayed to the jump and scuffle of some frolicsome members of brute society.

It was evening before the sleepers bestirred themselves, and even then they waited until the thick darkness brooded above them, and it was impossible to see a human form ten feet distant.

The pines and the hemlocks were moaning their unrest and forebodings when the muffled travelers stepped forth into the grim night. Silently they started to retrace their hasty path. Hour after hour they threaded a weary, toilsome, anxious way through the tangled thickets and overgrown trees. They were making steady progress, and the hope of their journey's end began to render their steps elastic and their tread more hurried.

On a sudden a hand came out of the night and seized hold of the foremost footman. There was an onset and a resistance so swift

that the second traveler fairly stumbled over
the two. No word escaped. It was a wrestling match in the dark and silence; then
through some strange witchery of hand or
spirit, the conflict was between the assailant
and the second of the assaulted party, while
the swift leader first seized had become lost
in the heavy shadows.

The fight lasted only a moment or two,
when the man who had the temerity to stop
these two travelers was flung heavily to the
ground, now at the mercy of his foe. There
was the ominous sound of gasping breath
and gurglings in the throat; the vanquished
man grew limp and nerveless; for a second
his victor peered down into the face of the
prostrate enemy; then, seeming to reconsider
or think better of his purpose, the traveler
sprang away from his unconscious victim and
plunged into the darkness.

The whaleboat was in good trim; the men
waited with sharp ears and keen eyes. It
was two o'clock, and no sign of a return;
half past two, and the first notes of the on-
coming day broke the hush of night; three
o'clock, and the eastern horizon showed pencilings of dim gray, when, hist! there was
the crackling of twigs, the hurried noise of

a swift approach : a solitary person pushed through the gloom and sprang into the boat. Every man was in his place, the oars were lifted, and at the motion of the unknown they stood out to sea; then, at the motion of the muffled figure, they rested upon their oars and strained their ears to catch any sound of man.

Full twenty minutes tardily passed, every nerve still stretched to interpret the various sounds that multiplied upon the land. At length a faint bird note, like the whippoorwill, drew from the throat of the mysterious passenger a strong, shrill response that hasted landward ; the oarsmen pulled for the shore, a form looming up in the distance ; then the belated comrade ran down to the little beach, tumbled into the waiting craft, and again they fled into waning obscurity, steering for the hospitable shores of Connecticut.

A few days later, it was reported in town that Duane Livingstone and Sherwood Spalding, both guests in the house of Judge Jones on Long Island, had come to blows over some personal matters, and Spalding had been seriously injured.

Sherwood wrote a letter to David Hardy the following month, and it befuddled him,

for it was the most curious medley of inco-
herent ravings imaginable.

" What can the fellow mean ? " said David
to his sister. 'As you value life, quit this
wicked business.'" He was reading detached
sentences and discussing them with Desire.
" Quit what business ? Does he think that I
am to be frightened out of standing up for
human rights ? " And David looked every
inch a man, as he spoke. "'I know it was
you. I recognized your walk, and dark as it
was, I saw the outlines of your features.'"
David was reading another sentence from the
mysterious letter. " Why, the fellow has
gone stark mad. If it's true that Duane
and he had a set-to, it's affected his brain."
Desire was spinning, and made no comments.
"'The best thing for you to do is to make
your peace with the king.'" He laughed
boisterously in reading the sentence. " What
do you think of that, Desire ? Make my
peace with the king ! And we know all the
time that God intends to see these colonies
free and independent States. They *are* free
and independent to-day."

David halted a moment to take breath,
then continued : "'I give you this final warning. You'll soon be without house and home,

and the clemency of your sovereign will have reached its limits.'" David stared at the paper, trying to solve the riddle.

"I think he must know something about the movements of General Clinton," finally observed Desire. "Give me the letter, and I'll see what can be made of it." But his sister did not throw any light upon the subject, and at last they consigned the mysterious epistle to the flames.

CHAPTER XIII

A FLEET SAILS UP THE SOUND

GENERAL TRYON was very busy these June days. Everything had been put into prime order, and a fleet was prepared to sail up the Sound with a good complement of well-trained troops.

The secret agent who served the patriots in New York, being thoroughly posted, had sent his warning to Washington; but the expedition which was on the eve of starting might be designed for one or another of the Connecticut towns. It was impossible to forestall the measure or extent of the intended depredations.

Word concerning the incursion had been passed all along the shore. Greenwich, Stamford, Norwalk, Fairfield, New Haven, New London, knew that something was in the air. But it was little that any of these towns could do by way of further preparation. The great portion of the male population was serving the popular cause beyond the borders of the

State. The handful of local militia trained at
every opportunity, and gathered such martial
resources as they were able to command.
Washington was over in the valley of the
Hudson with all available men, checking any
advance the enemy might attempt to the north.

Governor Trumbull had received appeal
after appeal from various ports of the State
asking help and protection, but his hands
were almost empty of resources, so he was
fain to strengthen his people with brave and
hopeful words alone. Did the foe turn the
tide of battle into Connecticut, as some prophe-
sied, the Continental army would come to the
rescue of this State, which had been so lavish
of her men and means; but for the present,
the men left to till the fields and gather in
train-bands would have to do whatever was
achieved by way of defense or resistance.

The towns alongshore were prosperous and
attractive centres of trade and activity. They
contained many pleasant homes and cultured
people.

New Haven was the seat of the second college in New England.

People living in these places came into frequent contact with the wide world, for their
ships sped to the uttermost parts of the earth,

and brought to them the fruits of every far-
away civilization.

Connecticut was famous for her numerous
sea captains, men of large experience and considerable wealth, who built their substantial
homes on some outlook over the sea and settled
down to the calm enjoyment of life's late
afternoon.

There were many scholars and men of
affairs among her citizens, descendants of an
unmixed, honorable English ancestry, the bone
and sinew of an intellectual aristocracy destined to exert controlling influence in the
great nation that was rising into being.

Fairfield in 1779 was outstripped in numbers by several neighbors, yet it had attained
fair prominence as a business town, there being
forty-eight shops and stores within its limits,
a large amount of shipping connected with its
harbor at Black Rock, and interminable legal
activity in the county court house. All western Connecticut gravitated to Fairfield as the
county seat, the centre of refined and culti-
vated society, the local source of important
movements, the headquarters of military life
in the section, the town which represented the
wealth, energy, enthusiasm, and leadership of
a vigorous and intelligent patriotism.

FAIRFIELD BEACH

One hundred and forty years had passed since Roger Ludlow fathered the settlement. Five generations of men had made the place their home and given their worth to its development. Lying contiguous to the Sound and stretching back into the adjacent hills, laid out in large squares intersected by rectangular streets, shaded by regal oaks and elms left standing when the place was cleared or planted later by industrious hands, there was an air of repose and comfort about it, a brooding spirit of intelligence, hospitality, cheerful ease, sweet content, and good taste, that won every heart and made all feel at home. There was a freedom and an amplitude to the characteristic life of the town, a high mood of conservative friendliness and rational enjoyment, almost unique. People were extremely social, and this sociability was tempered with all the refinement, the gracious courtesy, and the fine moral sensitiveness of the Puritan gentry at their best.

For many years, the men of mark in the colonies had been attracted to the aristocratic, beautiful country town. It made no pretensions to opulence or greatness. It was obscure. Yet people learned to love Fairfield, and to find in its varied landscapes, agreeable prosperity, genial citizens, and high-spirited life that which won their interest and loyalty. The Adamses, the Warrens, Otis, Paine, Quincy, Gerry, Roger Sherman, Oliver Wolcott, Benjamin Franklin, Thomas Jefferson, Lyman Hall (he studied medicine here, and married for his first wife Mary Burr), General Putnam, Silas Deane, President Burr, Lafayette, John Jay, Livingstone, and Schuyler, — well-nigh all the statesmen of the country, and many a commanding officer in the army, carried pleasant reminiscences of Fairfield with them, having shared at some time or other its generous fellowship.

The Connecticut parsons and statesmen, or poets like Barlow and Humphrey, or scholars like Johnson, Edwards, Dwight, Clap, delighted in the congenial atmosphere of the town and frequented its open homes. Newfield was awaking to the importance of its harbor, and the signs of alert enterprise appeared on the surface of its life, yet her homage to Fairfield continued unquestioned.

The Meeting-house Green was a scene of countless notable gatherings, the place for trainings, the centre for the distribution of justice, a trysting-place for friends and lovers, a spot made sacred by the tread of our grandest men, the very elect of the western world. With what veneration the people of sentiment and imagination regarded the few ancient trees that still graced the open acres in the middle of the village ! The court house stood near the centre; in front of it, and to the right across the road, was the plain, substantial meeting-house of the Prime Ancient Society, with its many windows, and its slender, graceful spire piercing the sky. Along the edges of the square, fringing the road that bounded the interior plat of green, were placed a few houses, — the home of the late Rev. Noah Hobart, the town ordinary, and that public necessity, the jail.

While there was no display or lavish expenditure in public edifice or private dwelling, there appeared to the observer many evidences of quiet wealth or generous competence. Good order, thorough workmanship, and an excellent condition of things were in constant evidence. People took pains with their property. Thrift was a word often suggested. One felt instinctively that, although war raged in the land, the spirit of industry still prevailed, and these people were doing their best to brave the situation and carry their heavy burdens.

On the night of July 3d, David was disturbed by a pebble tossed against his bedroom window. Desire heard it and responded on the instant. David quickly dressed himself, and hastened to admit the midnight visitor, Desire following him to the door. For half an hour the three held their whispered consultation, and then the visitor departed.

"David," said his sister, "why did he run such a risk in coming to us? I do not see that anything can be done, and now he must return to Huntington, and, mayhap, fall into the clutches of the enemy."

"He has done what seemed to him for the best. His judgment may be at fault, but I shall never doubt his integrity or patriotism hereafter."

There was a long silence, and then Lois crept into the room, the three sitting down in dumb consternation; for the midnight caller had come to tell them that Tryon was on the wing, and that the British were arranging to celebrate the Fourth of July (the day on which America had declared her independence) by swooping down upon the Connecticut towns and making the long-threatened raid.

There was nothing to do but watch and

wait. It was still possible that Fairfield might escape " The Firebrand." (This was the new title that Desire had given General Tryon since his descent upon Danbury.) New London was an important shore town, the depot of small war supplies. New Haven was large and flourishing, widely famed for its share in resisting the king's measures. It must be that the enemy had them in view.

The Rev. Andrew Eliot preached to an anxious congregation on Sunday, July 4th, 1779. The coast guard did not report any foe in sight, but it was known that Tryon was moving up the Sound.

Mr. Eliot spoke patriotic words to the assembled people, prayed with the fervor of an old-time prophet for the success of the American arms, and besought the mercy of God upon the distressed worshipers.

" It is awful to think that we are facing destruction and nothing can be done to avert it ! " exclaimed Desire, as she walked out of the meeting-house with Mrs. Thaddeus Burr. " Does it not appear to you that Governor Trumbull might help us in our extremity ? "

" My child, the governor has strained every nerve, for he has been the fast and sustaining friend of General Washington. Did he have the power, this coast would be lined with men-of-war for our defense; but his hands are tied, and we must not ask him to do the impossible."

Mrs. Burr spoke with an air of conviction and authority. Her husband was a member of Governor Trumbull's Council of Safety.

" If they land off our shore, what shall you do?" asked Desire.

" I shall remain in my home and try to protect it."

But this was a bold and perilous thing to do, and Desire was hoping that things would not come to that pass.

" I hear the neighbors saying that it will be better for us to go back into the hills, and Duane advises it, if worst comes to worst."

They were standing on the Green, the sky clear, the air balmy and fragrant, nature adorned with all the luxury of summer beauty. It was the beginning of wheat harvest, a season of extraordinary labor and festivity. Never in the memory of the oldest inhabitant had there been such a season of plenty.

The afternoon service was conducted under the same tense feeling. Every ear was listening for some news of the fleet; and when the people dispersed, it was to hasten down to the shore or away to the hills, in order that they might scan the open waters of the sea.

It was night when General Tryon, joined by Sir George Collier, the commodore at Huntington, sailed past Fairfield with his two men-of-war and forty-eight row-galleys, tenders, and transports.

Monday was another day of uncertainty and foreboding, and the night was spent in vigils. Then word came that New Haven was given to the flames by "The Firebrand."

Tuesday the townspeople began to pack up their valuables and such stuff as was easily transportable. The night was sleepless and feverish.

Wednesday the beach was lined with restless walkers, eyes ever turned toward the east.

It was four o'clock in the morning when the British fleet hove in sight. A single shot fired by an American cannon announced their advent. Then the fog settled down upon the scene, and there was faint hope of escape or relief.

The fort at Grover's Hill was garrisoned by twenty-three men under command of Lieutenant Jarvis, while the small band of militia under Colonel Whiting gathered on the Green and awaited the onset of the foe.

The fog lifted, and the fleet moved in toward Kenzie's Point. Tryon sent on shore copies of the following address : —

To the Inhabitants of Connecticut, — The ungenerous and wanton insurrection against the sovereignty of Great Britain, into which this colony has been deluded, by the artifice of desperate and designing men, for private purposes, might well justify in you every fear which conscious guilt could form respecting the intentions of the present armament.

Your towns, your property, and yourselves lie still within the grasp of that power whose forbearance you have ungenerously construed into fear, but whose lenity has persisted in its mild and noble efforts, even though branded with the most unworthy imputation.

The existence of a single habitation on your defenseless coast ought to be a constant reproof to your ingratitude. Can the strength of your whole province cope with the force which might at any time be poured through every district in your country? You are conscious it cannot. Why, then, will you persist in a ruinous and ill-judged resistance?

We had hoped that you would recover from

the frenzy which has distracted this unhappy country, and we believe the day to be now come when the greater part of this continent begin to blush at their delusion. You who lie so much in our power afford the most striking monument of our mercy, and therefore ought to set the first example of returning to allegiance.

Reflect upon what gratitude requires of you. If that is insufficient to move you, attend to your own interests. We offer you a refuge against the distress which you universally acknowledge broods with increasing and intolerable weight over all your country.

Leaving you to consult with each other upon this invitation, we do declare that whosoever shall be found and remain in peace at his usual place of residence shall be shielded from any insult, either to his person or his property, excepting such as bear offices, either civil or military, under your present usurped government, of whom it will be further required that they shall give proofs of their penitence and voluntary submission, and they shall then partake the like immunity.

Those whose folly and obstinacy may slight this favorable warning must take notice that they are not to expect a continuance of that lenity which their inveteracy would now render blamable.

Given on board his Majesty's ship Camilla, in the Sound, 4th July, 1779.

George Collier.
William Tryon.

A copy of this document was placed in the hands of Colonel Whiting, who returned his answer by the Rev. Mr. Sayre under a flag of truce : —

Fairfield, July 7th, 1779.

Sir, — Connecticut having nobly dared to oppose the usurpations of an unjust and oppressive nation (as flames have preceded the answer to your flag), we hope they will still continue, as far as in their power, to protect persecuted and oppressed innocence.

Sam. Whiting, Colonel.
Sir George Collier and Governor Tryon.
Per Mr. Sayre in flag.

David Hardy was with the militia on the Green, and one of the addresses came into his possession. He smiled grimly at the proffers of mercy, and settled himself to the stern task of resistance.

CHAPTER XIV

" THE FIREBRAND " KINDLES FLAMES

EVERY horse and cart in town had been busy all day Wednesday, and through the night, carrying household stuff away to concealment in the woods. Desire and Lois, with the help of Minto and Chloe, packed up the linen, the wearing apparel, the books, the family heirlooms and valuables, and sent them up to General Silliman's on Holland Hill, where they were stored in one of his slave cabins. The whole town seemed on the move, a general deportation to the wooded hill country, amid gravest fears and sorriest anticipations.

"Desire, it's like a hundred funerals," said Lois, as she wiped the rebellious tears from her wild eyes. " I feel as if my heart would break. Do you think they'll set our house on fire and leave us all homeless and unsheltered ? "

"Child, that is what ' The Firebrand' comes here to do. He'll punish the people of Connecticut so that they will cry for mercy, I suppose he thinks. We are to be made an example, and when other States see how we are humbled and distressed, they will all prostrate themselves at the feet of the enemy and sue for peace."

" You don't believe that we or anybody else will ever sue for peace, do you, Desire?"

There was a flash of the eye and a curl of the lip that revealed what the elder sister believed as she answered Lois : —

" Sue for peace?   Never, so long as there is left an acre on which we can fight our foe, and a man or a woman to handle a musket ! "

It was evident that Desire Hardy was one to fill the breach or discharge the office, when the sterner sex failed.

" But oh, Desire, I cannot bear to leave the dear place.   It's the only home we have ever known, and every room and nook and cranny, every piece of furniture and old keepsake, is a reminder of happy, happy hours. It's cruel, it's wicked, to drive unarmed, helpless people into want and beggary ! "

" Lois, say it not again.   It is holding out against the decrees of God.   I know how you love the old place, and that your heart bleeds, but have you not been told a hundred times

that it is part of the price which we must pay
for liberty? Others have suffered and will
suffer. Are we better than they, that we
ought to escape? It cuts me to the quick as
I hear the scattered shots, the muffled uproar,
and see that our town will be swept with the
scourge of fire and we left desolate, but I
glory in the spirit of our heroes; I say, on to
the end of the strife; liberty or death! But
here comes David."

The young man entered in great haste.
"Colonel Whiting bids me cross the country
and take the news of the enemy's landing
and inform General Washington of our condition. I must ride the old horse. Come with
me to the hills. It is not safe for you to stay.
It's a ribald, godless soldiery that's coming
up Beach Lane." David was making preparations for his ride while talking to his sisters.

"We will run over to Mrs. Burr's. She
has entertained General Tryon in her home,
and she thinks he will treat her with courtesy.
If needs be, we can slip away to General Silliman's later. I'm all the time thinking that
mayhap there will be something that I can
do. I hate to run like a whipped dog," said
Desire proudly.

"Good-by, sisters. God keep you. I'll be

back as soon as the old horse can return.
And I 'm hoping to bring Major Tallmadge."

Away sped the messenger, while the sisters
hurried to the house of Mrs. Thaddeus Burr,
the two slaves running to Holland Hill, where
they might keep an eye on the household
stuff that was hidden from the enemy.

The march, march, of approaching hosts
sounded above the din and confusion of
many voices, the lowing of cattle driven
toward the back country, the shrill cries of
frightened children, and the babel of all sorts
of noises made by the mixed companies of
people, as they withdrew from the town and
searched for secure retreat above or beyond
the cross currents of hideous warfare.   Then
followed the crack, crack, of the muskets, the
booming of cannon from Grover's Hill, the
shouts of defiance sent from the hoarse
throats of the militia on the Green, the sound
of a charge, wild cries, thick utterance of a
single piece of ordnance aimed at the enemy,
sudden uproar of hundreds upon hundreds of
quick shots, the murderous clash and jangle
of assault: the British were in possession of
the Green, the patriot defenders of the town,
overwhelmed in numbers, driven into retreat
and dispersed in many directions.

"There was only a handful of them," said Mrs. Burr to Desire. "And I hear that General Tryon commanded three thousand troops. What could be done to resist such a force?"

"Well, our men made their stand even when they knew that defeat was inevitable. They are brave fellows, and they shall be honored for their daring," exclaimed Desire.

The riot of war was surging around them as they spoke. Several neighbors, unable to flee to the country, had taken refuge at the mansion, and they made a distressed company. Still Mrs. Burr held out hopes of security.

"I have met several of the officers," she observed repeatedly, "and they are gentlemen. I cannot think they will be rude to us."

"Here they come," cried Lois, as a dozen men sprang into the front door and pounded the floor with the butt end of their muskets, shouting for Mr. Burr.

"Here, you damned rebel, where is your husband?" One of the ruffians was accosting Mrs. Burr, who drew herself up with dignity and stared him out of countenance.

"Ah, my sweet, what pretty buckles you

wear!" The fellow stooped down before
Desire and tore the silver ornaments from
her shoes, while another redcoat seized the
elegant jewels from the foot-gear of Mrs.
Burr.

"Fine curtains, boys!" exclaimed a jestful
son of the English aristocracy, as he reached
up to the heavy damask drapings of the parlor windows and wrenched them from their
fastenings. "Make me think of home," and
he jauntily threw one over his shoulder and
tossed a second to his nearest comrade.

"Give up your firearms, old woman,"
shouted the leader of the band.

Mrs. Burr was in the prime of life, a person
of regal manners and presence, refined and
gracious, with high forehead, shapely features,
lustrous eyes, and sensitive mouth, a sweet and
beautiful embodiment of the highest type of
womanhood. She had never been addressed
with other terms than those of deference,
respect, or affection. But it was Desire that
interrupted the boisterous demand : —

"Tell me where the arms are kept, and I
will get them for these creatures."

There was a dangerous light lurking in the
eyes of the speaker. Nothing of fear was seen,
rather a challenge or a curse. The intruders

EUNICE DENNIE BURR

did not stay to bandy words with the lady or any of her attendants; they scattered through the house, breaking china, overturning furniture, ransacking drawers, stealing small objects of value, making their way, at the last, to kitchen, storeroom, and cellar, where they helped themselves to food and drink, and feasted for an hour.

When one set of despoilers left the premises another followed, so that there was no respite for Mrs. Burr. It was past midday when there occurred a brief diversion.

"I believe it is General Tryon himself that is coming," exclaimed Desire, as she surveyed the scene from one of the front windows, and saw the showily dressed, pompous gentleman tramp across the yard and enter the house.

Mrs. Burr and Desire both hastened into the hall below.

"I have the honor to address Mrs. Burr," he said, bowing with studied politeness.

"This is not such an occasion, your Excellency, as when you were pleased to accept our poor hospitality a few years ago." The lady bowed, speaking with agitation which she labored hard to control.

"No one regrets the cruel exigencies of

war more deeply than I, madam. I must request you to hand over to me whatever papers and documents you may have within your house." Underneath the exterior of formal courtesy there was a strong current of vindictive feeling.

" The house contains no papers, either public or private, save those which concern my husband's estate." Mrs. Burr had regained her self-possession, and answered with an air that was queenly.

" The very papers that we want, madam. We want them, and we want the estate, too, and we shall have them both, I trow." There was a note of exultation in his speech. " I infer that you have not read the address which was scattered through your town before the troops landed and were subjected to the indignity of resistance on the part of your militia?"

" *I* have read it, sir, and I have likewise heard the reply which Colonel Whiting sent you."

Desire had descended to the last stair when she injected herself into the conversation. Her entire person expressed scorn, wrath, repulsion. As Tryon turned to the speaker, he uttered an exclamation of astonishment, and stepped back a pace.

" And who are you, I pray, that dare beard me in such terms? By the eternal heavens, methinks it is the counterfeit presentment of Duane Livingstone!" The man passed his hands over his eyes, as if to make sure that vision was not obscured.

Desire remained speechless.

"I will find the papers for you, sir," exclaimed Mrs. Burr. "They are all arranged in this secretary." She advanced into the adjoining room, followed slowly by Tryon, who still gazed upon the young lady in the hall.

When they emerged, Desire had withdrawn upstairs. General Tryon took his papers and carried them hastily over to the court house.

An hour later, a fourth set of half drunken brutes entered the Burr homestead.

" Come, come," said the foremost of the band, " show us what you 've got worth taking, and hand it over without further parley." They were standing near the door in the rear of the hall. " Do I not see a watch with its furnishments upon your person?" and the fiend grasped Mrs. Burr by the wrist.

"You villain, loose your hold upon my arm!" cried the lady. But he struggled

with her, threw her down upon the floor, and
tore the very clothes from her bosom.

"Wretch, let go! let go!" shrieked Desire,
as she seized the brass-handled poker standing
by the hearth, and swung it above his head
with such force that he sprang one side with a
curse, and started to pursue her up the stairs,
while Mrs. Burr escaped into the back yard.

At this moment an officer appeared, and
sent the fellow with his companions away
from the place.

Late in the day, General Tryon called again
with Captain Chapman, a Tory citizen of
Stratford, who had cast in his fortunes with
the enemies of his native land.

"I had supposed, sir, that it was an army
of men, and not a horde of wild beasts, which
had taken possession of our town. I have
been subjected to the grossest indignities,
your creatures attempting to take the very
clothes from my person, and rifling me of the
ornaments which I use as articles of dress."

There was the flush of righteous anger
upon the face of the speaker, as she stood
forth the bold accuser of Tryon.

"These are hard and grievous days," observed Captain Chapman sympathetically.
"We deplore these stern circumstances."

"You must carry with you a brave heart, Mr. Chapman, to have the audacity to enter my house at this time, when you recall the many courtesies we have extended to you in years past."

"Madam, madam, forbear your unkind speeches. I am here not to gloat over your misfortune, but to render any service in my power."

"See that I am treated with the respect and consideration due my sex and station! See that my home is preserved from further spoliation, and that the few people who have fled to my protection are saved from the abuses that have already been heaped upon me!"

The lady was addressing General Tryon, who winced under the just charges which she brought against his men.

"Madam, you shall have sentries placed before your door."

The order was immediately given, and the watch placed over the premises.

The night was one of indescribable horror. The Hessians had been let loose for plunder. They surged up and down the streets like an angry tide, making the darkness hideous with their mongrel speech, rough oaths, and brutal tricks.

The slave of a citizen living on the main street fired a shot from an upper window and killed a British soldier. His comrades rushed into the house, seized the colored patriot, carried him out to the Green, soaked a blanket in rum, wrapped it securely about the victim, and then set fire to the poor wretch. While he writhed in the flames consuming his clothes and scarring his flesh, the redcoats gazed upon the scene with savage zest. Everything which the people left in their homes that might please the cupidity of the raiders was taken. The few women who ventured to stay in town in order to save their property were most shamefully maltreated, being compelled to fight like tigers in numerous cases for the defense of virtue itself. Occasional shots were heard all through the night. Liquor flowed in rivers, so that a large proportion of the soldiery became grossly intoxicated before the morning. When a house had been sufficiently plundered, and there was nothing left to feed their rapacity, the enemy applied the torch, beginning this latter part of their work an hour before sunset at the house of Mr. Isaac Jennings. By nine o'clock, half a dozen buildings in different parts of the town were ablaze.

"The Firebrand" had taken up his head-quarters in the home of a Tory family on the Green. Here he was beset by the faithful wives and mothers that remained in town, and appeal after appeal made to stop the firing of homes. Mr. Sayre lent his supplications to those of his neighbors.

"No," Tryon cried, with an oath, "you are a pack of rebels, and deserve to be hanged, drawn, and quartered. Don't talk to me of mercy. Have n't you fought the king like devils? Did n't you fire upon my men after I had offered you peace and clemency? Are there not a score of killed or wounded among our troops? Is not this place a vile den of arch traitors, engaged in hellish conspiracy? I 'll put a firebrand in every house, store, shop, barn, shed, and building that curses the ground of Fairfield. Don't try to parley with me longer."

And then the edict went forth that every-thing was to be destroyed, so that by mid-night the heavens were one vast, seething maelstrom of flames.

The horror of the scene was intensified by a frightful thunderstorm, which broke above the town in the night. It had gathered from the four quarters of the heavens, and massed

its forces for a riotous onset. The rain fell
in deluges, the thick blackness being pierced
by such vivid flashes of lightning that one's
eyes were blinded ; the crash and roar of the
thunder drowned all notes of misery and ex-
cess that filled the air ; and yet the awful
work of destruction went on. House after
house was given to the flames. When opposition was encountered, little mercy was shown.
The slave of Mr. Lewis was bayoneted while
trying to save his master's property. Mr.
Solomon Sturges, an esteemed citizen, was
stabbed repeatedly. Several bodies were cast
into the cauldron of fire.

Toward morning, Captain Chapman and
General Tryon called again upon Mrs. Burr.
It had been a night of awful strain and agony
for the people housed in the stately mansion.
From the windows on every side they saw the
dwellings and property of friends vanish in
the furious conflagration. The lurid glare
made the night like day. The shriek of some
person in distress, or the groans of the dying, fell many times upon their ears. The
hour before sunrise Mrs. Burr was summoned
below to meet her callers.

"I beg pardon for this early intrusion,"
said General Tryon, "but my work will be

finished soon, and we shall reëmbark. I do not like to burn churches and meeting-houses. I have therefore ordered that they be left uninjured. And I have promised to save the homes of Mr. Sayre and Mr. Eliot."

The speaker paused, evidently awaiting some word of gratitude from the lady he was addressing.

"It is kind of you to spare our houses of public worship, your Excellency," answered Mrs. Burr, in strained and wearied tones. "I thank you."

"With your permission I will seat myself at this desk and write a protection for your home."

He moved across the room with condescension and sat down.

"May I ask for pen, ink, and paper?"

There was silence in the room, broken by the scratch of the quill, and the ominous rise and swell of the conflagration raging throughout the town.

"Madam, it irks me to observe your distress. But I have served you to the extent of my authority."

There was a pause, interrupted by an hysterical laugh. General Tryon lifted his eyes and beheld Desire standing in the doorway.

Captain Chapman bowed deferentially to the newcomer.

"Madam, may I inquire the name of the person that honors you with her company?" There was a shadow upon his face, and his tone of inquiry was rude. "I trace a startling resemblance to a gentleman of my acquaintance in New York. I have reason to suspect his loyalty to our sovereign, and I swear that I saw him on the hills of Danbury two years ago fighting with the rebels. It is not possible" — he hesitated a moment, gave an unpleasant look toward the individual standing in the shadows, and then continued — "that Mr. Duane Livingstone is a magician, and has the power to transform himself into the semblance of one of the gentler sex?"

"It is Miss Desire Hardy," suddenly explained Captain Chapman, "the daughter of the old schoolmaster. I will vouch for her identity."

"I thank you for the protection which is granted me," said Mrs. Burr, with sudden spirit, evidently wishing to divert attention from Desire. "I trust that it will avail, sir."

General Tryon had risen from his chair, when one of his subalterns entered the house, crossed the room, and whispered in his ear.

"I bid you good-day, madam, and hope that the time will soon come when we shall again meet in amity as loyal subjects of his gracious Majesty our king."

Without tarrying to receive her devoirs, the three men hastily withdrew from the apartment.

Intelligence had come to Tryon that all western Connecticut was rising in arms. It was expedient for him to end his task and set sail for Huntington. Firing the remaining buildings in the early light of the day, the word was at length passed for the troops to make their way to the shore, the sentries placed to guard the home of Mrs. Burr being withdrawn. No sooner were they gone than roving bands of stragglers appeared.

"I have a protection from General Tryon," exclaimed the lady, when these ruffians dashed into the house and began their final work of demolition.

"Tryon be damned!" they shouted. And as Mrs. Burr was in the act of showing the brief writing to them, they snatched it from her hands, tore it into fragments, and continued their desperate conduct. As Mrs. Burr had stayed in her home with the hope that she might save it, and as General Tryon had at last pledged her that the torch should not be applied, little or nothing had been removed except what the British miscreants had stolen. Now the creatures in possession had full swing, and were altogether heedless of orders or consequences. They seized the lady's pocket-book, taking it forcibly from her person; they rifled her of the gold buttons used to fasten her garments, and threatened in foulest language life itself. In the extremity of their terror and anguish, the women all fled to the meadows at the rear of the mansion, and no sooner were they hidden from the sight of the ravishers than smoke was seen to issue from the windows. A few moments later, the entire house was wrapped in flames.

There, in the welcome seclusion of the marsh grasses, the friends gave way to tears, while their moans were caught up by the breezes pushing in from the sea, and made to blend with the wild, doleful notes of the raging fire-storm, and the hoarse, fiendish clamor of the departing Hessians and refugees.

CHAPTER XV

DAVID HARDY returned from his forced ride across country in the forenoon of Thursday, the 8th of July. He had seen General Washington, and Major Tallmadge was dispatched with a body of light infantry to aid the militia in driving Tryon and his army from the Connecticut shores.

As the enemy withdrew, the little fort on Grover's Hill, which had never ceased to throw its shot into the ranks of the British through the night and morning, still continued to harass them. A company of redcoats had been sent over to Black Rock to dislodge the patriots, but without success.

Erected in 1776 to protect the town and harbor against the petty incursions of Long Island Tories, supplied with cannon from the furnaces of Salisbury, this battery, with its barracks and defenses, had become a pet with the people, and on numerous occasions resisted the assaults of the enemy prowling in these waters. While the fort, during the burning of Fairfield, availed naught in the preservation of property, still it was a factor in the heartening of the people, and from this point of vantage and others the Americans, who had responded to the summons of Colonel Whiting and his subordinates, poured in their vexatious fire, so that the retreat, while conducted with military precision, was subject to severe distress. But the wounded were taken along by their comrades, and a fair-sized company of fresh refugees joined the fleet.

The course pursued by Mr. Sayre, having alienated the entire community, forced him to leave Fairfield.

"It was in the midst of hostilities, while the flames were raging and the bullets flying," observed Mr. Eliot to David on his return to the scene of desolation, "that Mr. Sayre came out with a flag of truce. We had gone back into the hills and the woods skirting the town. What was Tryon's proclamation to us? And was not that a strange hour and occasion to speak with us concerning clemency? We sent back a very spirited reply. And we were justly indignant that Mr. Sayre should have consented to bear such a message to us. Dire threats were made against him, and I hear this morning that he and all his family have retired on shipboard, although I was told that Tryon said, 'You may go on board the ships, sir, but I cannot promise you any assistance.'"

David had ridden to Holland Hill, and he had met the minister as he moved rapidly among the friends that he was comforting.

"Where shall I find Desire?" said her brother, who was. looking in various directions, with the hope of distinguishing her among the people.

"Why, Desire stayed with Mrs. Burr, and so did Lois. I tried to get them to come back here to the Heights, but Mrs. Burr believed that she might save her home, and the girls chose to remain."

"And was the Burr mansion left untouched?" continued David anxiously.

"I cannot say. The sky has been so obscured with thick clouds of smoke that it was impossible to measure the ravages of the enemy. But I will return with you, and we will find the children. Poor Mrs. Silliman did not venture to stay in her house, so she put the horses to their big wagon and started for Trumbull, when the first booming of cannon announced the landing of the enemy;

but the general's house is filled with his friends. Captain Bartram is there, sadly wounded. My wife and three children and several of our neighbors came with me. What a night we have lived! First we saw the flames issuing from some dwelling back of the meeting-house, then I recognized Sheriff Abel's place, and then it was a barn in the western part of the town, and a little later several of the shops along the main street. By midnight, it seemed as if half the village was on fire, and it boiled and seethed like an immense cauldron, the crackling and hissing of the flames sounding in our ears at Holland Hill." The two men were now hastening toward the desolated place.

" Did not the train-band attack the enemy? Could n't our men do anything to stop the depredations of the savages?"

" No, David; we were only a few men, and they were a host. To be sure, our soldiers have been watching through the day and the night, picking off a redcoat now and then, and doing whatever was possible to annoy and disconcert them; but the enemy have had their own way, and we've been almost helpless in their hands."

As they were talking, the fresh winds from

the north came with their cool breath and brushed some portions of the thick, brooding blackness away from the landscape beneath them.   What a sight it was that unfolded to their view!

"Mr. Eliot, methinks they have obliterated the town," said David, with emotion. "Colonel Gould's house ought to be there," — he pointed to a mass of charred ruins near the creek that ran in from the sea, — "the Green ought to be over there," pointing to the southwest; "but there is n't a distinguishable object visible.   Everything is gone.   Not even a barn remains to guide the eye."   The young man stopped again to master his feelings.   "Oh, is n't it pitiful — pitiful!"

"And I believe the meeting-house has gone too," suddenly exclaimed Mr. Eliot.   "General Tryon promised Mr. Sayre that both the sanctuaries should be preserved.   Is it possible that he is such a miscreant that not even a place of prayer is sacred to him?"

The sense of loss was overwhelming to the minister.   He had put confidence in the pledge of the British officer, and believed that God's house would be respected.   As his eyes swept the eastern portion of the town and Green, it struck him again with awful force that the cruelties of war are beyond human language to depict.

Nearing the village, they were joined by small bands of people who had been hovering nigh in hopes that the enemy would soon drop their work and put to sea; so it was a considerable company that hurried by the smoking heap where formerly stood the Gould homestead and made for the Green. On every side it was the blackest desolation. Charred timbers lifted their repulsive forms into the air; great chimneys stood forth smoke-marked and solitary; withered, leafless trees kept sentinel along the streets; gaping cellars, smouldering masses of wood, blighted gardens and fields, scorched door-yards, stretched in the distance as far as the eye could reach; and beyond were wreaths, eddies, clouds of smoke, and the gathering whirlwinds of ashes, sweeping now one way and now another. The enemy had landed in two parts of the town, coming together as they completed their work, so that the entire village was devastated.

"Mrs. Redfield saved her house," said one of the boys that David met, as he came to the Green. "Mrs. Nichols put her fire out with her dye-tub, and General Tryon stayed in the Bulkleys' house, and there are two other

houses on the Green, and Mrs. Rowland drove
the Hessians away from hers, but everything
else is burned."

The people were now trooping in from many
directions. The sound of firing ceased, for
the British had embarked and gone across
to Huntington. Major Tallmadge and his
infantry arrived, and their tents were filling
a part of the Green, the commanding officer
making his headquarters in the convenient
mansion that had been used by Tryon; there
was the subdued tumult of horses, wagons,
hurrying feet, crying children, anxious parents, hungry men and women, heart-broken
home-lovers, sick, wounded, and distressed
people who knew not where to lay their heads,
or from whence would come the food to keep
them from starvation.

"Oh, David, David, have you come at
last?" cried Lois, as her brother picked his
way through ruins and reached one of the
sheds on the Burr place standing near the
marshes. "It has been the awfulest night
of a lifetime. We've been robbed, beaten,
insulted, and driven into the fields, and we're
almost dead. Mrs. Burr and Desire are there
in the hut trying to do something for the
sufferers brought to us. You never saw such

savages in all your life. There was nothing
too wicked for them to stoop to do. Why,
they took the rings off Mrs. Burr's fingers,
and stole my beautiful brooch that Aaron
Burr sent to me and they burned one of our
soldiers alive, and they stabbed several slaves .
with their bayonets so that they died; and,
oh, what did n't they do that was inhuman
and devilish!"

"Why, child," said David, "I'm thankful
to see you alive again. I told you not to stay
in the town, but to go to General Silliman's.
They 're a pack of fiends. I knew it, for I
saw them at Danbury and Ridgefield."

And then David met Desire and Mrs. Burr,
and the story of their agony was told.

Later in the day, Major Tallmadge called.
So unexpected had been the firing of the
Burr house that its mistress, having saved
nothing from it, found herself in extreme
need. The clothes, torn and soiled, which
she wore, and a few pieces of old furniture
that had been cast into one of the sheds,
constituted the capital on which she was to
begin her new housekeeping.

"I can offer you this bench, Major Tallmadge," said the lady, as he lingered at her
door and entered into conversation.

COLONEL BENJAMIN TALLMADGE

The gentleman was a tall, robust, manly young soldier, with delightful suavity of manner and a most genial flow of spirits.

"Mayhap he would prefer this tub," said Desire, whose sense of humor was keen, even in the midst of poverty and distress.

"You honor me," replied the brilliant, popular officer. "Let those who better deserve it enjoy the luxury of a bench or a tub. I will stand, ladies."

The cloud was already lifting from the countenance of Desire. The safe return of her brother, and the sense of security which comes with the knowledge that the worst has been suffered and there can be no repetition of the woeful experience, served to cheer and sustain her. Sleep had not visited them for several nights, so that eyes were heavy and deep furrows appeared on many a face. The bitterness of loss and insult remained keen. The nervous strain through which they had passed showed itself in tense speech and excited action.

But Desire was not one to give way to trouble. In fact, the dark, tragic hours served to bring into exquisite relief certain beautiful traits of character. Now was the time to rise above the prevailing sorrow and wretchedness, manifesting to friends one's superiority to circumstances. She was so fagged that her limbs rebelled when she moved from place to place in her attendance upon the sick and aged, yet she resolved that it should not be observed. She was hungry, and provisions were so scarce that it was an open question whether they would have anything to eat that night, yet she showed no signs of hunger. On the contrary, their common need made her inventive of expedients.

"David," she said, "I wish you would go over to what remains of our place and see if they burned the corn which we left standing in the field back of the barn. If you will find our hidden treasures, we can sup like princes. Be careful and don't tread on any household stuff, for I threw a lot of bedding and furniture among the thrifty stalks. If it is n't all consumed, we shall have to depend upon it for comfort these many days." ·

David and Lois went over to the cornfield. It was one of the things left intact by the despoilers. While they were searching for provisions, Minto and Chloe appeared on the scene.

"De Lo'd be praised," exclaimed the faithful old colored woman. "Here's Mas'r David an' Mis' Lois. Oh, chillun, we 's been worried to death 'bout you. An' what 's cum ob Mis' D'sire?"

" De Lo'd hab mehcy on us," cried Minto. " I 's been awfully 'minded o' de day ob judgment. Whar' is Mis' D'sire, Mas'r David?"

" Oh, she 's safe and sound down at Mrs. Burr's. But we 're almost starved to death. We have n't had much to eat for an age. Come, now, turn to and search the field, and look out you don't smash anything that you find underfoot. We 've stored our household goods here, you remember."

" Shall I go fo' de cow? She 's back in de wood-lot, sah," said Minto.

" Why, yes, that 's the very thing," exclaimed Lois. " How good a cup of nice, fresh milk would taste!"

So Minto retraced his steps into the woods, David dug potatoes, while Lois and Chloe, picking a careful way amid the lush greenery of the field, searched for a pot of butter, a piece of dried beef, and some odds and ends of Indian bread and doughnuts that had been recklessly tossed into a big brass kettle. The simple fare was a godsend. They hastened down the street with it, and came to the hut on the Burr place with all the exultant pride of a hunter who returns home laden with the riches of abundant game.

" Now we are to feast," shouted David, when he was within the hearing of his sister.

Despite smoking ruins, worn bodies, loss of worldly gear, sound of dismal grief, or awful reaction of mind, there was a cheerful party moving about the hut.

Chloe washed the soil from the potatoes; David and Major Tallmadge made the fire where the roots were to be roasted and the kettle boiled; Lois borrowed the sword of the officer, and, unbeknown to him, sliced off strips of dark crimson beef; Desire told where she had concealed some of her precious linen (such as had not been carried to Holland Hill), so that a spotless, beautiful cloth was spread; salt and pepper were found; Minto arrived with his pail of fresh milk; and then all were ready for the feast.

They seated themselves in the back yard, where the grass was unscorched and a noble elm sheltered them. The sun was going down behind the low hill in the west. The sky had partially cleared, and the salt winds, speeding to them over the marshes, drove away the odors of burning homes, barns, and produce. The hum and tumult of voices

fell upon their ears with not ungrateful ca-
dence, while the sweet calm of a beautiful
midsummer twilight settled down upon the
strange scene. Never did the lordliest fare
taste better to the most favored diner-out
than did stale Indian bread, chipped beef, hot
roast potatoes, golden butter well salted, fat
old-fashioned doughnuts crisp and light, with
tin cups brimful of milk, taste to these homeless, thirsty, distraught people.

"How good it seems to take a few mouth-
fuls that are not embittered by the insults of
inhuman foes," said Mrs. Burr, who was pre-
siding over the feast with all the fine grace
and dignity that had marked her when she
entertained the great and good of the land
in her now desecrated mansion.

"Let us think of our mercies," replied
David. "We can live on potatoes all summer. It's a flourishing field that we own.
And the cow remains. It's a wonder that
the miscreants did n't kill every piece of stock
in the neighborhood. And Desire has saved
all her linen. We can make it up into frocks
and dresses. And the sheep-shearing will
give us all the wool we need; and we can
camp out under the trees that passed through
the fire unscathed, or burrow in the ground

until we make some log huts and begin where our forefathers did a hundred and fifty years ago."

" I think it 'll be fun to live out of doors all summer," interrupted Lois. " It 's so delightfully simple and primitive ! "

The conversation flowed along, their spirits soothed and strengthened.

But it was a night of tears, bitterness, and pain to the great mass of the people. As they came back to the village with the few articles which they had carried with them into their retreat, it was to find their homes annihilated. And it was women and children that necessarily bore the brunt of the distress, for the men were away in their country's service.

The majority of the people stretched themselves upon the ground near the ashes, still hot and smouldering, and there, roofless and supperless, gave way to sleep.

Major Tallmadge, Mrs. Burr, Desire, and David talked into the night ; then the hostess withdrew to her hut, the commanding officer to his headquarters in the Bulkley house, while the Hardy young people spread their bedding along the edges of their cornfield, thinking it wise to look after the little property which was left them, since the fire had attracted to the town various suspicious characters, and there had been losses at the hands of other than British vandals and robbers.

CHAPTER XVI

ONE MYSTERIOUS PASSENGER

TOWARD morning, David was aroused by stealthy footsteps near him. He listened intently, crept in the direction of the open land, and peered through the gloom. Soon the form of a man loomed in the distance; then, by the dim light against which the visitor stood as he appeared along the horizon, David recognized the motions of Duane Livingstone. The two young men were soon clasped in each other's embrace. They tried to be quiet in their communications, but the sharp ears of Desire detected them. It was only a moment before she was by their side, taking part in their suppressed conversation.

"Duane, Duane, you ought not to have done this thing, and you know it!" whispered the girl, with every evidence of agitation in her voice. "Why will you run such risks? I cannot for the life of me see how you stole into the village. Every road and spot is picketed, and Major Tallmadge is taking the greatest pains to preserve order and keep us free of intruders."

"Why, Desire, do you suppose I could stay on Long Island when I saw the smoke of Fairfield filling the heavens? I knew what it meant. I told you it was coming. Why did n't you flee?"

"It's like a Hardy to flee in face of danger, is n't it?"

One might feel the flash of Desire's eyes, even if he could not see it.

"But what good was there in your staying? You could do nothing. The place was consigned to the flames weeks ago. Judge Jones has told General Tryon many times that more than half the inhabitants of the town were Tories, but he never believed it. He 's been determined to destroy Fairfield ever since the burning of Colonel Delancey's house in Westchester. That incident seemed to inflame him as a red flag does a wild bull."

"Duane, you had no business to come here to-night. I wish you would go away. You 'll surely be seen in the morning. We have n't a corner where we can hide you. Major Tallmadge's infantry and hundreds of the militia are here, or in the neighborhood. Oh,

Duane, I wish you had n't come! It adds to our worry and perplexity."

The cousin was deeply moved by this outburst of feeling. He bent over Desire, and whispered something that David did not hear.

"Oh!" groaned Desire, and then, lifting her head suddenly, she peered into the encircling gloom to observe if any listener was visible.

" David," continued Duane, "you must hide me through the day. I can't return to Huntington to-night. It is too late. I 'll promise to get away some time within the next twenty hours."

There followed a long consultation within the curious solitude of the cornfield. It was necessary to awaken Minto, Chloe, and Lois, and tell them of Duane's presence, so that some of them might stand guard for the rest of the night, while David or Desire held further talk with their troublesome visitor. For the young man was not a welcome comer at this particular time.

The impression had gone abroad that Duane Livingstone was at heart a Tory, although his family continued stanch patriots. The feeling against Tories in Connecticut had grown strong since the capture of General Silliman by a band of men who were known to come from this very section of the country. The recent raids along the shore had now fanned the flame of hatred to a sort of frenzy. While Duane Livingstone was well known and popular in town, having been treated with justice and courtesy, when a guest, throughout the early years of the struggle, yet now it was the height of folly for him or any other person bearing his reputation to appear in these borders.

It was nothing less than madness which had driven him to face such a risk.

While they were fixing some sort of a hiding in the middle of the cornfield, Desire led David aside, and told him that he must carry a message to Major Tallmadge.

" Why, you don't mean to tell him that Duane is here," exclaimed David, with terror in his voice.

Desire shuddered, reaching forth a trembling hand to her brother.

" Hush, David, hush ! How your words startled me ! You don't know what you are saying."

" Why, of course not," cried the brother eagerly, — " of course not. What was I thinking about ? " There was a note of regret and deprecation in his voice. " What an absurd question ! "   .

" You must hand this little packet to Major
Tallmadge at once. Put it into his hands
yourself, and say that a friend gave it to you
for him."

David was off on his errand in a moment,
the packet being duly delivered without question on the part of giver or taker; fifteen
minutes found the messenger back again in
the cornfield, sharing the wait and the watch
with the other members of the family.

On this Friday, it seemed that every returning man, woman, and child came to the Hardy
place in order to condole with the young
folks, or get their sympathy, or ask their
advice, or borrow a little food. It required
the five of them to hold people beyond the
pale of the inviting field. It was one of the
few pieces of grain or other growing stuff
near the town that had escaped devastation.
While the ears of corn were not ripe enough
to be good eating, yet one must not be critical when confronted by hunger; and in case
this resource failed, they could draw upon the
adjoining patch of potatoes.

A score of times some hasty friend, taking
it for granted that he was welcome to help
himself, plunged unbidden and unobserved
into the field, and when on the verge of

stumbling over Duane's sheltered nook, was discovered, diverted by some of the family, and finally drawn away from the place and made to stay in the open. The stress and anxiety of the hours was not less severe than on the days of the raid itself. It was only the swift, subtle ingenuity of the sisters which enabled them to get through Friday without the tragedy of Duane's capture.

The town was filled with people. The citizens and their families returned, and with them came every Tom, Dick, and Harry of the surrounding country; and with Tom, Dick, and Harry, womankind and children intent on witnessing the awful destruction which had swept over the place like a scourge. Then the militia continued to gather in larger force, and there on the Green stood the white tents of Major Tallmadge's troops, the men themselves busy furbishing up their arms, putting things into proper trim, serving as guard throughout the town, moving hither and thither with an air of expectancy and determination that suggested mysterious events.

Before night settled down upon the throngs of people, it was whispered about that "The Firebrand" had simply withdrawn to Huntington to get his men into condition for another foray. New Haven and Fairfield had served to whet his appetite. He was now like a savage brute that had tasted blood, so that every cruel instinct in him was aroused and tigerish. He must gorge himself with inhumanity, suffering, and desolation. Some thought that New London must be the next point of attack, and a messenger had been sent to warn the people of their peril. Others believed that one of the nearer towns was destined to receive the blow.

Little sheds and huts began to appear in different parts of the village, the citizens taking odds and ends of boards, half charred bits of timber, the branches of trees, sticks, and stones convenient to their hands, and working them into these rude temporary shelters. By night, quite a large number of families had provided themselves with some covering. Into these strange abodes they brought the little stuff that had been saved from the flames; on the bare ground within them, or by their side, blankets were spread and rough couches fixed, where they were glad to throw their weary bodies with the setting of the sun, and sleep a dreamless or a feverish sleep, as the case might be.

The Hardy family watched the descent of

the sun with painful solicitude. It had been the longest day within memory, — a day of infinite finesse and difficulty.

"Thank God for the on-coming darkness," cried Desire, when the shadows thickened. "We must give him a good supper." She was talking with Chloe.

With all their keeping guard over the cornfield, they had been able to bring together enough stuff to make a cabin, and into this playhouse of a dwelling they had put a part of their domestic possessions. The kettle was boiling over the fire at the rear of the cabin, an odor of fresh vegetables and frying chicken diffusing itself upon the calm evening air.

"See that the corncakes are kept hot," continued Desire, "and when everything is ready, I'll take them in this pan over into the corn."

It was delicious fare on which Duane Livingstone feasted that Friday night, July 9th, 1779. David, Lois, and Minto continued their watch, Chloe prepared more corncake and chicken in her open-air kitchen, while Desire carried her pan of food, covered with her homespun apron, into the thicket, and there, amid shadows, served the young man,

with an air of mixed cheeriness and distress
that gave sweetest relish to every mouthful
of food.

" You 've brought me a perfect banquet,"
whispered Duane, as he smelt the chicken,
felt the crisp hoecake, and bit into the lus-
cious, butter-smeared vegetables. " And what
are these mellow, fragrant little things in the
bottom of the pan? Desire, methinks they
are berries." He put one into his mouth and
let the grateful juice season a fresh bite of
the chicken. " You dear child, you 're my
providence. Are the berries red like your
lips?" He tried to look through the gloom
into her face.

" Now, Duane, we must get you away from
this place as soon as your feast is ended. I
never spent a more wretched day in my
life."

" And I 've made you wretched. Forgive
me, Desire. There, that piece of chicken
did n't taste half as good as the first."

He hesitated in his eating, and waited for
the girl to continue.

" Oh, do eat your feast and get what pleasure you can out of it, Duane, and don't mind
any hard or disagreeable words I may let fall.
These are hard times, and we 're not always

responsible for what we say. I want to see you safely landed on the other side, cousin, and " —

" Don't cousin me, Desire Hardy. If I 'm nothing more than a cousin to you, the jig 's ended. I don't care what becomes of me. I 'll go and deliver myself up to your great friend, Major Tallmadge. They tell me he 's a most dashing fellow, quite the peer of Aaron Burr in his good looks and many graces."

" Duane, you must hush. Somebody 'll hear us. It 's been almost impossible to keep folks out of the cornfield by day, when we could see them, and now it is night, any number of men might steal in here and surprise us, and work their will upon you." She trembled with fear as she spoke.

" Well, Desire, I 'll go; I 'm sorry that I 've worried you. But how could I keep away at this time ? "

The first exhilaration of his feast had passed. Appetite was now sated, and he must think upon the perils that beset him.

" Everything has been arranged for your trip across the Sound," said his companion eagerly. " But you 'll have to submit to one condition that will humble your pride, I sup-

pose. You 'll do it for my sake, won't you,
Duane ? "

There was tender appeal in her voice.

" Desire, I 'd do anything for your sake, —
anything reasonable that did not reflect upon
honor, and *that* you could never ask of one.
What is it ? "

She whispered the condition, and he drew
back with repugnance.

" Child, child, why do you ask such a
thing ? " he said, with startling vehemence.
" I am ashamed to think of it. It *is* humili-
ating. I can't do it."

" Duane, there is nothing mean or disgraceful about the condition I propose. It
will enable us to get you away without trouble.
You must do as I say."

He was silent for a moment.

" Desire, kiss me. I 'll accept the condition."

There was a playful seriousness in the
answer, and the compact was sealed.

" Good-by," she said, when their interview
came to an end. " David will bring the
things to you. Remember, you are not to
speak a word except in an emergency. No
conversation ! The whaleboat will be at Pine
Creek, and will leave you at the point men-

tioned near Huntington, and " — Duane
stood close by her side and held her hand
for a moment, as she whispered; then, as she
drew it away and turned into the greater darkness, she continued, with a spice of mischief,
" It was only a cousinly kiss, you know," and
disappeared.

It might have been an hour later that
Desire Hardy and her brother were seen passing down the main street toward Pine Creek.
They met various acquaintances, but did not
stop to do more than answer some question
or say a brief good-evening. They were evidently in considerable haste, for their interview with the pickets was the quickest possible.
By ten o'clock, they reached the short stretch
of beach on the west side of Pine Creek. The
lady stayed within the shelter of the trees,
while the gentleman picked a careful way
to the edge of the water, softly imitating
the notes of a whippoorwill. In response, a
dusky craft pushed along to the spot. Then
the gentleman returned to the bit of wood;
there was a delay of two or three minutes;
the man appeared a second time, wrapped in a
long military cape, and, springing into the
boat, he was off to sea.

Immediately, Desire returned to the village,

although, had a close observer been on the watch, he might have imagined that the Desire Hardy who came back seemed perhaps an inch shorter than the one who had left the homestead earlier in the evening.

"Now we must pray all night that there be no mishaps on the water, and that our cousin gets safely to the house of Judge Jones in good time to-morrow."

The Hardy family spent another restless ten hours waiting for the coming of the whaleboat with the word that the mysterious passenger had been left without adventure or accident on the Long Island shore.

CHAPTER XVII

A WRESTLING MATCH IN THE WOODS

MAJOR TALLMADGE had received secret intelligence that Tryon was to make Norwalk the next objective point in his destruction of the shore towns, so that the company of light infantry and a great portion of the state militia marched from Fairfield to the relief of the imperiled neighbor. Billy the Butcher crossed over to the fair village on Sunday afternoon, the 11th. It had been expected that a company of loyalists would rally to their support and join with the redcoats in their devastations. There were numerous Tories holding constant communication with the enemies of their country, serving the British marauders faithfully in this petty, malignant harassment of the patriots.

It was about nine o'clock in the evening when the enemy landed, and they lay upon their arms all night. In the morning, they made their way into the town, although Captain Betts and his company of Continentals tried to check their advance.   The militia was gathering, and Major Tallmadge was on the march, so that Tryon dared not delay his work.   No sooner had his minions entered the village than the torch was applied.   This was not warfare : it was vandalism and wanton cruelty to the defenseless.   But Tryon took his place on Grumman's Hill, overlooking the town, and there, seated comfortably in his chair, surveyed the hideous work.

Nearly everybody fled from the village, for people had learned that " The Firebrand " did not spare even women and children from insult and terror.   As the troops of Major Tallmadge and the state militia were delayed, the setting fire to the buildings and shipping was not a long task.   The first blaze appeared about daylight, and by the middle of the forenoon the conflagration was in full blast.

" I 'd like to burn the house of every traitor in the land, and teach them that the penalty of rebellion is no light matter."

Tryon addressed his refugee friend Sherwood Spalding, who was standing by his side.

" But there are many brave and loyal men who suffer with these people, your Excellency. And the homes of the Tories are dear to them."

"I know it. They are involved in this common disaster, and I am sorry for it, but there is no help that I can suggest. Spalding, what do you think of Livingstone? You have met him, have you not, at the house of Judge Jones?"

"I think, sir," and Spalding's eyes flamed with resentment and hatred, "that he is a dangerous man to have within the lines. His family are rank rebels. He may think that he can do business, amass a fortune, and keep on the fence all through the fight, but I doubt it. I believe that fellow ought to be watched. In fact, your Excellency, I've done a little watching of him myself; his movements are suspicious."

General Tryon was a man of quick insight and varied experience. The very intensity of feeling shown by Spalding suggested to his listener that some personal grudge was involved, so that the young man's testimony defeated the purpose which he had in view.

Spalding wished to get rid of Duane Livingstone. He would have been glad to see him in prison, or to hear of his sudden disappearance through the exigencies of war.

But General Tryon had a liking for him; and while he was angry because Duane did not come out like a man on the side of the king and identify himself whole-heartedly with the royal interests, yet he continued to look upon him with favor, and secretly to regard him with real affection. He had known him as child, youth, man; through all these years, the happy flow of good spirits, the gay, bright wit, and the frank, lovable nature of the young gentleman had been to General Tryon a source of real delight.

On two or three occasions, he had become suspicious that Duane sympathized with the rebels. But that was natural, under the circumstances. His family were ardent friends of the Continental leaders, several of them fighting in the ranks of the provincials; but Tryon had an idea that, while Duane was a man of courage and spirit, he did not screw himself up to the point where he would fight against his own kith and kin. Meanwhile, there was no doubt that the young fellow had a natural aptitude for trade, and was making money with the keenest sort of enjoyment.

"Why, Spalding, you speak as if you harbored some personal rancor. Is there a lady in the case?" The governor scrutinized his companion with sharp eyes.

" Well, sir," answered Spalding, blushing
under the keen observation of the questioner,
" he has a cousin in Fairfield whom he vexes
with his attentions. She looks near enough
like him to be his twin sister, but who wants
to marry a second self? I think he affects
a regard for her simply to annoy other men,
and hold them at a distance and torture them,
if possible."

" At least, that is the way the thing stands
in your case," said the general maliciously,
as he took his eyes off the young man's face
and swept with his glance the fascinating
scene stretching beneath him.

The conversation was interrupted at this
point by the approach of an aid, who informed Governor Tryon that the militia and
a small company of Continentals from Fairfield were drawing nigh. So the commanding
officer thought it best to bestir himself and
finish the work.

He had been playing Nero in a petty, foolish way, although the parallelism fell short
of the fiddlers and a few other notable ac-
companiments. But Tryon took a peculiar
delight in the service which he was now
rendering the king. He had these stiff-
necked, crafty Yankees on the hip, and he

was doing with them much as he pleased. How he reveled in their distress and anger! how he gloated over their losses and sufferings! how he cursed them for their meanness and obduracy, their swaggering independence and ingenious opposition!

" Did n't I say that I 'd make the damned rebels squirm ? "

This was the remark which sounded in Spalding's ears, as the general left his view point on Grumman's Hill and sent word for his men to return to their boats.

It was while Norwalk was burning, the royal troops getting ready to embark, and the patriots encircling the foe, that David Hardy ran across Sherwood Spalding. The two young men stood face to face. David's first impulse was to shoot the refugee; then he held back, remembering old times and former ties. They had played together since childhood, attending the same school, rowing in the same boat, swimming through the same surf, fishing in the same brook, — good friends until the war divided them. No, David could not shoot him.

Spalding was equally embarrassed. He had always loved David; he loved David's sister even better. You might as well ask a son to shoot his mother. So they stared at each other for a moment in the greatest dismay.

"Sherwood, I never thought to see you taking part in such a cruel thing as this!" exclaimed David. "You're a traitor to your native land, and I— I— ought to shoot you!" he continued, with hesitation.

"David, I've given you two or three warnings," replied Spalding. "The king is sure to win. I suppose I ought to make you a prisoner now, and drag you down to the fleet, and hand you over to General Tryon, but I hate to do it." He shifted from one foot to the other and leaned upon his musket. "I'm sorry you've lost your home, and that it is necessary to chastise you rebels in this rough way; but, David, keep out of mischief, and don't run over to Long Island any more, unless you come to join the royal cause and cast in your lot with us."

Spalding was talking rapidly. It was necessary for him to run for the fleet. If he was left on the Connecticut shore, the chances were that life would be of short or uncertain tenure.

"Spalding," said David hurriedly, but with conviction, "I must take you prisoner." He made a sudden spring for him.

" By Jove, David," cried Sherwood, " if
there's any prisoner to be taken, I'll take
you with me down to the boats."

Suiting action to their words, the young
men clinched with each other, wrestled vigor-
ously, and rolled over upon the ground down
into the underbrush, tearing their clothes,
scratching their faces, scattering their arms
and ammunition, continuing their set-to for
several minutes.

David had the easier task. It was simply
necessary for him to hold Spalding under
some restraint until help came or the fleet
sailed away, and the young refugee was his
assured prisoner. In order to secure David,
however, Spalding must drag him near
enough to the shore to make some of the
redcoats answer a call for help. He soon
discovered that this was a thing impossible
for him to do. So when, in the scuffle, David's hold upon him was slightly relaxed, he
made a sudden dash for liberty, and, having
shaken himself loose from his adversary, took
to his heels with all the speed of an Indian
runner, leaving musket and furnishings, with
more or less of his uniform, behind him.

" Well, perhaps it's as well that he escaped," soliloquized David, as he rose from

the ground, gathered up his arms and ammunition, and took possession of his foe's
belongings. "It would have been an unpleasant business to hand him over to the
authorities. Perhaps Desire likes him, and
would have felt sorry. I don't wish to be
mean, even to a refugee like Sherwood."

Coming out from the woods on top of a
hill, David saw the enemy in retreat. The
thick clouds of smoke that hovered above the
town concealed the extent of the conflagration, but there were only a few buildings that
escaped destruction. The losses were almost
as large as they had been in Fairfield; the
insult, cruelty, and wickedness fully equal.
Flames leaped through the blackness occasionally, seeming to David like red tongues
reaching into space that they might torture
the air itself. The roar and din beneath
reminded him of Milton's pictures of the infernal regions. This was making hell on
earth, and what other terms better describe
the hideous riot and agony of warfare?

The patriots gave the invaders not a little
annoyance, although the skirmishing did not
rise to the dignity of a drawn battle. General Parsons arrived with his Continentals, so
that a force of a thousand men hung upon

the skirts of the enemy. More than twenty British soldiers were killed, more than a hundred wounded.

But the fight was soon over, and David returned home. Drawing near the familiar place of Mr. Ripley, at Green Farms, he found the minister's house gone, his sanctuary a heap of ruins, and the whole neighborhood desolated. Entering again into the streets of Fairfield, he was met by eager questioners, anxious to know the fate of friends, or to inquire about the latest deeds of " Billy the Butcher."

" Desire," said he, sitting down beside the door of their cabin, wiping the sweat and dust from his grimy face, " it is sickening. God never intended that I should be a soldier. I 've not the stomach for it."

Then he told the story of Norwalk, ending with the meeting of Spalding and his escape. The tears streamed down the faces of his listeners as they heard his narrative. When would the wild work end ?

" I suppose it is Stamford next," said David, " although the enemy were afraid of us, and hastened to their boats when we gathered in force."

" Sherwood Spalding tried to take you

prisoner, did he, or make a turncoat and a redcoat of you?" It was Lois speaking in the midst of her tears. "I'd like to tell him what I thought about it," she continued. "He wouldn't dare to talk to me that way many minutes."

"Well, he didn't have a great while to talk with me," replied David, smiling, as he called to mind the scene when they grappled with each other and rolled over and over upon the ground.

"The wretches! Did you hear what 'Billy the Butcher' said to poor Mrs. Beers, with her babe in arms? 'You've got a pretty child; is it yours?'

"'Yes,' she said.

"'Are you willing it should be cut up and made a pie of? They say the Congress eat such pies, and they are very good.' And Mrs. Beers ran away from him with all her might. The brute! How I wish we had him here in this cabin!"

"Why, child," said David wearily, "what would you do with the man?"

"I'd do as Jael did with Sisera. I'd drive a peg through his forehead and nail him to the ground." Lois looked it, so savage and vindictive was her aspect.

" You ought to have heard what the hell-hounds (that's what Burr calls them) said when they set the meeting-house on fire! The sacrilegious wretches."

" What was it?" asked Lois.

" ' Now, God Almighty, come and defend your own house,' they shouted; then a dozen of them applied the torch, and danced about the sanctuary like a band of savages.

" I used to think that the Cherokees of North Carolina gave Tryon the very name that suited him," observed Desire. " 'The Great Wolf' is wonderfully expressive. And I thought the Sons of Liberty hit the nail on the head when they dubbed him 'Billy the Butcher.' But we folks in Connecticut must hold to the name that comports with his character as we see it. Don't you think 'The Firebrand' is best of all, David?"

" The very name! The very name!" shouted Lois. " Wolf! Butcher! Firebrand!"

" Why, Desire, we Yankees *are* ingenious. Yes, that's a happy title."

David smiled at the conceit. But he was too tired and worried to enter into the humor of the girls' bright sayings.

The prospects before them were poor. There was nothing but a mean, rude hut for shelter; their food supply was running low, a good portion of their crops ruined; David's hands were tied so that he could not venture into the world and try to earn a living for the family; Connecticut was now hard pressed, and many people had grown disheartened; the currency had depreciated to such an extent that it was not worth much more than the paper on which its good promises were printed; and the Tories were harassing the patriots by day and by night, gloating over the turn of events, and prophesying direst things to incorrigible rebels.

Only a few days previous to the recent descent of Tryon on the coast, a county convention had been held in Fairfield to discuss the currency question; while on July 1st, the town had appointed John Morehouse, Jr., and Nathaniel Seeley to provide clothing for the town soldiers in the Continental service, — to such straits had the men been reduced by war.

The selectmen had been requested to order ten men in addition to the former guards to look after the protection of the town. Thaddeus Burr, Jonathan Sturges, and Samuel Squire were chosen a committee to see the governor and the Council of Safety, and request that some vessel or vessels of force guard the coast against the further designs of the enemy during the summer season.

These were days of deep gloom. Governor Trumbull still braved the trials of his position, infusing his own spirit of hopefulness and confidence into wavering hearts. General Washington felt the need of diverting the enemy from further depredations upon the unprotected coast of Connecticut.

It was like the sun breaking through some rift in the clouds and lighting up once more the storm-bound landscape when news came that, on the morning of the 16th, "Mad" Anthony Wayne had assaulted Stony Point, killing fifty of the garrison, and taking prisoner almost ten times as many. General Tryon had remained at Huntington, preparing for another move alongshore, and the burning of other helpless towns; but the lively work of Wayne, and intimations of similar attacks in the neighborhood of New York, forced him to a speedy return, so that Connecticut was given a respite from The Great Wolf Billy the Butcher Firebrand Tryon.

CHAPTER XVIII

THE first weeks which followed the burning of Fairfield were filled with ceaseless activity. The guard was now increased to fifty men in the Prime Ancient Society, twenty-five at Green's Farms, and fifteen at Strathfield, although there was little probability that the foe would make a second raid on the town during the present summer. People set to work with all the energy at their command to make themselves temporary shelters, shops, stores, and barns. Religious services were held at private houses. The few days when citizens were able to think of little else than the stern necessities of life soon passed, and the sufferers recovered from their stunned and strickened state.

On the 20th of July, they held a special town meeting, when it was voted " that J. Lewis, Thaddeus Burr, George Burr, Samuel Wakeman, Jonathan Sturges (*et al.*) be a committee to put about subscriptions to raise

money as a reward for any person or persons
that shall captivate and take prisoner General
William Tryon, who commanded the British
troops when they burnt the town, and that
said committee issue a proclamation offering
such reward as shall be subscribed for that
purpose." Then it was voted that Mr. Andrew
Rowland, Jonathan Sturges, and Thaddeus
Burr draw up a narrative of the proceedings
of Governor Tryon in the destruction of the
town, and also point out his treatment of
the inhabitants that tarried in the town, and
the instances where he violated his own proclamation.

This proclamation which Tryon scattered
in his visits to the shore towns excited the
ridicule of its citizens.

"Talk about 'frenzy,'" exclaimed David,
"why, it is simply our enthusiasm for liberty."

"Yes, and see what he says about our being a monument of his mercy! It's a good
deal more like being a monument to his barbarity, I think," cried Desire. "Was n't it a
grand reply which Colonel Whiting sent to
old 'Great Wolf Billy the Butcher Firebrand
Tryon'?" interrupted Lois excitedly.

"Yes," answered Desire; "and Major Tallmadge has written us what General Washington said: 'It is truly ridiculous, and must tend to incense rather than intimidate,' he said. But the general admired Colonel Whiting's reply: 'It is laconic, but to the purpose.' I like to repeat it."

And then she took the words of the message, which had been memorized by many of the patriots, and said them over for the hundredth time: " ' Sir, Connecticut having nobly dared to oppose the usurpations of an unjust and oppressive nation (as flames have preceded the answer to your flag), we hope they will still continue, as far as in their power, to protect persecuted and oppressed innocence.' "

On Friday, the 30th, Parson Eliot met his people on the Green in front of the ruined sanctuary, and conducted a preparatory lecture. It was a pathetic scene. The listeners seated themselves on the down-trodden turf in a compact body, hearing his words with eager ears and loving hearts, for he was comforting them in their affliction and thrilling them with his appeals. "Not a house for my shelter," said he in the address, " two thirds of my personal estate plundered and consumed, a wife and three small children dependent on me for their maintenance. . . I feel myself in a state of uncertainty as to many of the necessities of life." Their eyes were filled with tears, for his poverty and losses were simply like to their own. Yet he loyally, trustingly continued, "I am ready to undergo any difficulties in the work of the ministry for your sakes." The elms did not even yield them a shade on that sorrowful occasion, for the leaves were sere and crisp with the blight of fire. Nevertheless, they were glad to meet in peace even amid scarred trees, scorched grass, and fitful ash-heaps. And when on Sunday morning, August the 1st, the people gathered at the house of Justin Hobart, one of the four in the centre of the town which weathered the fire-storm, their hearts went forth in gratitude. Pastor Eliot had recovered from the illness induced by the worry and strain of the conflagration, friends had rallied to their help and sent them needed supplies, prophets of light and hope spake often to them concerning victory and independence.

On August the 31st, the citizens voted to build a new town house on the same spot of ground where the late schoolhouse had stood near the old structure. This was one of the early manifestations of public spirit, —

an assuring forerunner of later and larger work.

All through the war, the Sound had been filled with British and American craft preying upon each other and the shore people, so that the unwary farmer or tradesman was never safe.

Connecticut privateersmen busied themselves in these skirmishes. Still, the annoyance visited upon the patriots by Tory raiders did not lessen. So on the 5th of September, Major Tallmadge (who had been honored with a separate command) undertook an expedition against the enemy at Lloyd's Neck, where there was a strong fortified post and five hundred troops. The patriots embarked from Shippan Point, near Stamford, in the evening, landing on the Long Island shore about ten. The attack was sudden and unexpected, nearly the whole party of refugee marauders and freebooters encamped behind the fort being captured, their boats destroyed, and huts razed to the ground, Major Tallmadge returning without the loss of a man.

"It was a real 'Sword of the Lord and Gideon' adventure," said David to the young hero.

They were taking counsel together within

the Hardy cabin; for the brilliant favorite of
Washington had hastened over to Fairfield to
look after some further details of the Secret
Service.

"Thank you for a good opinion of the
enterprise," was Major Tallmadge's reply.
"There's another task that might be done
on Long Island, which I think would result
to our advantage."

"You pique our curiosity, sir," exclaimed
Desire.

"We need General Silliman. He is a vigilant, conscientious officer, familiar with this
coast, and held in great esteem by the people.
But we have no man of equal position and
importance to offer the British in exchange."

There was that suggested by the manner
of Major Tallmadge which proved quite as
significant as words. David did not see the
drift of his thought, but Desire, gifted with
all the fine intuitions of a woman, was quick
to respond.

"I hear," she observed, "that Judge Jones
keeps open house at 'Tryon Hall.'"

"I believe you are well informed upon that
point," said Major Tallmadge, as he lifted his
eyebrows and shot a look of keen intelligence
into the face of the charming woman by his
side.

Days passed, with all the pressure of harvest
and the vexations of petty depredation along
the coast. Every night there were boats of
all sorts shoving off from Black Rock, Newfield, Stratford, Pine Creek, Compo, Shippan
Point, and a score of other places, which
made for the Long Island shore; sometimes,
they met a Tory foe in the middle of the
Sound and had a water fight, and again they
came to blows on land. Often, they fell upon
the marauders or their allies when the coming was swift and unexpected, so that the
work was done in briefest time, and the patriots sailed away on the sea before any alarm
had sounded.

It was therefore not an extraordinary event
when Captain Hawley and his chosen band of
helpers, one night in November, crossed over
from Newfield harbor to Stony Brook, disappearing in the darkness of the woods.

"We marched the rest of the night, and
then lay hid in the bushes through the day,"
said David, in telling his story to Desire and
Lois. "It was Saturday evening when we
reached Jones's place, and·I was so surprised
to see his elegant and commodious mansion.
Duane has never told us that the judge
lives in such handsome style and entertains

with such lavish hospitality. Why, the windows were all ablaze with light, and there were as many as fifteen or twenty of them in the front, I should think. He calls the place 'Tryon Hall,' you know, because he is a great friend of the governor's; and it was at Tryon's house in New York that Duane met Judge Jones and his family so many times, and began his friendship with the justice. Well, when we arrived, it was evident that something out of the ordinary kind was going on. We heard music, and then the patter of many feet, and the noise of many voices."

"'Boys, it's a party we've come to!' whispered Captain Hawley. 'I hope you're all dressed for the occasion.'

"'Yes, yes,' answered back the men, in stealthy, sepulchral tones. 'We're in full dress.'

"Then we surrounded the house, and some of the men climbed in at the upper windows and helped themselves to what stuff they could lay their hands on, and others went in by the back way and told the servants to keep still and they wouldn't get hurt, while some of us knocked at the front door and invited Judge Jones to accompany us on our return to Fairfield. He didn't seem to like

TRYON HALL.

it, and there was considerable excitement in the house. I wish some of our men had n't been so greedy, but they told Captain Hawley, after they crossed, that they would n't budge an inch, or do a thing to help, unless he gave them the privilege of taking any little keepsakes they might have a fancy for, and so they helped themselves to whatever they liked, while Judge Jones was preparing for his march. And who do you think was there at the house? Why, if you will believe it, Duane Livingstone and Sherwood Spalding. Captain Hawley saw them. Sherwood disappeared. I suppose he's in mortal terror of his life, for he knows how people feel about him here in Fairfield. But Duane faced the company, and was left undisturbed. I felt real sorry for Judge Jones. He seems like a fine, courtly gentleman, except that his Toryism is rampant. After we started on our tramp over the island, Duane joined me. He had managed to say, in the confusion, that I must lag behind and give him a chance. So he told me what little news there was, how hard he finds it now to get back and forth between city and country, and then he gave me a letter for you. Here it is."

The speaker handed a small, well-folded

packet to his sister, who received it with an assumed matter of fact air.

"I think Duane looks worn and troubled. He did n't seem natural and happy, as he usually does. I wish he 'd get off the fence and throw in his fortunes with the patriot army. That's the one thing that puzzles me about him. I used to think he was the bravest, frankest kind of a fellow. And I can't help believing it now. But how shall I reconcile his course with any standard of true manliness?" David spoke with genuine sorrow.

"Never mind about Duane," said Desire hurriedly. "Tell me how you reached home."

"Well, we traveled over little hills, through morasses, and by rough fields in the thickest forests. We hastened with all our might, for there are troops encamped in the neighborhood of Fort Neck, and we expected an alarm would be given and pursuit made. When it grew light, we were compelled to conceal ourselves and wait anxiously for the next night. Then we pressed on again, having only stale biscuit and poor cheese to eat, rending our clothes among the briers, cutting into the flesh, as you see" (David pointed to the interlaced red lines that disfigured his

countenance well-nigh beyond recognition),
" losing our hats and some of the spoil that
the men had taken with them, reaching the
shore after an awful night of toil and anxiety. But we had no serious annoyances
from the enemy. Two or three times we ran
against stray Tories, and once we thought to
have a brush with some of the refugees that
have donned the British uniform ; but at last
we came to our whaleboat, and thankful
enough we were to find ourselves once more
upon the water scudding over to our harbor.
Judge Jones acted sullen and aggrieved. I
suppose the falling into ditches, and climbing
over hedges and fences, and the eating poor,
scant fare, and having one's clothes half torn
from the back by briers and bushes, does n't
tend to make one cheerful, but he might at
least have borne his trouble with his usual
dignity."

" Oh, well, David, dignity will generally go
to the winds when it comes to scrambling
through a strange rough country on dark
nights."

" We took him up to Mrs. Silliman's after
we landed," continued the narrator. " As
General Silliman was in captivity on Long
Island, and Judge Jones had met him many

times and they had become quite friendly, it seemed the thing to do, and then Mrs. Silliman had invited us, for she thought it would give her a chance to ask about her husband. As we entered, Mrs. Silliman said to our prisoner : —

" ' The fortunes of war have brought you here under disagreeable circumstances.'

" ' Did they plunder when they took your husband?' he replied.

" ' Not much,' said Mrs. Silliman ; although you remember, Desire, that they *did* take whatever silver they could find, and anything else that was valuable to them and easily transported.

" ' Well, madam,' answered Judge Jones, ' they have plundered my house. I don't believe they have left my wife with a second sheet.'

" ' I am very sorry to hear it,' said Mrs. Silliman, ' and I hope it is not as bad as you fear. But I have prepared some refreshment for you, sir, and I shall be pleased to have you sit with us at our table.' Judge Jones thanked her and accepted the hospitality, although not with very good grace, and there I left him. But you know that he is not to stay here in Fairfield. They fear the Tories.

They are thick as bees in Newtown, and they use the harbor at Newfield as their special point of departure for parts unknown. Our neighbors have petitioned the governor and council to do something to stop the thieving and confiscating that goes on right under the noses of the people. I think they'll send our prisoner or prisoners (for we took a young man with Judge Jones) to Middletown, where he'll be out of the way and hard for the Tories to reach."

Desire had been fingering the small packet which David had discovered while fumbling in his pockets. She had taken it from him during their conversation, while in his absorption, having failed to note the fact, he continued to examine his clothes, seeming to have a faint impression that something was in some hiding-place and ought to be forthcoming.

"Don't bother yourself, David," said Desire at last, with a faint gleam of fun. "I've found it. I suppose you're looking after this?" She held up the article before her brother's face.

"Why, yes, Desire, where in the world did you get it? I put it here, or somewhere else."

As he made the remark, he laid his hand

first upon an inner vest pocket and then on the leg of his right boot.

"You gave it to me, Mr. Dreamer," said his sister laughingly. "David, some day you'll forget your name. We'll have to label you ; but, dear soul, you must be tired and hungry. Here comes Chloe to tell you that she's made some hot cakes and any number of nice things for you."

So while the young man was satisfying the cravings of a half-famished stomach, his sister, having withdrawn to her room, was deciphering the curious hieroglyphics in her letter.

CHAPTER XIX

It was a rude cabin in which the Hardy family lived through the autumn and winter of '79 and '80. A sum of money had been collected in the county of Hartford, according to the recommendation of Governor Trumbull, for the relief of sufferers in New Haven, Fairfield, and Norwalk, and a portion of it had been passed over to Jonathan Sturges for distribution; but David and Desire declined the proffered help. The season was the severest that had ever visited the country, Long Island Sound being frozen over so that men walked or drove from one shore to the other. In spite of the cold weather, there were numerous expeditions across this frozen sea, and the distress was well-nigh unmitigated.

In March, Captain Peter Thorpe was permitted by the governor to procure and export to the eastward (the ice having broken up and the cold being modified) twenty-five barrels of pork, thirty of flour, five hundred bushels of corn, two hundred of rye, and a thousand pounds of flax, to be exchanged for boards, glass, and other necessaries, so that a few of the citizens of the town might rebuild their houses or shops under the authority of the selectmen, and in accordance with the proper regulations of the naval office.

All trade had been at a standstill for years, and it was with the greatest difficulty that one bought the commonest articles used in building. Some of this stuff which Captain Thorpe was to get had been engaged by David Hardy. Terrible suffering through the winter months had forced him to accept the aid offered by Duane. The wind and the snow had played havoc with their cabin. There were days when they ate frozen food. Crowded into their hut, and crouching over the sputtering fire, they lived amid clouds of smoke, which filled the low spaces and gave them aching eyes and sore throats; but they were not worse off than their neighbors, so that in the fellowship of pain they encouraged each other, and bore up bravely for the sake of native land.

Cold might hold them in its vice-like grip, storms might rage and bury the hut in snow (then they were passably warm), poverty might

stint them to the coarsest, commonest fare;
nevertheless hope was swelling within the
breast. France had finally come to their
rescue in a generous way. Assurance was
now made doubly sure that the patriots must
win the day.

"I know it's hard," said Desire, as Lois
complained of her frost-bitten ears and David
referred to a frozen nose, "but we'll have a
better shelter next winter, and we shall soon
see the dawning of a true liberty day."

The faith and courage of this young woman
helped to sustain many a worn, depressed soul.
No soldier in the conflict showed a nobler
spirit of self-denial, or a grander purpose to
fight the issue to its victorious end.

The Hardy family might be living in close
quarters, subjected to unwonted deprivation,
yet their cabin was the centre of attraction
for the young patriots of the shore, and Desire continued to inflame these visitors with a
fresh and beautiful enthusiasm, for the cause
of human freedom. The Continental army
and its needs, the state of the local militia,
the stirring writings of Paine, the speeches in
the American Congress, the turn of events in
the south or north, — everything pertaining
to the great struggle was on her tongue's

end. She had familiarized herself with the
condition of the currency ; she talked with
intelligence concerning the difficulties connected with short enlistments, scant clothing,
raw troops, disaffected officers and privates.
In her serious, wise reflection, she had can-
vassed every question suggested by the dis-
couragements of the hour.

"I'm ashamed of my countrymen that
suffer under an attack of the cannon fever
and skulk away home," she observed to Major
Tallmadge, who made bitter complaints over
the frequency of desertions ; "but we must
remember that the majority of our soldiers
knew little or nothing about service. They've
been brought up to the plough. The shock of
warfare unnerves them, and they have yet to
learn that mastery of self which enables one
to resist the first onset of such a foe."

So Desire sought to relieve the burden of
chagrin and disappointment manifested by
some of the patriot officers, and to excite a
larger confidence in poor, weak humanity.

She was still the tireless comforter in
homes where sickness and sorrow came, showing infinite tact in her treatment of different
individuals, adapting herself to their moods
and conditions with delicate sympathy, bringing cheer and gladness with her presence.

This robust patriotism often suggested something of a masculine nature in her constitution. She had a forceful, startling way of expressing an opinion on public affairs. In her championship of independence and urgency to drive the British from the land, she was charged with unsexing herself, defying the rigid conventionalities of good society. There was a strength of mind, a loftiness of purpose, a conception of duty, a superiority to circumstances about her that reminded close observers of some ancient hero and martyr.

And yet Desire had all the fine sensibilities, the subtle graces, peculiar to the highest type of womanhood. It was simply that in her absorbing devotion to country she had passed for the time being beyond the recognition of sex. A patriot was a patriot, whatever might be the cut of the garment or the cast of the mind. She was sweet and gentle in the home, her heart yearned over the little circle grouped about her; but she felt a call to take some part in the enfranchisement of her country. If she was not permitted to shoulder a musket and march to meet the foe, she might kindle a flame of patriotism, or fan it into a little conflagration, among the people that touched her life.

Perchance, while rendering this service to the progress of liberty, there might come the opportunity to do some better work, and give life itself if need be. That was her spirit and vocation these days, and she represented a class of patriots that served to infuse fresh zeal and determination into thousands of hearts when the tide seemed to turn against the new States, and a few men would fain have entered into compromise with the oppressor.

The exchange of General Silliman and Judge Jones having been arranged, the latter was brought to Fairfield; but in the passing of papers, David was sent as a messenger to Lebanon, and his sister accompanied him. They traveled on horseback. Although they knew the governor, this was the first time that his Excellency had entertained them in his home.

The house was a comely two-storied wooden structure, double doors admitting the visitors to a hall running through the centre. It was set low on the ground, the big chimney towering above it, — a square, roomy, simple dwelling, having the appearance of comfort and prosperity. The war office was near, a low, hipped-roofed structure, with attic, three windows, and a door in front, one window in each end, a great chimney, and an old well-sweep standing guard on the left.

Governor Trumbull was seventy years old at this time, a small, finely featured man, antique in his dress, formal and dignified in manners, didactic and methodical, a lover of business and action, absorbed in public affairs, devoted to his country with a passion that was electric and masterful.

"I have considered the matter," said he to David, when his message — both spoken and written — had been delivered. "I have referred it to my council, and we are ready to do all in our power to expedite affairs."

As he spoke, the elaborate wig upon his head shook itself loose from the powder freely scattered over it. He wore fine ruffles on his wrists and in his bosom, a thick, high neck-cloth supported his chin, while his wide-skirted coat was buttoned nearly to the top, now and then a space being left open through which the spotless linen under-trimming appeared. A benign, firm mouth, keen eyes, high forehead, prominent nose, and spiritual countenance impressed one with the extraordinary character of the man.

"Methinks I have often heard our friend,

Mr. Thaddeus Burr, speak of Desire Hardy. Even the members of our Council of Safety must turn one side on occasion and confide to each other the homely gossip of town or domestic circle." While speaking, the good man smiled paternally upon his lovely guest. "But it is not often, child" (no wonder that the governor addressed Desire with this familiar term, for she appeared as fresh and girlish in his presence as a maiden in her teens), "that I hear a gentleman speak with such loving praises concerning our patriotic girls. Mr. Burr tells me you are the stanchest defender of the true political faith in all the country round."

"I fear, your Excellency, that my friend speaks with overmuch kindness. He is a very gallant gentleman, the soul of honor and courtesy. Mayhap in the natural warmth of his heart he puts too high a value upon the poor services that I may render our beloved country."

"Thou art a modest-spoken maiden," continued the governor, "but I have heard other wise observers give their testimony. I thank God for such loyal souls among our women. They are to us a mighty stay and support, the solace and inspiration of our life." Deep

emotion was manifest on the part of the
speaker, for a goodly report had come to
Governor Trumbull. The names of David
and Desire were both familiar to him. He
knew that on many occasions they had served
their country with rare fidelity. And now
he stood before them like some patriarch
bestowing a blessing upon the souls that had
proved worthy of his love. " Virtue ought
to be the object of all government," he continued reverently. " It is such a government
that we are founding in America. The men
and women who give themselves to the task
will command the gratitude of all coming
generations. My friends, remember that the
business of religion must be our daily concern. The people who love righteousness
and exalt God are the people who ought to
do the most and the best for the freedom of
the individual and the glory of a nation."

These lofty sentiments gave the travelers
something to think about on their return
to Fairfield. There was much pleasant con-
verse before the horse was brought to the
front door on the following morning, and
the young folks became deeply interested in
the company that gathered in the hospitable
dwelling of this noble friend of liberty; but

time was precious, and they tarried no longer than circumstances dictated.

"I met you at one wedding festival in Fairfield," said Governor Trumbull to Desire, as the brother and sister bade their host farewell; "and if God spares my life, I shall hope to meet you on another such occasion."

The grave and beautiful courtesy of the old gentleman touched the heart of the young woman. The light of an ardent faith in the coming greatness of her country illumined the face of Desire.

"May God speed the day when this land shall be freed from the oppressor, and a million happy homes adorn the fair landscape," was the lady's reply.

"Amen," said Governor Trumbull. "May God bless you, and make one of those happy homes your own."

And so the travelers hastened from Lebanon to Fairfield, enriched by the good man's benediction.

The governor and his council demanded the following parole of Judge Jones: —

"I, Thomas Jones, of Long Island, do acknowledge myself a prisoner of war to the United States of America, and do on my sacred honor engage and promise to say nor do nothing contrary to the interests and independence of the said United States, and I promise to go from Fairfield to Lebanon, in the State of Connecticut, to Governor Trumbull and wait his further orders."

Thaddeus Burr was a witness to the paper.

When the time came to exchange General Silliman and Judge Jones, the general set off from Long Island with his escort of redcoats, while the judge sailed from the Connecticut shore with his escort of patriots. The boats met in the middle of the Sound, and it was the hour for dinner.

They hailed each other.

"Is General Silliman in that boat?" shouted the leader of the patriots.

"Yes," was the answer. "Is Judge Jones in your boat?"

"Yes."

The two craft came to close quarters, and the prisoners arose and saluted; then followed hand to hand greetings and a moment of excitement and confusion.

"Mrs. Silliman has sent a turkey for you to feast upon, general," said one patriot sailor.

"And will Judge Jones stay with me for an hour and join in the feast?"

The happy commander of state militia was

speaking to the justice of the Supreme Court of New York.

"You honor me," was the cordial reply. "It gives me great pleasure to celebrate this event by dining with my esteemed friend."

And soon the two gentlemen, with David Hardy and Sherwood Spalding, were doing credit to the fare which the foresight and kindness of Mrs. Silliman had provided.

The conversation turned on Governor Tryon, and Judge Jones waxed eloquent in his eulogy.

"He is governor no longer," remarked the judge. "Bitter foes have sought his removal, and now that Robertson succeeds him, affairs will run less smoothly than when General Tryon was at the head."

"It may be that we are unduly prejudiced against him," replied General Silliman, "but to the people of Connecticut he seems anything but an exemplary man. His course in our State has been marked with great unkindness and barbarity."

"Simply the hard necessity of warfare!" exclaimed Judge Jones, with warmth. "Tryon is an honest, worthy, true-born Englishman, whose word is as sacred and binding as his obligation. He is beloved, esteemed, and almost adored by the people of New York. Why, sir, when he was governor, he heard all complaints with the utmost patience, his ears were always open as well to the rich as the poor, he was easy of access, kind, charitable, humane, and benevolent, a gentleman of activity, but sincere and honorable."

David's eyes glittered threateningly during the speech, while General Silliman smiled with an air of generous indulgence.

Doubtless Judge Jones had seen the best side of The Great Wolf. So far as the eulogist knew, he had never appeared in his rôle of Billy the Butcher; and Judge Jones doubtless felt that as a Firebrand, Tryon was simply doing his duty in Connecticut.

"Why, sir," continued this brave apologist of the royal governor, "he despised, abhorred, abominated all kinds of peculation, and never did a mean act while in office. I consider him a valiant soldier, a man of strict integrity, and a good Christian."

As Judge Jones was now the guest of General Silliman and the patriots were jubilant over his return to Fairfield and his post of duty, there was nothing for them to do but listen with incredulity or astonishment to such praise of the British officer.

"Well, sir," answered General Silliman, "I perceive that our views on Governor Tryon do not coincide. But I think we agree that this day is a happy one for both of us. I have not seen my little son Benjamin, who was born after I had been taken to Long Island. And I know that my faithful spouse is awaiting my return with full heart."

"And I, sir," exclaimed the judge, "shall receive a royal welcome from my family and friends, and once more shall find myself in the current of public events, although held in check by force of circumstances. Yes, it is a day of gladness for both of us. Yet methinks that clouds shut out a great part of the light, and the storm shows no sign of passing." He turned toward David, abruptly changing the subject of conversation. "Your likeness to your cousin, sir, is remarkable. I think it would be impossible for me to tell you apart."

"It is often observed," replied David gravely, "sometimes I fear to our mutual embarrassment."

"And there is a sister, if I mistake not," continued the judge. "Did I not see her with Mrs. Silliman in Fairfield?"

"My twin sister," said David courteously.

JUDGE THOMAS JONES

"A very decorous, lovely young woman," continued the judge. "What a strange coincidence that you three people should be such images of one another."

"I think it would be hard to find a young lady and gentleman more unlike in nature than Miss Desire Hardy and Mr. Duane Livingstone," interrupted Spalding. "The lady is the brightest and noblest of her sex."

There was a moment's break in the conversation; Judge Jones had entertained Duane Livingstone and Sherwood Spalding many times at Tryon Hall, and had observed that the best of feeling did not exist between them.

"I've got your musket and a few other things which you dropped in the woods on the edge of Norwalk," whispered David to the Fairfield Tory and refugee.

Spalding moved uneasily in his seat, and the color mounted his face.

"Keep them for me, my friend," was the reply, made in undertone. "Some day I'll go over and get the stuff."

There was a significant nod of the head, and an air of provoking confidence on the part of the speaker.

"Yes, you'll find them ready for you when you come;" and David's manner was that of warning or challenge.

CHAPTER XX

THE summer was another season of depression. Little occurred to strengthen the faith of the patriots, and there were weeks which never discovered a single rift in the war clouds. Men deserted shamelessly from the American army, and others entered into secret correspondence with the enemy, simply biding the time for their defection.

There was a great deal of public wrangling and private jealousy among the patriots, so that one did not feel sure of his man, and often the true hearts found themselves in gravest perplexity, for they did not know whom to trust. But there were many stanch souls that never wavered in their assurance of success.

"In a series of marvelous occurrences during the present war," Governor Trumbull had said to Desire and David, "he must be blind who doth not see the divine ordering thereof."

" Yes, your Excellency," had been the answer of the young woman, " God is manifest in this conflict not less than in the wars of ancient Israel."

General Silliman was now in command of the shore forces again, and the early events of the conflict seemed on the verge of a repetition in Connecticut. The jails and prisons were filled with Tories from other States. Every bay and harbor on the coast was the scene of frequent incursions and excursions. The inadequate protection of the shore towns was a constant invitation to " The Firebrand " to repeat his cruelty and barbarism.

Nevertheless, there was a small circle of enthusiasts in Fairfield that waxed stronger and stronger in courage, and they held uninterrupted communication with the patriot leaders.

Aaron Burr, now a man high in public esteem and fertile in resources, sent an occasional missive into the Hardy household, relating his adventures, breathing forth love, patriotism, ambition, spurring on the little company of kindred spirits to fresh effort and devotion. One day, when they were in the midst of building their modest cottage, the stuff having come to them through Captain

Thorpe, Burr appeared on the scene in all
the radiancy of his fashionable clothes, gay
manners, and high spirit. He was only five
feet and six inches in height, but there was
that in his person which made one forget or
ignore his small stature. Slender, symmetri-
cal, well poised, with fair transparent com-
plexion and a commanding aspect, forehead
prominent, nose rectilinear, betraying haughti-
ness, eyes dark hazel, glowing with ardor and
scintillating with tremulous sensibility, lips
thin and flexible, voice manly and melodious,
speaking with great animation and frankness, all devotion to the ladies, gazing at
them with a sort of rapture, using the most
captivating gestures, and talking with a natural and insinuating eloquence, — he was a
young man to win instant attention in any
company, and cause great flutterings of heart
whenever thrown into the society of the gentler sex.

Burr's visit to Fairfield was during this
period of depression ; and his unfailing flow
of humor, his dashing, riotous spirit of adventure and hopefulness, did much to dispel
any gloom that chanced among the Hardy
patriots. He was aided in this delightful
task by Major Tallmadge, who still made fre-

quent visits to the town, and held closely in
hand the agents engaged in secret service for
Washington.

Tallmadge was quite the contrast of Burr
in respect to size, looks, and manners. Yet in
personal charm, soldierly mien, and gayety of
disposition, one noted a marked resemblance.
The home that entertained two such guests
was bound to grow bright with the cheeriest
fellowship, and any life caught in the current
of their youthful exuberance and *bonhomie*
must needs shine with peculiar brightness.

"Ah, David," said Burr, "you made a mistake in not joining the Continental army. We
young bucks saw lively times, and I hear that
you have been wasting your martial energies
in petty warfare along the Connecticut coast."

"Why did n't you stick to your regiment,
then ?" inquired David, with some degree of
asperity.

Burr, having left the army, was now living
at his ease.

"Oh," was the ready answer, "illness
forced me out of the ranks. I was obliged
to preserve my health." It had been cur-
rently reported that the proud young officer
did not like some of his superiors.

"And pray, sir, is not David fighting as

truly for his country when engaged in protecting our homes and serving loyally in the state militia?" It was Desire that put the question to Colonel Burr.

"My charming cousin," exclaimed the gallant officer, "I wish a thousand times that I had such a brace of sisters to protect. My patriotism would multiply a hundredfold." He smiled in his subtle witchery.

"It is a noble service which many of the train-bands have performed under the lead of their captain-general, our great war governor, Trumbull," said Major Tallmadge. "Connecticut has distinguished herself most honorably. Washington leans upon his good brother 'Jonathan.' The virtues of such a patriot, forwarded by the noble support of kindred spirits in this commonwealth, have been an unfailing resource and encouragement to the Commander-in-chief."

"I know it, I know it," interrupted Colonel Burr, with enthusiasm. "I am proud of such men as poor David here, who wants to preach the gospel of peace, and yet boldly takes up arms and fights the devil with a matter of fact instrument like a musket. David, you've done your duty. You ought to have stayed on your native heath and

met the aggressor when he came to despoil
this fair land. By Jove, my boy, I'm going
to speak a good word for you when the war
is ended, and see if we cannot put you where
your shining qualities are credited for their
full value."

There was a frank, generous expression in
the speaker's face that won instant confidence.
But David smiled in an absent, deprecating
way, seeming to feel the kind intentions of the
speaker at the same time that his mind wan-
dered to other and more engaging themes.

"We'll set up David as a teacher of philosophy or some other profound subject by
and by," said Major Tallmadge. "He has
been a faithful, courageous member of the
train-band, but war is not in his line. It is
only the exigency of the situation that makes
it bearable for him. Let us pray that the
day of peace shall speedily dawn upon us."

"It is true," observed Desire, with a color
of sadness in her words, "David is a man
of peace. His heart is with his books. And
I am often made wretched because I have
to send him into the strife. Not that he is
unwilling, or lacks the zeal of service. Far
from it. You know, gentlemen, that a more
unflinching, a more devoted patriot is hard

to find." Desire paused a moment in her praises. "But his tastes and aptitudes do not run to fighting. He sometimes gets absorbed in less tangible things." Desire had a whimsical expression upon her face. "He forgets himself and works away bravely upon some metaphysical contention, and unless somebody keeps watch over him, the enemy, methinks, might bag him as the hunter does his game."

They all laughed, David looking indulgently upon his sister, only half heeding the words which she had spoken, his mind wandering upon the political aspects of public affairs, shaping the course of events in case the war ended and the people were brought face to face with the questions of a new government.

In the midst of this conversation, one summer evening, as the shades had thickened into darkness, Chloe entered the room and motioned for her mistress to come out. Excusing herself for a moment, Desire followed the slave.

"What is it?" asked the young woman, with eagerness.

"Minto here say dat Mas'r Livingstone be mighty sick in de ba'n."

Desire waited not for any further words of explanation. She ran through the night toward the rough shed which had served as a shelter to their stock and a granary for their corn and grain. It was at best a poor, mean makeshift of a place, crowded with produce and implements, hastily constructed, and very insecure. Here she found Mr. Duane Livingstone, lying weak, bruised, wounded, and unconscious upon the hay.

"What does this mean," cried Desire, as she tried to pierce through the blackness and distinguish objects before her.

"Mas'r Livingstone, he stagger into de ba'n like a drunken man, and call me and say tell my missis, an' den he fall down in a heap, he do." And that was all the information to be elicited from Minto.

The first thing was to bring the young man back to consciousness and learn what ailed him. Desire's experience among the sick and wounded soldiers had taught her how to deal with ordinary cases. So she dispatched Chloe to the unfinished house for the simple remedies which they kept in stock, and soon the efforts of the mistress with her two faithful helpers were rewarded by signs of returning life.

David and Lois had been left to entertain their visitors, although the sudden exit of Desire proved disturbing to the other members of the party. When a few minutes passed and the young lady did not return, Aaron Burr declared that he must now go over to his cousin's, where he was to spend the night. Mr. Thaddeus Burr had built a humble, tidy cottage as a temporary resting-place. There he continued to exercise such hospitality as his curtailed income and narrow circumstances permitted. It was not the old-time, affluent open house to a constant train of passing friends and grateful dependents, but it was the same genial spirit and gracious courtesy, extended freely to whomsoever might happen along the way, and choose to submit unto the plain fare and meagre quarters.

Major Tallmadge remained. When at length Desire reëntered the room, it was to excuse herself for the night, on the plea that her presence was needed elsewhere. As Major Tallmadge bade them good-by, perceiving that it would be agreeable for him to withdraw, she accompanied him to the door, handing into his keeping a bit of carefully folded paper.

No sooner were the visitors gone than all was commotion in the house.

"Duane lies helpless in the barn," said

Desire excitedly. "He must be brought here and hidden while we nurse him back to life. We shall be forced to let Dr. Allen into the secret, for I fear that some bones are broken, and his injuries very severe."

It was decided to carry him to the attic, as that place offered the best facilities for concealment. So the room was hastily prepared, and in the uncertain yet friendly darkness, Minto, Chloe, and David bore their unexpected visitor to this primitive resting-place. Here the doctor examined him and applied the remedies which his case demanded, announcing that the gentleman was elected to a siege that must extend through weeks.

Duane Livingstone, so well known in Fairfield, had been observed with the keenest interest. The fact that his family took sides with the patriots prejudiced his Connecticut friends in the young man's favor, and it had been a long time before the people of Fairfield could believe that this handsome, gallant scion of a worthy stock was casting in his lot with the oppressors of the land. But when once this impression went abroad, Livingstone's friends along the main steeled their hearts against him. So he had been a proscribed character many months, although it was impossible to bring specific charges of Toryism against him. The most that could be said in his condemnation was that Tryon still reckoned him as a friend, and was known to see him frequently, and the associations of the young man were chiefly among the Tories of New York and Long Island.

After the burning, Desire and David had earnestly besought him to make no further attempts to visit them. His life was menaced, and they feared that in his secret coming their own friends and neighbors might become the instruments of death or injury to him. Had he appeared at their door when Colonel Burr and Major Tallmadge were their guests, these men would have been in duty bound to put him under arrest; had they seen him bruised and wounded, his face and clothes smeared with blood, his condition would have rendered an investigation necessary, and proved exceedingly embarrassing to all concerned.

Duane acted contrary to the wishes and commands of his cousins. He had again crossed the Sound and attempted to steal unobserved into town, but the coast guard was still on duty, and he was unfortunate enough to run across one of them. Duane had landed at Pine Creek, the boat which brought him having turned about and shoved off to sea. He was picking his careful way through the swamp and the woods when the guard challenged him. In his efforts to get away undetected he had slipped and fallen, so that the sentinel was upon him in a second. A rough, wild scuffle had ensued, in which Duane was worsted, having his musket wrenched from him, his ribs broken, his face badly disfigured, and his whole system thoroughly shaken up. By a tremendous, final effort he had torn himself away from his assailant, and actually escaped in the dark, dragging himself stealthily, with great pain and loss of blood, to the family homestead. This was the plight in which Desire found him as he lay unconscious upon the fresh hay.

"I suppose," said Colonel Burr on the following morning, when he called to say farewell to his cousins, "that you hear occasionally from that elegant gentleman, Mr. Duane Livingstone. What a pity that he did n't have backbone enough to stand by his country."

"Well, now, Aaron," replied David, "you must n't be uncharitable. Remember there 's another side to the question. Duane lived in England a good many years, and may have imbibed considerable English spirit, although, mind you, I'm not upholding him. I simply point out that extenuating fact."

"Ah, David," said Burr, with great good humor, " when I go astray, I want you to sit on the bench and judge me. I think you'd find something to say in behalf of the Devil himself, if his Satanic Majesty was on trial. You're a good boy, David. Heaven was made for people like you. When you get there, keep me in mind, and press my suit with the Great Judge."

There was jest and earnest in the words of the speaker. It was hard to say which predominated.

"I have never met the gentleman," remarked Major Tallmadge, who had likewise called to say his last words before returning to Washington's headquarters. "I hear nothing against him save that he is a stickler for neutrality, and a neutrality that can stand the test of Tryon's favor has too much British color to suit me. I can't help but suspect it. I am told that Mr. Livingstone makes hay while the sun shines, and is really amassing a good fortune. Well, confusion to our enemies and sweets to the sweet!" — a senti-

ment which met the approval of the gentlemen, and occasioned no dissent on the part
of Desire and Lois.

"I should be extremely sorry to hear that
Livingstone had ventured into Connecticut,"
said Colonel Burr. "Some tanner might get
hold of him and tan his hide. If you ever
write to him, David, tell him to fight shy of
the shore patriots."

One might have suspected from the tone
that Burr had some special purpose in giving
such a warning. There was noted in the face
of Desire a fleeting expression of annoyance
or confusion.

"Oh, the man is shrewd enough to keep
himself away from the clutches of these high-
strung, stiff-necked Yankees," exclaimed Tallmadge. "And he may not be so far gone in
his Toryism as some of his old acquaintances
try to make us think. He may be making
money in order to defray the expenses of
rebellion against the king."

The major laughed heartily at his happy
conceit.

The conversation moved smoothly along,
while Mr. Duane Livingstone was lying helpless and battered upon a rough cot in the
attic. It required all the self-command and

assurance of the cousins to conceal the anxiety that was preying upon their minds.

When Colonel Burr departed, it was with a consciousness that, whatever power he exerted over the gentler sex, it had been used in vain with Desire Hardy, — not that she was deficient in sensibility, or averse to the attentions of men : she impressed him as a young woman whose soul was absorbed in the struggle waging through the land, as one so consecrated to the cause of liberty that any lesser passion was held in abject slavery to it.

CHAPTER XXI

THERE followed days and weeks of tender nursing. Work on the house was delayed because the sick man could not bear the racket of saw and hammer; it was easy enough to find plausible excuses in this time of harvest and constant skirmishing with the enemy.

Through the unfinished roof the sunshine and the fresh air entered the attic. The loosely matched boards of the floors and the thin, unplastered walls gave the patient every opportunity to hear what was said and done in the little home. This condition of things did not prove a source of annoyance; on the contrary, it became a means of entertainment and diversion. The cousins could not say to the numerous visitors who frequented their home, "Hush," "Do be quiet," "Don't speak above a whisper," for that would have required explanation; so they let conversation take its natural course, and the fortunate or unfortunate eavesdropper above gleaned whatever satisfaction his peculiar situation afforded.

There were times when he heard that which amused; then again some friend or neighbor said things that made his ears tingle, giving him food for serious reflection.

Duane Livingstone himself was a not uncommon topic of conversation; and if ever a man received a careful and exhaustive analysis of his character, and was subjected to the frankest, most critical examination in respect to motives, actions, and prospects, that man was the prisoner of circumstances in the attic. He might blush with shame when they called him traitor, or give way to nervous tremors when some one suggested that he be tarred and feathered; but Desire's wise speeches, her brave and beautiful defense of him, the passion of personal loyalty into which she was betrayed on two or three important occasions, more than offset any trivial discomfort caused by a candid expression of the visitor's opinion concerning Duane Livingstone.

David, Lois, Minto, and Chloe had their share in winning the young man back to health, but Desire was head nurse, and she ruled with perverse tyranny. It seemed to be her purpose, when Duane began to mend and was comfortable, to pass the care of him over to the other members of the family, the excuse being that more important duties demanded her attention. The patient fretted because she neglected him, but it availed nothing.

When once the household had settled down to the routine of his sick room, Duane was anticipating many quiet, happy hours with Desire. Had she not shown real, deep affection for him? Did he not detect tell-tale evidences of an attachment that was more than cousin love? So he blessed the fate which drove him into this despoiled town and handed him over to the watch-care of these tender-hearted patriots.

And yet his dream seemed likely to prove naught but a castle in Spain. Desire was occupied with other things. People were coming every hour of the day to ask her help or counsel. Every soldier in town appeared to think that he was not thoroughly prepared for duty until he had talked with this young woman and caught something of her ardor and devotion. There were hours when Duane was feverish with jealousy; then his sober second thought showed the absurdity of it.

The more men the merrier, and the less likeli-
hood that she cared particularly for any of
them.

The thing which chiefly vexed the invalid
was Desire's perverse effort to keep some third
person in the room whenever she sat with him.
Duane would devise a score of errands on
which to send the intruder, but Desire herself
was the one who invariably chose to discharge
these trivial offices. When, by chance, they
two were left together, the conversation was
sure to run in certain political or warlike channels, so that there was never the opportunity
for words of endearment or heart confidence.

The shrewd and specific way in which Desire inquired into the haunts and associations
of her cousin would have suggested to an
observer that she had some deep purpose in
view. In these weeks, she learned everything
about his habits of life, the characteristic
phrases he used among his associates, the
nature and condition of his business, his relations with the men through whom he was
working in the amassing of his fortune, the
names and peculiarities of many prominent
or obscure Tories on Long Island and New
York, the places where he stopped in his trips
to and fro between New York and Hunting-

ton, how he carried his money, what he paid for things, a hundred kindred matters. Was her interest so great in the young man that she must devote all her time with him to these careful inquiries? Was it because he was Duane Livingstone that she delighted to pry into the innumerable details of dress, conduct, manners, business, comrades, and experiences?

Duane had ventured down into the chamber below the attic on several occasions; he was beginning to chafe over his limits and talk about making a break for liberty, although the doctor said it would be weeks before he was fit to leave the place.

On one evening in early October, he was sitting with David. Desire and Lois were spinning, sewing, knitting, or doing some of the many household tasks which fell to their lot. There was a knock at the door, and the voice of Major Tallmadge fell upon their ears. A moment, and greetings were exchanged; then the young officer was heard to throw himself into a chair before the blazing fire.

"You are weary," cried Desire, startled by the worn and painful expression upon his face. "Chloe, make a glass of flip for the gentleman."

Major Tallmadge was not himself. He

gazed at the fire, then he looked upon the sisters. The old bright, merry spirit was gone. There were lines of sorrow and trouble written into cheek and forehead. The atmosphere of depression and suffering which he brought with him diffused itself through the room.

"I fear me that you bring us doleful news," said Desire, interpreting the mood of her visitor.

"My God!" exclaimed the man, in a voice hoarse with anguish, "how cruel and diabolic a thing is war!"

"Pray relieve our anxiety, sir."

"Have you not heard that Major André of the British army was arrested as a spy?"

"Oh, yes, we have known it these several days, and the awful treachery of Benedict Arnold, a Connecticut man, I am ashamed to confess."

"André was hanged on the 2d of October."

The silence was unbroken save by the crackling of the wood on the hearth and a sudden, heavy fall in the room above.

"What is that?" exclaimed Major Tallmadge. Springing to his feet, he looked inquiringly toward Desire.

"Something has toppled over," answered

the young woman huskily. She arose from her seat, as though she would prevent any interference or investigation on the part of her guest. " David is in his room. Perhaps he has stumbled in the dark. Excuse me for a moment; I will see."

She took a fresh candle from the kitchen and climbed the stairs with slow step. Duane had fainted. David was using all his art and skill to bring the young man back to life. Desire ventured to stay long enough to see that her cousin was regaining consciousness, then she returned to the room below, remarking that David begged to be excused; he would see Major Tallmadge in the morning.

" You were with Major André," said Desire, with assumed calmness, as she took up the thread of conversation.

"Yes, I had been skirmishing with the enemy and capturing cowboys, and on the evening of September 23d, I returned to the regiment near Northcastle. After I had disposed of my detachment, I was informed that a prisoner had been brought in that day by the name of Anderson. Three men had fallen in with him on his way to New York; and finding in his boots suspicious papers, they brought the man to Lieutenant-Colonel

Jameson, who soon sent him on to Arnold at West Point."

"What did Lieutenant-Colonel Jameson do that for?" inquired Desire excitedly.

She had regained her self-possession, and was now following the narrative of the speaker with the closest attention.

"I have n't been able to find out," was the reply of Major Tallmadge, "but I did not fail to state the glaring inconsistency of this conduct in a perfectly friendly manner, of course, to the ranking officer of the day, and I finally obtained his reluctant consent to have the prisoner brought back to our head-quarters."

The interest taken by the auditors in Major Tallmadge's story was painful. He was not aware that Minto and Chloe stood at the kitchen door with drawn faces and staring eyes, or that David Hardy and Duane Livingstone were seated in the room above him, listening with bated breath.

"As soon as I saw Anderson, and especially after I saw him walk (as he did almost constantly) across the floor, I became impressed with the belief that he had been bred to arms. It was deemed best to remove the prisoner to Salem, and I was to escort him.

I was constantly in the room with him, and he soon became very conversable and extremely interesting."

Major Tallmadge stopped to wipe the sweat from his face. The room had grown warm, or his emotions had given him a fever.

"It was very manifest that his agitation and anxiety were great. After dinner, on the 24th, perhaps by three o'clock, he asked to be favored with a pen, ink, and paper, which I readily granted, and he wrote a letter to General Washington. In this letter he disclosed his true character to be Major André, adjutant-general to the British army. When I received and read the letter (for he handed it to me as soon as he had written it), my distress was extreme, and my emotions wholly indescribable."

Again there was a pause in the narrative, unbroken by his hearers.

"Lieutenant-Colonel Jameson's letter, telling of André's capture, had gone to Arnold, and he escaped to the Vulture on the morning of the 25th. I took Major André under a strong escort of cavalry to West Point, and the next day we went down the Hudson to Haverstraw and on to headquarters. A court of fourteen general officers was ordered to sit

and hear the case. On the 29th, General
Greene, the president of the court, reported
to the Commander-in-chief that they had come
to the conclusion that Major André ought to
be considered as a spy from the enemy ; that
agreeably to the law and usages of nations, in
their opinion he ought to suffer death. The
next day, General Washington approved the
finding, and ordered that the execution should
take place at five o'clock in the afternoon on
October the 1st."

The narrator lingered for breath. Desire
and Lois did not take their eyes from his face.

" A vast concourse of people assembled to
witness the solemn scene, but the execution
was postponed in consequence of a flag having
arrived from the enemy; but no satisfactory
proposition was received, and the next day
was named for the execution."

There was another pause, longer than the
previous ones. Major Tallmadge was en-
deavoring to control his feelings.

" He was in truth a most elegant and ac-
complished gentleman. It may sound strange
in your ears when I repeat it, ladies; but I
say it, with God as my witness, that for the
few days of intimate intercourse I had with
him, which was from the time of his being

brought back to our headquarters to the day
of his execution, I became so deeply attached
to Major André that I can remember no
instance where my affections were so fully
absorbed in any man." Tears filled the eyes
of Major Tallmadge, while his voice trembled.

"After he was informed of his sentence, he
wrote a touching and finished letter to Washington, requesting that the mode of death
might be adapted to the feelings of a man of
honor, but his request could not be granted.
I walked with him to the place of execution,
and never discovered any evidence of fear.
When he came in sight of the gibbet," —
Major Tallmadge again stopped, and, lifting
his hand to his eyes, seemed trying to shut
out the awful vision, — "he appeared to be
startled, and inquired with some emotion
whether he was not to be shot. Being informed that the mode first appointed for his
death could not be consistently altered, he
exclaimed, 'How hard is my fate!' but
immediately added, 'It will soon be over.'
Brave, ingenuous soul! I then shook hands
with him under the gallows and retired."

Was Major Tallmadge morbid and distraught that he told this tragic incident to
Desire and Lois Hardy? Was the horror of

it a burden that he must share with these
lofty patriotic spirits?

"When I saw him swinging under the gibbet," he continued, with husky voice and
quivering lips, "it seemed for a time as if I
could not support it. Oh, the agony of that
moment! The spectators were overwhelmed.
There was not a hardened or indifferent one
in all the multitude. May I never look upon
the like again! May God preserve from such
a fate any great soul known to me!" The
soldier groaned in bitterness and horror.

A spasm of sharp pain darted across the
face of Desire, while Lois wept in terror and
sympathy. A moment passed, when Major
Tallmadge leaned his aching head upon his
hand. Then he seemed to shake himself free
of the gloom, the hideous memory, the awful
sorrow of the occasion. The telling of it had
relieved him. A new light came into his face,
and he gazed questioningly at Desire Hardy.

"It is like a nightmare," she observed.
"It takes one back to our friend, Nathan
Hale. I thank God that in the necessities of
this terrible circumstance Major André was
well treated, and all possible done to mitigate
his suffering."

"They didn't treat Captain Hale that way,

did they?" cried Lois, grateful for an opportunity to say something in order to relieve the tension of her mind. "I remember how the infuriated English officers cried, 'Swing the rebel up! Swing the rebel up!' It makes my blood boil with indignation. I feel like saying all the imprecatory psalms."

"And yet," observed Desire, with quiet manner and measured words, "a patriot would even die for one's country on the gibbet, if needs be."

There was a deathlike stillness in the room, Major Tallmadge being the first to break it.

"I ask no friend of mine to run the risk of an ignominious death like that of the lowest criminal in order to aid me in any campaign. It is brave beyond words, but I dare not prefer such a request." There was an air of warning and determination about him that went further than anything he might say.

"Major Tallmadge, I bethink me that our blessed Lord died the most shameful and iniquitous of all deaths. Shall we refuse to follow in his footsteps when it is the will of Heaven?"

"I perceive," said the soldier, with awe and reverence, "that the spirit of the martyrs is abroad in our beloved land. America shall be free!"

CHAPTER XXII

DESIRE ON THE MOUNT OF VISION

THE ethics of the Secret Service was often discussed in the Hardy family, for there was diversity of opinion on the subject. Colonel Burr had observed in one of his serious moods that all was fair in war. When it came to a question of advantage over the enemies of one's country, the patriot might resort to whatever ruse or deceit he pleased.

David had combated this position, saying that while ambuscades and strategy were legitimate, anything that reflected upon personal honor was unpardonable. A man might go into the enemy's camp as Captain Hale did, and get all the information possible. That was taking great risks, but it involved nothing that was inherently against conscience; but when a man, professedly the friend of a people, was all the time plotting against them, making his associations one means of foul betrayal, David contended that his course ought to put him beyond the pale of respectable society.

It was hard to draw the line.

" I cannot see how an honorable man such as I take Major André to have been could have entered into negotiations with a traitor like Benedict Arnold," observed David on the morning that followed the visit of Major Tallmadge.

" Well, David, I think your sense of honor is too keen. Major André believed that he was in the right, and that the rebels (as they call us) ought to be subdued and brought back in allegiance to the king. He was consummating a bargain by which a supposed misguided American was to be won over to the side of his rightful sovereign, put in a position where he would help speedily to bring all of us to our senses, and hasten on the war to its end. I don't see that Major André is to be blamed. The renegade Arnold was the man of base mind and conduct."

Desire spoke with clear and definite conviction. Long months had she reflected upon the various phases of experience suggested by the example of Nathan Hale and other men engaged in the like service.

" Well, it is very perplexing to me," answered the brother. " I don't think I would ever hesitate to penetrate into the enemy's camp, get all the information possible, do what I was able to do in order to bring confusion upon them; but when it comes to dealing with traitors, or betraying the confidence of friends, I declare myself to be unequivocally opposed to it."

"I think that is Duane's opinion too," said Desire. "I have heard him say many times that while a man undoubtedly will be able to learn more or less concerning the state of things in an enemy's camp by simply keeping his ears open and his mouth shut, yet he has no right to betray friendship, or resort to other dishonorable means."

"I suppose the difficulty will lie in the ideas of different individuals. One man would esteem one thing honorable, and another would stamp it on the instant as dishonorable. Conscience is a curious faculty, and I would sooner rely upon the judgment of the average child than on that of the majority of men, when it comes to the matter of deceit or evasion."

"David," replied his sister, "I 've been studying the wars of Israel. God will make the wrath of man to praise Him. The Old Testament worthies adopted measures that seem harsh and cruel; but don't you find the

same thing all through life? Is n't sickness
or accident sometimes a dreadful thing?
We'll try to find out what is right, and then
do it; but it seems to me that there are times
when the right means the doing of things
that are an awful strain upon body and soul,
reason and affection."

The three or four days that passed after
the story of André was told by Major Tallmadge fostered a spirit of unrest in the Hardy
household. David was more absent-minded
than ever, revolving over and over his tragic
case, and searching history for any parallel
incident, consulting philosophy and litera-
ture for problems in casuistry, growing more
troubled and perplexed the further he pushed
his investigations.

Duane was not as well; his wounds and
bruises began to annoy him again; he was
nervous and fretful. So bold and careless
had he become that on several occasions neighbors had had their suspicions aroused, and put
embarrassing questions to Chloe and Minto.

But the greatest change was observable in
Desire. Her mind dwelt on Hale and André.
She spoke with enthusiasm concerning their
willingness to serve the cause they loved,
even when they knew that possible disgrace

and contumely might become their lot. In
her talks with Duane, a line of conduct had
been distinctly indicated and agreed to. They
were one in their views as to the rights and
the wrongs of secret service. The man engaged in such a perilous undertaking might
proceed with pure heart and clean conscience
unto certain well-defined limits. Passing said
line, he involved himself in moral obliquity.

All the inmates in the home noted the
change in Desire. The first thought was that
perchance the shadow of André's death was
upon her, for a strange, inexplicable seriousness marked every mood and action. Later,
a certain grand, exalted manner manifested
itself, so that, all unconscious to Desire, a
barrier was separating her from the other
members of the household.

She had many things to say concerning
love of country, and they were said in a way
to thrill one's heart. She pictured that which
in her imagination she conceived this land
must become with the help of time and favor-
ing circumstances. The names of ancient
heroes were upon her lips, and she recited
their achievements with natural eloquence.
When neighbors spoke upon the darkness
which enshrouded the country after the treach-

ery of Arnold, she cheered them with her
noble faith, and infused a new spirit of confidence and sacrifice into their circle.   Meeting
with the men who had put everything into
the struggle, and whose hopes of life centred
in the independence of the States, she encouraged them with beautiful prophecies of
speedy peace, returning prosperity, and sub-
lime achievement, in which all the nations of
the world must ultimately rejoice.   Her mood
was not so much one of patriotic fervor as
that of moral grandeur and seer-like inspiration.

"I 'se afraid to touch her," whispered
Chloe to Duane. "She be livin' wid de
angels in de clouds."

"David," said his cousin, with deep concern, "methinks Desire has climbed some
mount of vision. I am distressed to think
what might happen to her in case the patriots
suffer defeat."

"Duane, have no fears on that score."   The
suggestion had aroused David from his growing absorption in the purely speculative.
"America will have her freedom ; and Desire — why, she 's heart and soul in the
struggle, a better patriot than two thirds the
men in the field, a clear-visioned spirit that

gains more by intuition and foresight than nine
tenths of men ever get by study and experience. Duane, she ought to have been a man.
She'd have made her mark in this conflict.
She's got the intelligence and acumen of the
best scholar in politics you can find; she's
sound on every question of state; she's a
natural leader and inspirer of men; she's
ready to give life itself for the sake of country. A thousand times I've wished she was
a man so that she might serve the cause to
best advantage."

There was a glow of unstinted love and appreciation in the countenance of the speaker.
It was the sweet, spontaneous tribute of a
brother to one dearer to him than life itself.

"I've never regretted that I was a man,
Duane," he continued, "but how I have
wished that Desire could have had my chances!
There's Tallmadge and Burr and Hamilton
and half a dozen other bright young men
that would have been distanced by her long
ago; and here the child stays tied down by
narrow circumstances and her sex. It's one
of the inscrutable things of this most puzzling
and inexplicable world."

"Ah, David," answered his cousin, with infinite yearnings and outreachings betraying

themselves to any ears save dull ones like David's, "I thank God that Desire is what she is. She's doing well enough. By and by the good Lord will open the way for her, and she'll do greater things. But to my mind, young man, the woman who makes a home, and brings under her sway the needy world, is a person doing quite as much for men as some gay coxcomb of an Aaron Burr."

David looked with wide-extended eyes into the face of his cousin. Why did the invalid show such heat and passion?

The faithfulness of Desire in the home was like the service of sunshine and shower, — one took it in the course of nature and made no comments.

But this extraordinary, vitalizing patriotism was something to be remarked and exalted. It transformed the woman into a kind of goddess. David loyally elevated his sister to this unique pedestal. He had ceased to think of her as one submitting to the common homage of love, or yielding to any witchery of men.

"Duane," said his cousin severely, "Desire has long ago risen above the ordinary passions of a woman's heart. I suppose she does love her family, but her passion is the passion of a patriot." His frame swelled with pride, as he uttered the words. " I believe she'd like to die for America; and now we are speaking upon the subject, that must be the matter with her, these days since Tallmadge was here. Did you ever see such faith? Why, Duane, you must have a heart of stone not to be won by it and join the patriots in their struggle. I'm glad to have you with us, and you know how much we all love you; but it passes my understanding that you can see the suffering inflicted upon these colonies, and come into contact with such a glorious lover of country as Desire, and not be moved to cast in your lot with us."

Duane made no answer, and David left the room.

There was an atmosphere of suppressed excitement in the home the ensuing day. The face of Desire glowed with a light that seemed preternatural. Her voice was low and sweet, but every word which she spoke was surcharged with feeling. Little opportunity was given for conversation, since every member of the household was intent upon some necessary task. Even the invalid was allowed to help, in order to pass away the time, although his face expressed dissent and wretchedness. The unwonted activity was a prelude to succeeding days of quiet, for it had been decided that Lois and Chloe were to take charge of Duane and the home, while the other members of the family made a brief excursion into the country. It was not an unusual thing for the young folks to go to Hartford, New Haven, or Waterbury. They had friends in all these towns. And when one went away during troublous times, it was not expected that his business or pleasure would be noised abroad through the neighborhood; so the young travelers quietly took their leave.

Never did Washington feel greater need for secret intelligence in respect to the condition and purposes of the enemy. If it is always darkest before day, there might have been assurance in the heart of many a patriot that the day was at hand, for public affairs and private inclinations foreboded dire evil. The Commander-in-chief was alive to the situation, and every nerve was strained to meet the threatened disintegration.

In his management of the Secret Service, Major Tallmadge had resorted to a variety of means and agents. He met some of the men engaged in this perilous business and gave them personal orders. There were other individuals unknown to him, who did their work as they chose, and made their reports in writing or through some confidential go-between.

A large portion of the intelligence received by the way of Fairfield came from a patriot whose identity was hidden beyond the possibility of disclosure. Major Tallmadge did not wish to know the individual. It was enough for him and for Washington that a mutual friend vouched for the absolute fidelity of the person, and that the revelations coming through this channel had always proved correct and valuable.

One thing in connection with this particular agent had been mentioned; namely, that the letters or documents generally passed through several hands in their transmission from New York to Fairfield; it was in connection with the bringing of these missives that a whaleboat had been kept for the service of Major Tallmadge in Black Rock harbor. The city agent was supposed to be a gentleman who did not find it possible to leave home, and was therefore forced to rely upon confederates. The letters were generally in cipher, although invisible ink was used a part of the time, so that when Governor Tryon blundered into the finding of two or three precious letters, he was none the wiser, never discovering the key to the smooth-reading epistles that provoked his curiosity.

Occasionally, these letters passed as communications between lovers. A cursory glance over them led one to infer that he had stumbled upon some clandestine love correspondence. Great was the amusement of the Commander-in-chief and those admitted to his confidence when these ardent, beautifully phrased epistles were read. The person who devised them must have been not only shrewd and highly imaginative, but one thoroughly versed in affairs of the heart. There was a ring and air of genuine love-making in them that often startled Washington. Could that sort of thing be simulated so tenderly, naturally, in order to carry secret intelligence to the patriots? Certain words and letters in certain relations conveyed the news which was designed for the help of the American army; but in construing this deftly concealed message, many a time did the chief and his assistants pause to note the delicate sentiment, the noble spirit, manifest on the surface of the writing.

"The ladies are our stanchest soldiers," said Major Tallmadge to Washington, after reading one of these interesting epistles. "They not only have to fight the battle at home, but they must nerve their husbands, sons, and lovers to fight in the field abroad."

"We are great debtors to the fair sex," answered the general. "Their patriotism is indeed our stay and inspiration."

CHAPTER XXIII

IN THREE PLACES AT THE SAME TIME

THE achievements of the women during the struggle for American independence is a theme for some future historian. When a Georgia giantess was put in charge of the fort which sheltered all the women and children of her neighborhood, during the absence of the patriots engaged in a distant skirmish, the redcoats arranged for an assault, thinking to find the fort an easy conquest. This woman donned the uniform of an officer, bade the other women clothe themselves in male attire, distributed them in conspicuous places along the works, put the cannon into action, and when the enemy approached opened fire. Then the royal troops, discovering that the fort was garrisoned, withdrew. This giantess represented the indomitable courage and fidelity of her sex.

Desire Hardy gloried in the devotion to liberty observed among her compatriots, and every incident of war shared by womankind

was a fresh incentive. What zeal and patience, what energy and shrewdness, what consecration and sacrifice, marked their course!
Working in the fields, melting pewter into
bullets, feeding and clothing the men, playing the part of messengers, carrying a musket when necessary, taking care of the sick,
editing and printing newspapers, arresting an
army, as did Mrs. Murray, in New York,
working as Daughters of Liberty to teach
and defend the great principles at stake,
denying themselves all luxuries and many
necessaries of life with sweet composure, —
the record is matchless. " Our ambition is
kindled by the fame of ancient heroines,"
said one of these great souls to Desire.
" We should at least equal them, and sometimes surpass them, in our love for the public good." Miriam, Deborah, Esther, Judith,
the mother of the Maccabees, were all familiar to the thought of Desire Hardy.

She read about the siege of Fort Henry,
Virginia, in 1777, when savages assailed the
little company of patriots. The powder being
suddenly exhausted, Elizabeth Zane arose in
her strength and ran the twelve rods to the
powder house and brought back into the fort
a keg of the precious stuff, thus saving the

garrison. She talked about Catherine Green, of Rhode Island, who gave up her beautiful home for a hospital when smallpox scourged the army in that State; the ladies of Philadelphia, who ministered with unstinted generosity to the suffering patriots during the campaigns in New Jersey and Pennsylvania; the maiden who carried a message across country, and when arrested and put in the guard-house, swallowed the precious paper; Dame Batherick taking her redcoat prisoners at Lexington; Esther Gaston shaming some runaway men, saying, "Give us your guns, then, and we will stand in your places."

Desire was familiar with these incidents and hundreds of others. They all served as fuel added to the volcanic fire of her passionate nature. When she said good-by to Duane and Lois, they were hushed into the most quiet and commonplace words of farewell. It is true that they were puzzled respecting her absence. Desire said that she had work to do which called her away from home. They must trust her and bide the time of a return. There was a loftiness of mien, a concentration and consecration of purpose evident, a greatness of soul that brooked no restraint. It was the culmination of that

masterful enthusiasm which had done so much
to inspire people and shape the course of
events in her narrow sphere.

It was four o'clock of a bright, gorgeous
October afternoon that a gentleman dismounted before the door of Tryon Hall, the
home of Judge Jones on Long Island. This
was the fortunate, or unfortunate, hour when
the judge and his lady had been accustomed
to enjoy their outdoor airing.

"Ah, Mas'r Livingstone, it be you, is it?"
observed the slave that hastened to hold the
bridle of the young man's horse while he dismounted and made known his errand. "De
jedge and lady am a-walkin' in de woods."

"Ah," said the gentleman, "I shall not
see them, then, for I must hasten on to meet
a comrade with whom I am traveling. Any
letters or packets, Sambo?"

"Yes, sah," was the reply, "I 'se got a lot
ob 'em."

"Bring them to me, Sambo, and there's a
piece of silver for your pains. I'll look after
my charger," continued the gentleman, with
a peculiar twinkle in his eyes.

The letters and packets were speedily delivered and tucked away in various pockets,
some every-day remarks made concerning the

day and the family, and away sped the gentleman on his journey to New York.

" Give your master and mistress my compliments, and say that I hope to pass this way again before a month is gone," was the parting word.

"Seems like he be in an awful hurry," grumbled Sambo, who was fond of Mr. Duane Livingstone. " If de gem'man go to New Yo'k, he might trabel wid Mas'r Spaldin'. I heard 'im say he be goin' to de city too."

But the gentleman evidently had more congenial company in view than Mr. Sherwood Spalding, judging from the pleased expression on his face as he departed from the precincts of Tryon Hall.

On the same evening, two or three hours later, Lois Hardy and Duane Livingstone might have been seen taking a walk over Round Hill.

" I 've been shut up in this place about as long as a human being can stand it," observed the young man to his cousin, when the shades of evening fell. " Lois, let 's take a walk. I 'll put on that suit I gave David last summer. He 's been wearing it lately, and if anybody asks questions, you say David has returned for the night and must

go away again in the morning. That's easy
enough to do. You see I'm dying for fresh
air and exercise."

Both Lois and Duane had their absent
ones in mind. The harmless diversion of an
evening walk might help to lessen anxiety,
although it was contrary to the orders of
Desire for the young man to leave the premises, or show himself to a person beyond their
home circle. But the temptation was great,
and the objections or perils seemed trivial.

It was a calm, delicious air, odors of wild
grapes diffusing themselves over the hillside.
Never did life seem more precious or beautiful. The tonic of October weather imparted
something of healthful impulse to the young
man. The sense of freedom made his pulse
beat faster. Then he grew vexed to think
that he had remained in Fairfield while
Desire mayhap was needing his protection or
restraint. And while they were walking along
the crest of the hill, whom should they hear
through the grateful, deepening night but
Major Tallmadge.

"Now," said Lois, "we must return straight
home. He'll be wanting to see David and Desire, and you'll have to stay in the barn until
I send Chloe to bring you into the house."

" Where 's David ? " asked the major, when Lois admitted him to the unfinished dwelling, " and your sister ? "

" They are visiting, and I don't know when they 'll return," was the reply.

" Ah," said the caller reflectively. He sat for a few moments talking with Lois, evidently keeping up another distinct train of thought, not making himself especially agreeable. He seemed anxious and disturbed.

" And you don't know when they 'll be home ? " he repeated, quite as much to himself as to his companion.

" No," she said. " Desire was on her high horse when she went away. She acted like one transported to the third heaven, if you know what that means. I should think from her manner that she expected to be offered up as a voluntary sacrifice. And I am quite sure that she 'd like it. Such talk as we have had in the house these last days since you were here I never heard in all my life. Desire ought to have been a general or a statesman. She 's got patriotism and faith enough for a whole State."

Major Tallmadge looked more anxious and harassed as Lois continued.

"I must go," he said, with puzzling constraint in his manner.

On that same night, the servant in charge of the Livingstone dwelling in New York (a domicile rented since the great fire, and inhabited chiefly by Duane and the several slaves) admitted a young gentleman and his attendant.

"How glad I is to see you," said the domestic. "You's bin away de longes' time," and he hastened to usher him into the house and follow him to his room. "We's 'pared to gib you a hot supper, mas'r," the servant continued. "You mus' be done gone sta'ved."

"No, Jock," said the gentleman quietly, "I'm tired and sleepy, and I must keep still all day to-morrow. You mustn't tell anybody that I'm here. My business is private, and I shall stay in my room most of the time and cannot be disturbed. I've picked up a man in my travels," — the speaker pointed to Minto, — "he'll wait on me. Take him with you now, and send me any letters or packets that have been waiting."

No extra lights appeared in the Livingstone headquarters that night, and had the house not been closely watched by observers, one would naturally have concluded that the occupants of it still remained away.

But Sherwood Spalding, with his confederates, had exercised surveillance over the place for many days. The Tory refugee from Fairfield was moved not so much by jealousy as distrust. While it was evident to him that Duane Livingstone transacted considerable business and amassed no mean sums of money, yet he believed that the young man had been accustomed to take a surreptitious part in the war, and that such a service was in fact the chief object held in view.

There were times when he thought that the prosperous fellow was a secret ally of Tryon, keeping ostensibly on the fence in order that he might serve the royal cause to better advantage; but he finally reached the conclusion that Duane was really an enemy of the king, and ought to be suppressed. Sherwood Spalding took it upon himself to ferret out the secret life of the unsuspecting young merchant, and bring him to that punishment which he was convinced Livingstone deserved.

During the weeks that his victim lay on the sick bed in the home of the Hardys, this watch had availed nothing. The house was untenanted save for the colored care-takers.

But now, at last, virtue had its reward. Sherwood had seen the young man enter the place. He proposed to face him down, accuse him of his duplicity, then hand him over to the proper authorities.

A little before nine o'clock that night, Spalding crossed over the street and rapped sharply upon the door. No attention was paid to the caller. He repeated his loud summons. Still it was unanswered. A third time he plied the knocker. At length, the ancient serving-man raised a window on the third floor, asking what was wanted.

" Come down and open the door, you black devil," answered the caller angrily.

" Fo'ks gone away," croaked Jock.

" You lie ! " shouted Mr. Sherwood Spalding. The head of the servant slowly disappeared, and the window was put down.

The insistent caller waited a brief time, expecting that Jock would descend and unfasten the door, but no sounds of footsteps greeted his listening ears. Becoming impatient, he pounded upon the door, making the knocker resound through the house, shaking the very front of the establishment in his wrathful vehemence. But there came no response to all this rudeness and commotion.

" I 'll face him, if I have to climb in a window or break a door down," was the passionate exclamation of Spalding, as he withdrew from the scene and called his associates to a hasty council of war.

" I know he 's there, for I saw him enter; he 's afraid to meet me," said the valiant refugee.

" Send for an officer and half a dozen men and surround the house," counseled one.

" Batter down a door and rush in upon him before he slips away," said another adviser.

" Make an entrance through a window quietly, feel your way to his room, and there have it out with him. We 'll be on the watch to see that he does not have a chance to escape."

" That 's a good idea," answered Spalding, after a moment's deliberation. " I know his room. There 's an easy way of entrance to it from a trellis. I 'm in for it, boys. One of you watch in the front, and the other follow me to the rear of the house." And so the council broke up, and the men proceeded to action.

Sherwood Spalding would hardly have ventured upon these summary measures except

that he was positive as to the complicity of
Duane Livingstone in certain schemes detri-
mental to the royal cause; he felt assured
that the evidences which he possessed would
be sufficient justification of his course when
the matter was brought to the notice of General Tryon or other officers in the British
army.

His men were placed according to the plan,
and Spalding climbed the trellis, which reached
to the second floor on the rear of the house.
It was a hall window which he tried. Through
some carelessness of the servant, it had been
left unfastened, so that he entered without
difficulty. The darkness and silence within
suggested a mistake on his part. Could it
be possible that his eyes had deceived him,
and that it was two servants he saw enter the
place? Yet he was ready to swear that,
through the dim light of the evening, he
detected a white man, Duane Livingstone.
There could be no doubt that he was in
hiding. Spalding now had the man where
he could lay hands on him, and drag him to
justice.

Groping stealthily across the hall, he stood
before the door leading into his victim's room.
He lifted the latch; the door yielded to his

touch. A candle flickered in its socket on the table. The fire on the hearth was dying, so that it did little to drive away the gloom of the place.

Standing by the door, which he had closed, Spalding cast his eyes over the room in search of the gentleman whom he sought. For a moment, it appeared that the intruder was the only occupant of the chamber; but as he peered more intently through the dim light of the apartment, an old settle against the wall took shape before him, and — he started nervously as he made the discovery — there was a cloaked form lying stretched upon it.

The two must have seen each other on the same instant, for as Spalding spoke, the figure reclining upon the settle sprang into the middle of the room.

"Livingstone, I've come to settle accounts with you. Don't think you can escape me. I've been on the watch for weeks, and my men are on hand to do king's service. And there's no use in making any fuss about the thing. I know you are a sly dog, and have pulled the wool over everybody's eyes, but we've got you this time, and you might as well throw up your hands and give in."

It was quite a long speech which the Tory

refugee made, and Mr. Duane Livingstone
seemed deeply impressed by it, for he stood
like a statue during its hasty recital. Mr.
Spalding advanced near to the middle of
the room as he concluded his address, and
standing face to face with the cloaked individual so lately resting on the settle, he did
not observe how another person had silently
opened the door, stepping close behind him.
Mr. Duane Livingstone (if this be he) made
no reply to his enemy's speech, but simply
lifted his arm, and motioned as though he
would fell him to the floor. How it was that
such an airy, distant gesture (for the gentlemen were still two or three feet apart) could
produce a result so marked and effective was
never explained to Mr. Spalding, but it suffices
to say that as the arm was swayed back and
forth in one swift movement, by some magic
this hound after human game dropped speechless and unconscious upon the floor.

"Hand him over to Jock, Minto," was the
order given by this strange antagonist. "We
must be soon going."

"O Mas'r Livingstone," exclaimed Jock,
when the silenced housebreaker was given
into his keeping, "what shall I do wid
him?"

"Let him go," said Minto, speaking for the master, who was making hurried preparations for departure.

In five minutes, Mr. Sherwood Spalding was left in possession of the Livingstone house, while the gentleman he had faced and threatened, having eluded the watchers, was gone on a journey.

CHAPTER XXIV

A PURSUIT AND A SKIRMISH

It was the night after the incident related in the preceding chapter that three gentlemen might have been observed in the neighborhood of Smith's Manor, at a point where the land projected into the South Bay. They did not appear altogether at home, and their movements would have been regarded as suspicious, had any Tory followed their track. They were evidently taking bearings, — spying out the land, — making themselves familiar with the situation.

The most easterly point was a triangular inclosure of several acres, at two angles of which was a strong barricade house, and at the third a fort, with deep ditch and wall encircled by an abatis of sharpened pickets, projecting at an angle of forty-five degrees. The fort and house were connected by a strong stockade, high, every post being sharpened, transverse rails bolted together holding the pickets and making a strong defense.

This fort, recently completed, was the depository of stores, dry goods, groceries, and arms. It presented a formidable appearance, being of peculiar importance for the reason that all Suffolk County could be easily supplied with provisions and the munitions of war from its resources.

Major Tallmadge had known that Fort St. George was an objectionable point in that part of the Long Island landscape, and as it drew near its completion, he proposed to General Washington that he be permitted to go over and demolish the works; but information was vague and inaccurate, so that the Commander-in-chief did not feel he was warranted in giving his consent to the undertaking.

The three strange visitors haunting the neighborhood were in quest of that definite knowledge which would serve the purposes of Major Tallmadge. By various means they procured a correct draft of the fort, made out an exact schedule of all the supplies, learned the size of the garrison, and also found that there was a large quantity of hay and forage collected by the enemy at Corum. A night and day were consumed in gathering these details. The following night, the mysterious trio, aided by well-paid agents among the farmers along the shore, hastened on their way to the rendezvous near Huntington.

They were drawing near the end of a most perilous and important expedition, one that had been surrounded with peculiar difficulties, and that could have been achieved only by consummate craftiness and intrepidity. It was so nigh the victorious finale that vigilance had been relaxed, and they ventured to exchange congratulations.

"How thankful we shall be, once safely embarked, speeding our way across the Sound," whispered the foremost traveler.

"Had we not been in the Lord's keeping, we should long ago have fallen a prey to the enemy," answered the second of the company.

"De Lo'd be praised foh his mehcy," muttered the hindmost man. Then a hush fell upon them, as they forged ahead through swamp and forest, open field and bush-besprinkled pasture.

The night was keen and crisp, frost stinging the face and nipping the fingers, so that the trio were glad to step lightly, swiftly, impelled by quickened beat of the pulse responding to the subtle tonic of the air.

" What shall we do in case the boat fails us ? "

" The boat will be on hand," was the emphatic reply.

" It cannot be more than a mile or two farther," whispered the first speaker.

" A mile, praise de Lo'd," croaked the rear guard.

" We 're coming to that marsh studded with underbrush. How I hate to pass through it. I feel as if every tuft of grass or old log was a stealthy Tory lying prone so that I might trip over him and fall into his treacherous embrace."

" Hush!" said the hindmost traveler, whose ears seemed preternaturally keen. They had entered the swamp, and there came floating to them faint, far-away sounds like the advance of a small troop through snapping, spiteful brush.

" We must turn back and skirt this ugly lot and make for the woods in the rear," said the leader of the party.

Like Indian warriors they crouched and crawled along their path, reaching at length the black shelter of the trees. Their progress would have been undetected except that they ran afoul of a dog, whose bark rang out discordantly in the night. It did not take a moment to pound the brute into the silence of death, but the incident drew the attention of their pursuers in that direction, and indicated that the game had finally been tracked.

It was a wild chase. The wearied trio at last separated in the fierce, frantic effort to elude their hunters and reach the point of embarkation. In a few moments, the woods and the country round seemed alive with troopers flying many ways.

The fugitives were familiar with the ground over which they ran, and they were spurred to superhuman exertions by the assurance that when they reached the goal assistance was awaiting them, and a fair chance of escape would be open.

Sherwood Spalding had been very busy since his adventure in the Livingstone house. The fact that his victim had slipped through his fingers and fled the city was, to his mind, the final incriminating circumstance. That Mr. Duane Livingstone was not vindictive and refrained from inflicting severe bodily injury upon him went for nothing.

No sooner had the Tory refugee returned to consciousness, and been allowed to withdraw peaceably from the house which he had entered like a thief in the night, than he reported to the general and demanded that men be sent in pursuit of Livingstone. After a day's delay, the order had been given, and a dozen redcoats went beating up and down the north shore of Long Island. Sherwood Spalding accompanied the band, and was the informing spirit of the adventure. The first trace of the fugitives was gained from one of the soldiers of the garrison at Fort St. George; but his information was so meagre and unsatisfactory that it did little except to confirm Spalding in his opinion that Livingstone must be somewhere along the shore opposite Stamford, Norwalk, or Fairfield, watching for a boat to take him across to the Connecticut side.

It was not until the tell-tale barking of the dog in the woods that Spalding and his troopers had any reward for all their pains. In the dim light of the stars they observed one or two shadowy forms shifting hither and thither amid the trees. It was not long before the pursuit waxed hot.

Off the shore faintly outlined against the eastern horizon, a large whaleboat was lying, every man in his place, alert and watchful, eyes turned toward Long Island, ears open to all sounds landward and seaward.

"What is that?" whispered the captain eagerly — excitedly.

"The report of a musket, sir," answered one of the crew.

"And there is a second and a third," exclaimed several husky voices.

"And I hear loud shouting," said another speaker.

"There's trouble on shore, my men," cried the captain. "A part of us must land and be ready to help."

A moment passed, and twelve sturdy patriots, fully armed, stood behind a rock projecting down upon the beach. A short distance in the rear, great frowning trees towered above them.

"There comes a man along the sand," whispered one of the boat's crew.

"And there come two more in the edge of the woods."

"And, by heavens! there's a dozen troopers in pursuit. Now we are in for it. Keep cool, boys!" muttered the captain. "Don't fire till I give the word."

The next two or three minutes of intense anxiety dragged themselves like hours. The

lone man on the beach was racing for dear
life, and two were in wild pursuit, making
evident gain.

"When those hounds get within shooting
distance, pick 'em off," said the captain to
two sharpshooters standing on his right.
"The rest of us will attend to the horde
coming out of the woods."

Another moment, and the clash of arms,
reverberation of muskets, shouts, cries, groans,
imprecations filled the air with the awful din
of conflict. A moment later, and the two
forces were grappling with each other in a
hand to hand encounter, and all was confusion
worse confounded ; for in the uncertain light
and sudden duel of men, it was difficult to
distinguish friend from foe.

The struggle waged fiercely for a few sec-
onds, one and another man being flung aside
dead or wounded. Then above the din and
turmoil of the fight the voice of Spalding
rang out strong and clear : —

"I have you now, my man " — blows and
metallic impact of steel upon steel. "You 're
fencing, are you, how 's that ?" — and the
stroke of a sabre resounded far and wide.
"I have you at my mercy, Livingstone " —
and there was a shot, a fall, a groan, a sudden

awful curse, hoarse and vengeful, when Mr.
Sherwood Spalding, who had been doing such
valiant work upon his bold yet unaggressive
antagonist, felt the butt end of a musket
touch his head, and on the instant sank beneath the crack of doom.   The man who
wielded the blow which felled Mr. Spalding,
did not stop to investigate the issue of his
work; but while in the very act of striking
hissed in his ears, "Dat no Mas'r Livingstone,
traitor, dat my " — and the last words were
running hoarsely, anguishfully through the
Tory's mind, as he reeled and tumbled in a
heap on the ground.

Minto dropped his musket, and, clasping in
his arms the limp form that Spalding's assault
had stretched low, ran like a deer for the boat,
followed quickly by the companion under
whose lead he had made a part of that memorable night march across the island.   The
fight did not continue, since the prime mover
in the pursuit — Mr. Sherwood Spalding —
was sleeping the deep sleep from which there
is no waking, sharing his long rest with several
comrades of the night.   The cessation of
hostilities came by swift mutual consent, for
while the remaining redcoats were blundering
through the darkness in search of the foe,

often mistaking one another for rebels, dealing their righteous judgments upon unoffending brethren, the patriots had retreated to the whaleboat on the plaintive cry of a whippoorwill twice repeated, and were already cutting the waters of the Sound in their swift course to the Connecticut shore.

CHAPTER XXV

It was on the morning of November 24th that Major Tallmadge called at the Hardy place to report upon the expedition against Fort St. George. Desire was reclining on a spacious settle drawn up in front of the hearth in the little parlor, now converted into a sick chamber. For more than a week she had been permitted to see her friends, and the doctor said that she mended rapidly.

"I hear your boats arrived off Fairfield beach at one o'clock this morning," said Desire cheerily. "I am waiting impatiently to hear the story of your adventure."

"*Our* adventure," remarked Major Tallmadge, with enthusiasm. "*Yours* not less than mine."

He seated himself near the settle, while David, Lois, Minto, and Chloe assumed positions in various parts of the room where they might watch his face and hear the narrative to the best advantage.

" Well, you know that the draft of the fortification and the schedule of munitions, supplies, and forces sent by the unknown patriot " — the officer smiled with charming naïveté — "satisfied Washington that my plan was feasible; so that permission was given me, and I brought my detachment of two companies of dismounted dragoons here to Fairfield, and on four o'clock of the 21st we embarked, arriving at ' Old Man's ' on Long Island about nine in the evening. By ten, we started across, and a pouring rain set in, so that we were obliged to go back to our boats, which we had placed in ambush, and there wait until the next night."

" That was too bad," exclaimed the invalid.

" Almost as bad as hiding in the heart of the forest one dismal night last month," interrupted David significantly.

" We marched over to Fort St. George the second night, and arrived at four in the morning," continued the narrator, with a contagious enthusiasm. " Just at break of day, I put my detachment in motion, having concealed two small detachments of men at different positions from the fort, where they were to remain until the enemy opened fire on my column. The pioneers who preceded

me had reached within forty yards of the
stockade before they were discovered.

"'Who comes there?' cried their sentinel,
and fired. Before the smoke cleared from
his gun, my sergeant had reached him with
his bayonet and laid him low. This was the
signal for all my men to move forward; and
how they did vie with one another to enter
the fort! So resolute were they that a break
was soon made in the stockade, where the
rear platoon halted to prevent the prisoners
from escaping. I led the column directly
through the grand parade against the main
fort, which we carried with the bayonet in
less than ten minutes, not a musket being
loaded. At the same instant that I entered
on one side of the fort, the officers commanding the two smaller detachments mounted the
ramparts on the other side, and the watchword, 'Washington and glory,' was repeated
from the three points of the fort at the same
time."

"Bless de Lo'd, bless de Lo'd! 'Washington and glory!'" interrupted Minto, in his
irrepressible excitement.

"'Washington and glory!'" shouted Lois
and Chloe. The mist of tears filled their
eager eyes.

"Grand watchword!" cried Desire, as the color mounted her pale cheeks and she raised herself from her pillows in emphasis of her deep feeling. "But we break the story," she continued. "Pray go on."

"We were elated with victory, and made our way to the centre of the fort; then a volley of musketry was discharged at us from the windows of a large house. We returned the fire, and then found it necessary to enter the place, break down the strong barricades, and drive the enemy from room to room. These men had fired upon us after the fort had been taken and the colors struck. According to the usages of war, their lives were forfeited, but I ordered the slaughter to cease. It was an extraordinary victory. We did not lose a man, and only one of our soldiers was badly wounded, and I have brought him back to Fairfield, where he will be committed to the loving care of your faithful nurses."

"Alas!" exclaimed Desire regretfully, "that I must forego the sweet pleasure of looking after your wounded patriot; but Lois will do her part."

"Ah, my friend," replied the officer, weaving infinite praise, sympathy, admiration, into the words with which he addressed the invalid, " you have served far beyond the measure of common soldiering and simple devotion to liberty. You have won a well-merited repose."

" We are waiting for the rest of the story," said Desire quietly.

" When we secured our prisoners, it was discovered that some of the redcoats were getting the shipping under way. Their boats were loaded with stores, so we brought the guns of the fort to bear upon them, and they obeyed orders; then we had to destroy the immense quantity of stuff that was accumulating. Shipping, provisions, munitions of war, all sorts of dry goods, were committed to the flames. A few valuable articles were placed on the shoulders of the prisoners, who were pinioned two and two together, and thus carried across the island to our boats. The work of capturing and destroying the fort was finished at eight in the morning, and we put about to recross. I took with me a dozen men to burn the magazine at Corum, having mounted horses which we captured at the fort. It was three hours later that we rejoined our comrades, having achieved our purpose, burning everything at the magazine, and riding sixteen miles through the enemy's country on this little diversion. Arriving at the appointed rendezvous, we found everything in good order, and having rested awhile, we resumed the march and reached our boats at four o'clock; and here we are back to Fairfield by midnight, bringing my men in fine condition, escorting as prisoners of war one lieutenant-colonel, the commandant, one lieutenant, a surgeon, fifty rank and file, with a host of others in the garrison."

"'Washington and glory!' say I," exclaimed David jubilantly.

"Hallelujah, hallelujah! Bless de Lo'd!" cried Chloe, with genuine religious fervor. "De God ob battles am wid us, a pillar o' cloud by day, and by night de glorious pillar o' fire."

"And now that I have told my story," observed Major Tallmadge, "I am wishing to hear a good report on your part," turning toward Desire with keen, questioning glance. "In fact, your report should have come first, but such impatience as you manifested was not to be gainsaid. Please tell me what the surgeon-general says concerning Miss Desire Hardy."

"Oh, my patient is doing finely," inter-

rupted Lois, in the most matter of fact way.
"The dislocated shoulder and the broken
arm are getting into prime condition. It's
only the bullet wound that bothers us, and
the doctor says that will heal in good time.
I suppose it will be some weeks before Desire
can lord it over us in the old-time way and go
adventuring up and down the country like
some love-lorn lassie gone daft; but she's
coming along. No fears for that child. I
can't find out what she's been trying to do.
I've tried to make her confess to masquer-
ading like some of our bold female patriots at
Groton, but she only smiles and keeps still.
Perhaps you know, Major Tallmadge?" and
Lois waited for some reply.

"Well," she continued, "you 're as close-
mouthed as she. Never mind. I 'll find out
some time. I'm not one to have the wool
pulled over my eyes every day."

Desire seemed to grow restless and looked
pained.

"Dear soul!" exclaimed Lois, flinging herself down by the settle, and touching with
ever so tender a touch the prostrate sister,
"don't mind what I say. You may have all
the secrets you please, and I 'll never pry into
one of them. You 're the sweetest, noblest

girl in all the world, and you shall go and
get all your limbs broken and your body
riddled with bullets, and I'll not say one
word about it until you say I may, so long as
you get well and grow to be your own dear
self again."

As Lois spoke, the tears ran down her
cheeks, and she kissed Desire over and over
again, while Major Tallmadge sat silently in
his chair, albeit strangely agitated and distressed.

"I thank you," answered Desire, when she
finally broke the stillness. She was now
speaking to the major. "I grow strong and
happy each day. I see the beginning of the
end. Mark well my words." The prophetic
fire transfigured her countenance. "It may
be that another year shall roll round before
the clouds break, but the conflict is drawing
nigh its end. Great Britain will come to
terms of honorable peace, and America shall
be free;" and then in tones of wondrous
sweetness, with rich pathetic power, she repeated four stanzas of "The American Patriot's Prayer:" —

> "'Parent of all, omnipotent
> In heaven and earth below,
> Through all creation's bounds unspent,
> Whose streams of goodness flow,

" ' Teach me to know from whence I rose,
    And unto what designed ;
No private aims let me propose,
    Since linked with human kind.

" ' But chief to hear my country's voice,
    May all my thoughts incline ;
'T is reason's law, 't is virtue's choice,
    'T is nature's call and Thine.

" ' Me from fair Freedom's sacred cause
    Let nothing e'er divide ;
Grandeur, nor gold, nor vain applause,
    Nor friendship false, misguide.' "

" Noble sentiments," said Major Tallmadge, " and never repeated by lips more worthy."

" Well," observed Lois, " if the struggle is near the end, we 've made our record here in Connecticut. Poor General Putnam, he 's gone, but for a time he was a tower of strength ; and General Wooster, he gave his life for his native land ; and what a roster of soldiers we 've furnished General Washington, beside taking care of our own State."

" I am glad that Colonel Humphrey made use of our slaves," remarked Desire. " I shall always think of Minto with unbounded gratitude."

The servants had left the room at the conclusion of Major Tallmadge's narrative.

" The loyalty and courage of our colored

people has been one of the beautiful incidents of war."

"Yes, I've heard General Washington remark upon it," said the major.

"And we must n't forget the poets that have sung liberty into the hearts of our people," continued Lois. "Joel Barlow, John Trumbull, David Humphrey, and Timothy Dwight, — why, such men do more to fire the souls of patriots than all the loud-mouthed speakers in the land !"

"You are loyal to your native heath, Lois," observed Desire, with pride.

"And so are you," interjected the sister.

"True. Connecticut compares most favorably with other States both in the number and the quality of the men she has furnished in this great liberty fight. Massachusetts may claim precedence, but Connecticut certainly comes next. I call Governor Trumbull the backbone of help and sympathy for General Washington. Our generals have been his right-hand men. Our statesmen have given wisdom, nerve, stability to the councils of Congress. Silas Deane may poke fun at his co-worker, Roger Sherman, but they both are great men in their way, bent on doing their duty, and we have others like them."

" Ah," cried David, who did not wish to seem indifferent to the honor of his State, " it 's our ideas that have done the work. We 're a remarkably ingenious and thoughtful people. We are self-made above many others. Our ancestors have insisted upon education for the citizen. We have been great lovers of liberty since the time that Samuel Hooker set his seal upon the court of the colony. We 've got the best government among the States. It 's a genuine democracy, and we can give a model to Congress itself when it comes to the pinch."

" Well," remarked Major Tallmadge, ready to share this State eulogy with his friends, " Connecticut has been most generous and willing in her contribution of supplies; and another feather in her cap is seen when I point to the great number of ships and boats of all descriptions which she has given to fight the country's battles and prey upon the enemy's commerce, — nearly 180, carrying almost 1400 guns, with more than 6000 marines; and she has paid great sums in taxes, — a splendid showing."

Desire was happy in this laudation of Connecticut.

" I would not have you forget," she said,

"that much of the spiritual force which has diffused itself through the conflict came from this State; then consider the energy, the good sense, the sterling virtue, the magnificent faith manifested by our goodly company of patriots. Governor Trumbull is a typical man of the State, a man of fine and noble spirit, given to the affairs of this world and the next, combining the two in such way that he brings things to the issue of a grand and blessed harmony."

"Very true," interrupted Lois; "but it's as well that our mutual admiration society holds a secret session. All the same," she continued, with spirit, "this panegyric on Connecticut is deserved. I'm glad *I* was born in the famous little colony."

But this jubilation over victory and glowing exhibit of patriotism was too great a tax upon the strength of the invalid. Major Tallmadge withdrew amid the liveliest congratulations, and the household settled down to such a level of peace as seemed possible during these piping times of war.

CHAPTER XXVI

"HAVE I NOT SERVED SEVEN YEARS?"

THE news of Cornwallis's surrender traveled to Fairfield on the wings of the wind, and the lads wished to celebrate the auspicious event. Since the old town was burned, poverty had prevailed to such an extent that little or nothing had been spared for such unnecessary pleasures as a village festival or jubilee; and it might truthfully be remarked that the occasions for any such rejoicing had been few and far between.

But the surrender of Cornwallis meant that the war could not survive for long. The prophecy of Desire was coming true. The beginning of the end was now an acknowledged fact.

When the boys discussed among themselves the particular form to be given to their celebration, they came over to consult Desire and Lois Hardy.

"They 're as good as boys any day," was the generous praise awarded them by their common admirers and devotees, the sprightly, high-spirited lads of the village. " Why, they can ride and row, shoot a musket and run a race, hoe corn or mend a harness, like any man in town; and they 're as lively as crickets," continued the youngsters.

" Well, I suppose," said Desire, who was now her old self, " that you want a bonfire, although it is n't but two years since we saw the biggest, grandest, saddest one that it will ever be our lot to look upon."

" Yes, yes," replied the boys, " we must have a bonfire."

" Well, you can find enough charred sticks and timbers to supply you with all necessary fuel," continued Desire. " All you 'll have to do is to set the stuff well agoing, and it will burn with the fury of '79, methinks."

" But you must do something more than make a vast conflagration of old ruins," observed Lois, with enthusiasm. " What would you say to an effigy of old Tryon, — ' Great Wolf Billy the Butcher Firebrand Tryon' ? "

" That's what we 're after. Good! good!" shouted the boys. " And you 'll help us make it ? " The remark was addressed to Lois.

" Oh, yes," answered this popular maiden. " I 'm always ready to serve my country ; "

and the roguish expression in her eyes said
that she was not the less prepared to serve
companionable lads like the committee in
consultation.

So it happened on an Indian summer's
night in November, 1781, that the volatile
and patriotic youth of Fairfield raised a
rickety, fantastic gibbet on the Green (permission having been granted by the selectmen), and decorated it with a well-stuffed,
wondrously bedizened figure of the despised
and hated monster who had subjected so
many patriots to his cruelties.

The bonfire illumined the Green, and gave
a weird, ghostly appearance to the extrava-
gant performances of the boys. The townspeople, old as well as young, naturally gravitated to the scene. The British might still
be in possession of New York, and Long
Island flourish with Tory sentiment and spirit,
nevertheless independence was in the air. A
few months, and the redcoats must depart
for good. The gray light on the eastern
horizon forecast the full-orbed day of peace.
So the staid, serious people of this New England town could afford to thrust dignity one
side for a night and join the frolic of the
rising generation.

A new court house had been reared near the middle of the Green, and three or four small dwellings on the edge of the open, added to the four left standing after the burning, gave an appearance of recovery that was not altogether dispelled by the gaunt black chimneys which towered above the ruins that framed the public common. A broad fringe of men and women moved along the edges of the familiar place, stopping now and then to peer into the ashes of the meeting-house, or comment upon the great losses which hampered them in work.

"They have swung the old wretch aloft," said Lois to David, as they stood in front of the Bulkley house. "How I wish it was really the man himself brought out of these headquarters!" She pointed over her shoulder to the dwelling that had sheltered Tryon when he was destroying the town.

"Snarl and bite now, you Great Wolf," shouted one of the boys.

"Looking for another butchering job, Billy?" mockingly asked a second youngster, as the effigy twisted itself around and faced the north.

"How do you like that?" exclaimed a third tormentor, as a rotten egg struck the figure square in the face and trickled down upon the gorgeous waistcoat.

" I wonder what we 'll do with the Tories when peace is declared," questioned a by-stander at the elbow of David.

" Do with 'em," replied a voice in the dark, " hang 'em, dang 'em ! " was the laconic reply. " Swing the devils over a gibbet like that ! " and the shadowy speaker pointed to the effigy.

" Hang 'em, dang 'em ! " shouted one of the riotous youths. The words were caught up by little knots of revelers until the refrain rang out with scandalous distinctness all over the Green, seeming to disturb the very ashes of the sanctuary by their profane vindictive-ness. " Hang 'em, dang 'em ! "

Little cross-currents of November air took the words and tossed them above the din and roar of the frolic. Ghostly presences seemed to flit about through the shades of night, bandying these awful words with each other.

" Try on ! Try on ! you Firebrand," ex-claimed a small boy, punning upon the sol-dier's name. " Try on that ! " and the small boy threw a dab of tar against the effigy, observing gleefully that it went straight for the middle of his waistcoat, where it stuck and spread.

"That's the thing! That's the thing! Try on a coat of tar and feathers!" suggested one of the train-band. And soon the dangling object was besmeared from head to foot with tar, and a plentiful supply of feathers was laboriously scattered over every inch of the repugnant, offensive effigy, while shouts of laughter, cries of "Hang 'em, dang 'em!" and loud, reverberating huzzas, filled the welkin.

"Now toast him!" exclaimed a husky voice in the distance. "Give him a taste of fire."

"Yes," was the ready answer, "send him home, down among the devils!"

"Fry him," shouted another man.

The excitement reached its height. Tryon's effigy had been taunted and humbled to heart's content. Rotten eggs dripped their vileness, tar and feathers coated the figure with their grotesque transmogrification. The bonfire burned low, so that it could easily be moved. It did not take many minutes to carry the burning pieces of wood to a place beneath the gibbet, and then heap high the pile with fresh fuel. A brief delay, and the mass was burning with redoubled fury; while amid the frenzied exultations of the boys and the resounding laughter of their elders, the tar and feathers, the stuffed boots and martial hat, the gay waistcoat and highly scented material which constituted the fictitious person of General "Great Wolf Billy the Butcher Firebrand" Tryon was ignominiously reduced to ashes.

"Mis' D'sire," whispered Minto, who approached at this stage of the festivities, "Mas'r Duane at de house. He wish to see you."

For more than a year Mr. Livingstone had avoided Fairfield, and this was his first appearance since he bade Desire Hardy good-by, a few days after she was brought home a wounded, shattered woman.

"Desire," exclaimed the young man, "you 've got my message about Yorktown?" This was his greeting.

"Yes, Duane," was the answer. "You see the town boys are celebrating the glorious event."

"You know what it means, child?" Livingstone spoke under strong emotion.

"It is the beginning of the end. America is free. Great Britain will make terms of

peace with us and acknowledge our independence." The speaker was aglow with passion.

"Yes, Desire, it means all that." How
sweet and tender in its manliness was his
voice. What depth of pure feeling did his
glad, eager, luminous eyes reveal! "And
does it not mean another thing for you and
me?"

It was a questioning intense, painful in
its seriousness, bringing Desire down from
her lofty pedestal of patriotic enthusiasm face
to face with an imperious spirit and life's destiny. The woman paled under the ardent
gaze of her lover. There was a sudden heaving of the breast, a pathetic sob smote the ear.

"Desire, Desire," continued he, with warning notes of fear, if not despair, sounding
through his words, "have I not served these
seven years! Do you love your country so
that no love is left for me?" He was watching the play of emotion in her countenance.

A sudden pang of jealousy pierced his
heart. It could not be that she really cared
for that Tory refugee, Spalding, felled like
an ox by the mighty arm of Minto.

Was it Aaron Burr? He had written
her numerous gay, lively, charming letters,

and often seen her in his visits to cousin
Thaddeus. But then Burr was a flirt, making love to every woman, and they all knew
it. Desire could not be such a fool as to give
her heart to that fickle gallant. And Burr
loved a widow, upon whom he was lavishing
his attentions. Had he not studied law with
Judge Patterson, and then with Thomas
Smith? Was he not expecting to be admitted
to the bar soon, in order (so it was reported)
that he might repair his wasted fortunes, gain
a good income, and then marry Mrs. Pre-
vost? It could n't be that Aaron Burr had
won the love of a sensible woman like Desire
Hardy.

But there were other gentlemen that
haunted the Hardy homestead, and chief
among them was Colonel Tallmadge. Livingstone had never met the man, but he knew
that he was the sort of a soldier and patriot
to command the homage of most women.
And Tallmadge had been a frequent visitor
and a not infrequent correspondent.

As these thoughts ran through his mind,
Desire remained silent, and her expression
gradually assumed that of a person surprised,
shocked, by the suddenness of some startling
announcement.

"Is it Colonel Tallmadge?" murmured Livingstone, putting his thought into speech, and talking to himself more than to the woman by his side.

There was a slight flush, a swift lifting of the head in anger, the kindling of a proud spirit.

"My cousin" (spoken with great dignity), "you are hasty in your addresses." By a strong effort she mastered herself, continuing with gentle reserve, "The news of Yorktown is still fresh. We have not had time to think upon it in all its bearings. Other days will follow, and — and" — she stumbled and hesitated — "there will be time to think everything over."

There was the faintest intimation of a smile upon her lips, and her eyes certainly beamed with friendliness.

"Forgive me, Desire, for all my boyish rashness and folly. We'll sit down and visit," for they had stood thus far through the interview. "And I'm your cousin to-night, if nothing more, so give me a kiss," a request which was granted on the instant, and an incident which appeared by no means to be devoid of interest to either party.

"I've heard from Tryon recently," observed Livingstone, in a matter of fact way. "He inquired for you and David."

"We've burned him here to-night," replied Desire genially. "The boys have had great fun. You did n't catch the refrain that's been sounding and resounding through the town the last hour, did you? It's a solemn warning to you, Duane." She was laughing merrily at her jest.

"Some new song of Barlow's or Trumbull's?"

"Oh, no; simply a concise, significant phrase. When Tryon was hanging on his gibbet, somebody asked what was to be done with the Tories in our midst, and some profane bystander sang out, 'Hang 'em, dang 'em!' and all the boys and perhaps a portion of the grown-ups have been singing it ever since. You'll have to look out for yourself."

"Desire, what do you say to taking Lois and David and going with me to Boston for a week or two? Now that Mrs. Hancock has invited you so many times and everything is quiet here in the north, and I've some business in that section, why not make the journey with me? I'm only stopping here for a day or two, and then I'm off."

John Hancock was the first governor of the State of Massachusetts. His spouse had not forgotten the happy days in Fairfield and the friendship of Desire Hardy. A pleasant correspondence had extended through the years, with varied and occasional renewings of personal intercourse when the Boston beauty revisited the scene of her nuptials. At the time news of Desire's injuries had reached the ears of the Hancocks, a most urgent request had been sent her to come and stay with them when able to make the journey. This was the first opportunity to gratify the wish.

It was a merry company that joined Mr. Duane Livingstone at Lebanon three days after the celebration on Fairfield Green.

Governor Trumbull and his council had issued a proclamation urging their fellow citizens not to raise a single cent the price of provisions during the passage of the French troops through the State on their march to Boston. The injunction had been obeyed, the people dealing generously with their foreign allies, so that a feeling of marked cordiality prevailed. The young folks noted it, and entered into the spirit of the times.

Was there not good reason for rejoicings? The fair prospects for peace filled

every patriotic heart with grand hopes. It
was not alone that war must cease, — all the
cruel butchery and woeful desolation, — but
from the ashes of conflagrations, from the
blood which encrimsoned many a field, there
must spring a new State and a people sancti-
fied to the championship of eternal liberty
and righteousness. Governor Trumbull had
issued his proclamation for a Thanksgiving, in
which he spoke of the promising and happy
turn of public affairs, the singular interposi-
tions of Providence, and the perfect union and
understanding existing between the Americans and their allies. All these things quickened the hearts of the people, wooing them
into extraordinary merry-makings, wondrously
mitigating their distresses, inducing an atmosphere of cheerfulness which contrasted
boldly with the sorrow and depression of
seven years.

The gorgeous foliage of autumn had
withered and fallen, there were no flowers to
brighten field or forest, the landscape was
taking unto itself the barren, hostile aspect
of winter; yet it was the gayest, happiest
journey of life for these travelers.

They stretched it over four days, the length
of a stage trip. They lingered in every town

GOVERNOR JONATHAN TRUMBULL

where there was any excuse for delay. As the quartette ambled along together on their horses, the war and matters of state were discussed. Desire was reciting the part which Connecticut had taken in the conflict, going over the various episodes in the British attempts to annoy and humiliate the citizens of the little State, reviewing the incursions at Horseneck, North Stamford, Stonington, Darien, New London, and other places, eulogizing the Yankee soldiers and sailors, nourishing her New England pride with every memorable deed and service which she was able to recall.

But there were hours when David and Lois dropped behind or cantered on ahead. Those were the sweetest hours of the day.

Duane had learned his lesson. Desire was longing to be wooed and won in the good old-fashioned way. He had been too swift, eager, inconsequent, on the evening of the Yorktown celebration. All these years, when he was serving with the thought of Desire supreme in his soul, she had been absorbed in the struggle for freedom. Sex love remained in absolute abeyance. Men were fellow patriots with this martyr-spirited, extraordinary woman. She lived in the achievements of the statesmen and soldiers fighting the country's battles and shaping the nation s destiny. That work had now assumed such character that one might abide in the reasonable assurance that the end was victory for those exalted ideals which swayed the mind of the unselfish, liberty-loving comrade.

And now a man who had been true to her through long years, loving with a passion so pure and noble that no sacrifice became too great for him, — sacrifice itself being lost or glorified in devotion, — this man was come to awaken in her the responsive passion. She was to be made conscious of her woman's nature. It was a change — a wrench from the life which had completely absorbed her to another which made the same insistent demands, or greater.

Duane Livingstone, now reading her like the open pages of a book, set himself to the happy task of enkindling a flame as subtly strong, as intense, spiritual, and consuming, as that which mastered and purified his own heart.

There were memorable days in Boston. The governor's lady might have the guest to herself some little portion of the time, but Desire was unresistingly monopolized by Mr.

Livingstone. When the fair Dorothy observed this trend of true love, the way of courtship was made a path of roses.

"They were tragic days which drove us away from Boston," said Mrs. Hancock, "but it was a generous and delightful hospitality extended to us by Mr. and Mrs. Burr. What a summer of gayety and happiness, in spite of war and adversity!"

"Were they not sweet hours of hope, brave, gladsome hours of friendship, that we spent together?" observed Desire.

"Child," was the reply, "perhaps it was the atmosphere of love in which we lived." She gave the hand of Desire a gentle pressure, and smiled like one living over again the sweet, beautiful days of budding passion. "Was it not a kind and lovely thing to do, — the mothering of an exile and the giving her a wedding?" They were recalling past days. "Child, let us have a wedding here in Boston, and you shall be the bride."

There was a long, long silence; many thoughts of home, childhood, and mother; a swift panorama of years; at length a quiet, gentle, confiding assent.

So the Rev. Andrew Eliot came with Mr. and Mrs. Thaddeus Burr, that they might

share the joyous event.   It was not a case of
exile from home and the awful straits of war,
as when John Hancock married Dorothy Q.;
nevertheless, it was the bridegroom on both
occasions who gathered the silks, the laces,
the white hats, the gay stockings, the pretty
shoes, the exquisite fabrics and shining baubles
which graced the lady of his heart.

CHAPTER XXVII

HONORED BY WASHINGTON

"THE President will pass this way in October, and he has expressed a wish to meet 'D. H.'" It was Colonel Tallmadge speaking to David Hardy in the humble home which had been reared the year following the burning of Fairfield.

"I think the meeting can be arranged, colonel," was the reply ; "but tell me what the general knows concerning ' D. H.'" There was a note of curiosity in the question.

"Well, David," said the speaker, with a humorous twinkle in his eyes, "one or two of those love letters which passed through our hands were signed, unwittingly I suppose, by the writer of them, not the full name, simply the initials 'D. H.' It is almost ten years since they were written, and General Washington has kept them all. He may wish to give these unique epistles back to the writer of them."

David was bewildered.

"I'll arrange the meeting, colonel, but I don't seem to remember about the love letters," and the gentleman gazed abstractedly at his caller.

"A great deal has happened since those days," continued Colonel Tallmadge cheerily.

"Yes, to you and Desire and Lois and Duane and the country, but nothing extraordinary to me. Here I sit and study, or go out on the farm and work, and it's day in and day out. I'm fairly happy, colonel, however," a smile illumining his face. "What a fund of interesting reminiscence you must have to draw on for the pleasure of your friends!"

"David, you flatter me. I expect to become a garrulous old man, for I love to recall the days of yore. So much has been said about Washington's lack of deep feeling or his command of the emotions, that I must tell you how he said good-by to us when the army was disbanded and he left for Mount Vernon. We were at Fraunces' tavern, you know. We had taken some slight refreshment, when the general filled his glass, and, turning to his officers, said, 'With a heart full of love and gratitude I now take leave of you. I most devoutly wish that your latter days may be as prosperous and happy as your former ones have been glorious and honorable.' "

"Fine! fine!" interrupted David Hardy, kindling with his old-time enthusiasm. "I'd like to have been a witness to the scene."

"After the officers had taken a glass of wine," continued Colonel Tallmadge, now aglow with interest in his own narrative, "General Washington said (and I remember it as though it was only yesterday), 'I cannot come to each of you, but shall be obliged if each of you will come and take me by the hand.' General Knox was nearest to him. He turned to the Commander-in-chief, who, suffused with tears, was incapable of utterance, but grasped his hand, when they embraced each other in silence."

At this point, the reminiscent mood overwhelmed the narrator with its sacred memories. A moment elapsed before he went on with the story.

"In the same affectionate manner, every officer in the room marched up to, kissed, and parted with his General-in-chief. Such a scene of weeping I had never before witnessed, and I hope I may never be called upon to witness again," — the speaker's breast heaved with emotion, the eyes of David filled. "It seemed as if every heart was ready to burst from its wonted abode. Not a word was uttered to break the solemn silence that prevailed, or to interrupt the tenderness of the hour.

"David, we were parting with the man who had conducted us through a long and bloody war, and under whose conduct the glory and independence of our country had been achieved. The thought that we might not see his face again in this world seemed to me utterly insupportable; but the time of separation had come, and, waving his hand to his grieving children around him, he left the room, and, passing through a corps of light infantry who were paraded to receive him, he walked silently on to Whitehall, where a barge was in waiting. David, it was a heartrending scene. A few days, and we were all scattered, returning to our several abodes, beginning anew the vocations in life which had been laid one side while fighting for human rights."

"Oh, colonel, I can well believe that the heart of the old soldier was bleeding; and Colonel Humphrey has told me how General Washington returned to Mount Vernon, and how true and good he has been to all the brave, great souls that fought his battles. God bless him! And now we are to be honored with his presence."

" Yes," continued Colonel Tallmadge, " and I am sure that he has it in his heart to utter what will prove more precious than jewels unto ' D. H.,' for many times have I heard him say that when the opportunity came and it consorted with wisdom, he wished to meet my unknown patriot and render in person his thanks for many remarkable services."

The speaker gazed inquiringly at David; but the far-away look had crept into his eyes, so that he seemed like one wandering in dreamland or lost in deep reverie.

" David," said this friend, raising his voice and speaking with such emphasis that the man was brought back to himself, " you 've never been free and square with me on this matter, — not that you have done anything inconsistent with honor. Don't think I mean that, my man; but you have hidden away the facts and experiences clustering about your service for Washington and the cause of liberty with such modesty that not a soul knows our indebtedness to you."

David shifted uneasily in his chair, glanced out of the window and into the fire, then

turned slowly to his friend and remained
silent.

"Why not question Desire? She knows
all about it, and can tell what she pleases;
and methinks, colonel, that you came to her
five times where you came to me once."

"David, you 're the most subtle, reticent
fellow, I believe, in all the world. Don't try
to shift the responsibility for your noble services to the shoulders of your sister. She 's
done enough to put us under obligations without assuming the credit and glory belonging
to you; and mind, comrade, I 'm not prying
into your affairs. It 's your right to bury
these secrets with you when you die·; but I
would like to see people render you some part
of the praise which is your due."

The health of David Hardy had not been
good since the close of the war. Service and
exposure had crippled him, albeit he never
referred to his sacrifices or sought any pay
for his defense of the country. He was leading a bachelor life, under the foster care of
old Minto and Chloe, too feeble and diffident
to take up the work of preaching, growing
more and more indifferent to the world, becoming wholly centred in his favorite studies
and pursuits.

Public sentiment and the lively imagination of friends surrounded the recluse with the glamour of romance. It was whispered that he had been the confidant of Washington, one of his secret right-hand men, a quiet, tireless, sagacious agent, engaged in important matters of war and peace. The boys of the town looked upon David with reverence, repeating over and over to one another wonderful stories of hairbreadth escapes and unparalleled achievements, giving him credit for all sorts of good deeds and daring exploits. It was impossible to say how these tales became current, but many people knew that his sister Desire never denied their truth, and on more than one occasion had vouched for their historic accuracy.

Colonel Tallmadge had become familiar with these reports, and sometimes took pains to express his appreciation of the services rendered by David Hardy. Any revelation of private correspondence or secret service was unbecoming in him, but the impression prevailed that he might say not a little to enlighten people concerning the part which David had taken when he visited Long Island and New York as a spy.

Colonel Tallmadge, however, remained in

the dark, so far as the work done for Washington by the Hardy family was concerned. He had reached the conclusion that David was the one who had incurred the great risks and established a network of secret intelligence among his allies in the enemy's ranks, Desire being the helper through whom the brother had chosen to work. She had encouraged Colonel Tallmadge in this view of the matter; so when he told David that Washington was coming, and that the general wished to meet " D. H.," the colonel was puzzled by the vague, non-committal manner of his friend.

It was an important and extraordinary service which the unknown patriot had rendered the cause of American Independence. For years, this individual had transmitted to Washington exact information concerning almost every movement in the north planned by the enemy. The details of supplies, fortifications, number of troops, army life, and organization were passed through this trustworthy and invaluable channel of communication.

To employ agents in such a work, to sift and substantiate their reports, to organize and conduct a system of espionage, involved a large expenditure of money as well as a large investment of wit, insight, courage, personal force, and mastery. Colonel Tallmadge received from the Commander-in-chief small sums of money to carry on this work, but not one penny of it had ever been paid to an unknown patriot. The generous and splendid service done by this nameless person was counted simply as the meet offering put by a loyal spirit upon the altar of his country.

No account of perils, escapes, injuries, sorrows, or losses ever reached the ears of Washington. Not only was curiosity piqued, but a deep feeling of gratitude possessed the heart of the great soldier. He had treasured the curious love letters coming to him through the hands of Colonel Tallmadge, ultimately believing that, while veritable means of communicating important intelligence to him, they were also genuine expressions of a romantic passion existing between an unknown patriot and the unnamed object of his exalted, imperious love.

It was the evening of October the 16th that President Washington reached Fairfield on his journey through New England. He dined and lodged at "The Sign of the Sun," the tavern kept by Mr. Penfield, a popular host.

This was his first visit since the conflagration of ten years ago, and Tryon's scourge was manifest on every side. Washington took note of it. " The destructive evidences of British cruelty are yet visible in Norwalk and Fairfield," he wrote in his journal, " as there are the chimneys of many burnt houses standing in them yet."

The old army officers, the members of the Committee of Safety and Correspondence living, the men who had served in civil or military capacity during the period when the independence of the colonies was achieved, paid their respects to the great man; and then it was observed that he slipped away from the company gathered to do him honor.

Accompanied by Minto, Washington crossed the Green and was piloted to the Hardy homestead.

" His Excellency de President," said the faithful slave, as he ushered him into the plain little parlor, now adorned with a goodly portion of David's library.

Washington's face was an interesting study at the moment. Surprise, inquiry, pleasure, confusion and gratitude, recognition and perplexity, struggled for control. The candles flickered in their stands. The flames leaped high on the hearth and adorned the place with a ruddy glow. Shadows in their play shifted about the room. The Commander-in-chief was mystified.

"You are welcome, honored sir," said David, as he extended his hand.

"We are old acquaintances, I observe," was the courteous reply.

"Allow me to present my sister," continued David, "Mrs. Duane Livingstone, of New York, and her husband, my cousin."

"Friends whom I esteem," answered Washington, greeting them with marked cordiality, albeit amazement still the dominant expression upon his countenance.

There ensued a few moments of embarrassment. This was not the meeting that Washington had anticipated. David was like a man awaking from uneasy sleep, groping for his bearings; Desire, nervous and hesitant, moved by some deep, inexplicable emotion; Duane, sphinx-like.

Now that Washington saw David Hardy, he recalled his face and the numerous occasions when he had met him, but there was not manifest in his countenance that peculiar intelligence which the Commander-in-chief had pictured to himself; yet the initials " D. H."

fitted the man, and Colonel Tallmadge had
arranged this meeting.   It was not apparent
why Mr. and Mrs. Livingstone were present,
although the fact of their intimate relationship   was   perhaps   sufficient   explanation.
Washington had planned to meet the unknown patriot in strict privacy; but if the
brave man desired his sister and her husband to be present, no objections could be
offered.

Mr. and Mrs. Livingstone were people that
General Washington had known these several
years.   Could he forget the charming maiden
who drew the cooling draught of water
from a well in the rear of Thaddeus Burr's
mansion when he was passing through Fairfield on his return from Boston? When he
had first greeted her as a married woman, the
memory of that humble incident was revived.
Desire and Duane had been associated with
the people who gave shape to the new repub-
lic, so that the times were many when they
met in a social or public way the man whom
all delighted to honor.

Washington had prepared himself to face
a stranger.   He was in the presence of three
old friends.

The welcome having been extended, the

first embarrassment disappeared, and they were soon launched in conversation.

At length Washington unfolded a packet of letters. He did it with infinite tenderness, and the silence was broken only by the rustling of paper and the crackling of fire on the hearth. The yellow sheets showed evidences of rough usage, however gently Washington might handle them this night and spread the precious fragments before him.

They were various shapes and sizes, torn, defaced, discolored, wrinkled, creased, or faded. Some of them carried an address. Several were simply marked, " My Love." All except two went free of any signature. The tell-tale initials, " D. H.," had been written twice.

" These letters," said Washington, who now arose and stood in regal manliness before them, " I prize above any gems which gold can purchase. They have had a peculiar value for me, since they are part and parcel of the victories won by American patriots over British oppressors; but they have served the end for which they came into my possession. I have long wished to return them unto their rightful owner, for I believe that the intelligence designed for me was hidden in messages of love sent by 'D. H.' to the woman of his heart. The ingenious cipher used to convey secret news to me did not deceive in respect to the genuine character of the sentiments appearing on the surface of these epistles. To me they have been the most wonderful and pathetic expressions of an affection that I believe the sacredest, happiest in life."

The face of the great soldier was transfigured. His listeners stood before him in the subdued glow of the light, reflecting his own nobility of spirit and glory of aspect.

"I return these letters to 'D. H.,' the writer of them." As he spoke, they were pressed into the unwilling hands of David. "And I render my heartfelt gratitude to the unknown patriot, imploring the blessing of heaven upon him and those he loves."

It was one of the supreme moments of a lifetime.

"These letters," replied David, choking with the emotions welling up from his heart, "I writ not," and he pushed them gravely, insistently, back into the hands of the startled Washington. "There was, there is, a nobler 'D. H.' than David Hardy." He was speaking brokenly, joy, wonder, pride, striving for the mastery. "Methinks they belong to my sister, Desire Hardy Livingstone."

The great soldier seemed more deeply perplexed than ever. He glanced from brother to sister like one dazed; then, in response to the suggestion of David, he thrust them into the hands of Desire, a strange light suffusing his face.

"My words of gratitude and benediction have already been uttered in your hearing, honored and beloved madam," — he paused in the very stress of inexpressible admiration, — "but how feeble and inadequate they sound. A glorious work has been achieved by your sacrifices."

Words seemed to fail him, and Desire broke silence.

"Did not your Excellency wish to give these letters into the keeping of the writer?" She put the question in tender, pathetic way, catching the subdued enthusiasm manifest by Washington. "I did not write them." Again the stillness of night, a moment of intense suspense. "There was, there is, a nobler 'D. H.' "— borrowing her brother's language — "than Desire Hardy." And once more the tattered letters were given back to Washington. "There is another 'D. H.'

who well deserves all praise and reverence for his superlative love of country and a seven years' matchless fidelity, sacrifice, and perils on land and sea in behalf of liberty, albeit they were years of *secret* service, and the secret must remain locked forever in *our* breasts."

Washington turned to David. David gazed upon Livingstone. A great light was breaking; and Desire, in wordless, passionate, exalted homage, bowed unto her husband.

The general did not speak. He crossed the room to Duane Hardy Livingstone, gently deposited the letters in his keeping, then by a clasp of the hands and by unuttered prayers sealed in a covenant of love and secrecy his relations with an Unknown Patriot.

Late on the October night, far into the morning, that little room was like a Bethel. The fire on the hearth played fantastic pranks, adorning the place with exquisite tracery, flinging beautiful images against the walls, casting its golden glamour over each object touched by its magic pencilings. Two sons of Liberty and a daughter of the Revolution lingered long and lovingly amid the impalpable, beneficent shadows that filled the spaces with their indefinable glory. A bundle of

letters passed from one hand to another, and
many a kiss was printed upon the ragged,
glowing sheets. There was the murmur of
low, sweet voices woven into dearest, sacredest
reminiscence. They were living in the trans-
figuring atmosphere of a threefold love, —
the love of true heart for true heart, the love
of a patriot for his country, and the love of
man for God.

Washington and his company left " The
Sign of the Sun " at an early hour, having
arranged to breakfast at Stratford. When
they passed the Green, the soldier, wrapped
in profound meditation, was observed to lead
the way by a small, plain cottage. His men
respectfully followed. The gray of the morn
had been pushed one side by innumerable
shafts of roseate light. The humble homestead resting beneath the shelter of old trees,
now clad in all the rainbow hues of autumn,
never appeared more lovely and peaceful. As
Washington came abreast the place, he reverently uncovered, as one might pass in homage
before some monarch of earth. No word was
spoken. Simply the impact of the horses' feet
upon the hard ground resounded through the
crisp air.

There were unspoken words echoing through the soul of the Great Man; and when, in the ardor of his gratitude, these voiceless syllables formed upon his moving lips, the winds caught them and whispered to one another, "Ten thousand benisons upon the Unknown Patriot of our Land."

ELECTROTYPED AND PRINTED
BY H. O. HOUGHTON AND CO.

The Riverside Press

CAMBRIDGE, MASS., U. S. A.